Artificial Sunshine

Artificial Sunshine

A Social History of Domestic Lighting

Maureen Dillon

 THE NATIONAL TRUST

First published in Great Britain in 2002 by
National Trust Enterprises Ltd.,
36 Queen Anne's Gate, London SWIH 9AS

http://www.nationaltrust.org.uk/bookshop

British Library Cataloguing in Publication Data
A Catalogue record for this book is available from the British Library

ISBN 0-7078-0288-1

Picture research by Antonia Harrison

Designed by Newton Engert Partnership

Phototypeset in Caslon by SPAN Graphics Limited

Printed and bound in Italy, by G. Canale & Co. S.p.A.

HALF TITLE: Late nineteenth-century copper and brass electric light
fitting with vaseline shade, by W. A. S. Benson, hanging above the
Visitors' Staircase at Wightwick Manor, West Midlands.

FRONTISPIECE: The Great Parlour at Wightwick Manor, furnished in the
artistic tastes of the 1890s. On the left is the inglenook fireplace designed
by Edward Ould. The electroliers were designed by W. A. S. Benson to
recall Dutch brass chandeliers of the seventeenth century. On the table
is a lucerna, a multi-wick brass oil lamp.

Contents

In memory of my parents
William St John Dillon and Florence May Freeman Dillon
With love and gratitude

Acknowledgements

This book could not have been written without the help and encouragement of many people. My greatest debt of gratitude and thanks is to Dr Nigel Seeley, Head of Conservation at the National Trust, who first suggested that I write this book and who has remained steadfast in his support. When I first met Dr Seeley some years ago he was implementing a project whereby all historically significant, interesting and mundane technological installations and objects in National Trust properties would be recorded and photographed. I was subsequently invited to become a member of the Country House Technology Survey Team, whose ultimate aim is to build up a database of material that will be of use not only to the National Trust but also to all researchers. Although technological objects have increasingly become an area of interest and research, much remains to be discovered and analysed; and it is through innovative projects such as this that greater insight can be gained into the ways in which the introduction of technology into the home changed daily life. Dr Seeley offered invaluable assistance by reading the draft manuscript and making helpful comments and suggestions; however, any omissions and errors are entirely my own.

I am very grateful to those who shared their personal reminiscences and experiences of managing and living with different lighting technologies. I enjoyed a correspondence with Mr Jan Newman, who for many years worked at Arlington Court, a house lit by candles and oil lamps until 1951, and who permitted his recollections to appear in this book. Mrs Violet Liddle, who formerly worked for Mr and Mrs George Bernard Shaw, was also kind enough to write recalling her early experiences of electric lighting at Shaw's Corner. Others who also shared their memories were Mr George Wain, who recalled the gas and electricity installations at Cliveden, and Mr and Mrs Webb, who moved into Forthlin Road when the houses were newly built. My thanks to Lord Cawley for sending details of the electricity generation plant at Berrington Hall and to Mr T. W. Ferrers-Walker, who recalled the inefficiency of the electricity generation system at his former home Baddesley Clinton. I am grateful to Sir Richard Hyde Parker, who took time to show me the remnants of the gas lighting at Melford Hall. My thanks to Mr John Workman for his observations on Edison and Swan; and last but by no means least, Lord Faringdon, who arranged for me to see the spectacular light-fittings in the Faringdon Collection at Buscot Park.

The research for this book was considerably aided by the assistance of others and I am grateful to Brigadier Keith Prosser, Clerk to the Worshipful Company of Tallow Chandlers, who arranged for Jack Hall, the Beadle, to show me around the Company's very beautiful building that houses an interesting early lighting collection. Equally my thanks to Mr Percival at the Worshipful Company of Wax Chandlers for sharing his work on the history of the wax chandlers' craft and to Mark Young, the Beadle, for an impromptu guided tour of the Hall. Ms Susannah Heinemann of Price's Patent Candle Company kindly sent a history of the company, Ms Glennys Wild, Senior Curator, Birmingham Museum and Art Gallery provided information about the ventilating gas lights that continue to hang in the Industrial Gallery and Samantha Johns, Collections Assistant at Great Yarmouth Museums, gave the details about the candle brackets in the Conspiracy Room at the Elizabethan House Museum, Great Yarmouth.

I am indebted to those with specialist knowledge who have helped in unravelling problems and 'shedding light' on obscure questions and objects. My thanks to Brian Godwin, the National Trust Adviser on Firearms, for sharing his knowledge on strike-a-lights and to Martin Mortimer, Adviser on Glass Chandeliers. My thanks to Christopher Sugg of Sugg Lighting Limited, who has never failed to be interested or helpful on queries relating to gas lighting, John B. Horne for sharing his research regarding the gas installations at a number of National Trust properties, Trevor Pickford, Curator, the John Doran Gas Museum, Leicester, and Russell Ellis, industrial archaeologist, for sending quantities of useful material on all aspects of lighting. Dave Woodcock, Associate Curator at the Science Museum has been consistently helpful for many years, particularly in his ability to supply desperately needed information at short notice despite a heavy workload. At Hove Library, East Sussex, Linda Neale did her utmost to locate and retrieve rare and out-of-print publications and I am very grateful for her help.

Numerous members of National Trust staff were helpful in providing information and I am very grateful to Jill Banks, Archivist, for details of candle, rushlight, gas and electric lighting at Kedleston Hall, Adam Daber, Curator at Quarry Bank Mill, Styal for material relating to the gas installation, Michael Freeman for his thoughts on the gas lighting at East Riddlesden Hall and James Rothwell, Assistant Historic Buildings Representative, Mercia, for sending archive information on the lighting at Dunham Massey and Lyme Park. My thanks also to Maria Moffat and Neil Robinson for Mr D. C. J. Watkins's report on the electric lighting installation at Ickworth House and to Nick Ralls for Kate Atkinson's report on the installation at Lyme Park. Evadne Wright gave up her day off to show me around the Holy Austin Rock Houses at Kinver Edge and also suggested I meet with David Bills, a pharmacist in Kinver. Mr Bills, a local historian, very generously made copies available of his own research and other material relating to the history and habitation of the Rock Houses and I am very grateful to him.

I also want to express gratitude to the many National Trust staff who answered questions and who made time to take me round various properties. Their help in providing additional information has without doubt enriched the material in this book and my thanks go to David Adshead, Frances Bailey, Hugh Meller, Jeremy Pearson, Kevin Rogers, Kate Sharpe and Pamela Wallhead, Historic Buildings Representatives based at regional offices, and their fellow sunbeams at National Trust properties, David Adams, Canons Ashby, Janet Alcock, South Foreland Lighthouse, Pat Batten and Neville Blum at Waddesdon Manor, Stephen Bennett, Snowshill Manor, John Bignell and Philip Cotton at Cliveden, Merle Bowden, Penrhyn Castle, Bridget Carter, Wicken Fen, Graham Damant and George Potirakis at Wimpole Hall, Ruth Gofton, Standen, Harry Hall, Rufford Old Hall, John Halliday, Forthlin Road, Graham Hicks, Tatton Park, Chris Hoad, Arlington Court, Paul Holden, Lanhydrock, Howard James, Fell Foot, Stephen Pigott, the Treasurer's House, York, Elizabeth Proudfoot, Cotehele, Ian Russell and Stan Walford at Baddesley Clinton, Jo Seaman, Petworth House, Philip Warner, Anglesey Abbey, Kate Warren, Kingston Lacy and Michael Wynne and Kate Mayne at Chirk Castle.

At the National Trust headquarters, 36 Queen Anne's Gate, London, Margaret Willes, the Publisher, was long-suffering and tried very hard to be patient with this recalcitrant author who, as the deadline for the manuscript fast approached and went, required being brought sharply into line with a modified version of the stick-and-carrot approach, which meant withdrawal of the carrot and plenty of stick. Philippa Reynolds, Margaret's erstwhile assistant, was too kind and understanding for her role as 'enforcer' and her replacement, Antonia Harrison, who is in the same mould, has been very helpful. I am very grateful to Margaret for her support; despite the odds, she managed to keep her sense of humour even though, at times, the smile was wintry and the teeth gritted. Furthermore she also commissioned some of the beautiful photographs in this book that have been used with stunning effect by Gail Engert, the designer. At the National Trust Photographic Library there is a vast collection of images and Ed Gibbons, Robert Morris and the staff were of great help in locating and suggesting possible illustrations. In this context I am grateful to Francesca Scoones for access to the black and white illustrations in the archives and to Liz Drury and Pippa Thistlethwaite, who also kindly provided photographs and other illustrative material. My thanks to Oliver Garnett who alerted me to interesting articles and books. My thanks also to Pippa Pollard, assistant to Dr Nigel Seeley, for all her help. Pippa's speed and efficiency at doing tasks is truly formidable and her assistance has always been greatly appreciated.

Finally I want to thank my friends and family, who suffered through and eventually celebrated the labours of this book and who have by turns encouraged, cajoled and sympathised, but most of all were enduring in their support. My heartfelt thanks to Jane, Nathan and to my godson Alex Ching, Jane, Jim and Kirsty Pagan, Sharon, Paul, Nick and Elly Slade, Gillian Naylor, Chris Daley, Di Elliott, Michael Britnell, Tim and Catalina Flanagan, Yvette Queffurus, David Tanat-Jones and the Sisterhood, Cathy Caine, Tess Duncan, Anna Faulkener, Caroline Joffe and Vivienne Reid.

Introduction

Turning Night into Day

The days of my youth extend backwards to the dark ages, for I was born when the rushlight, the tallow dip or the solitary blaze of the hearth were the common means of indoor lighting. In the chambers of the great, the wax candle, or exceptionally a multiplicity of them, relieved the gloom on state occasions; but as a rule, the common people, wanting the inducement of indoor brightness such as we enjoy, went to bed after sunset.

Sir Joseph Wilson Swan (1828–1914)

Joseph Swan, who achieved fame with his development of the electric lamp, rose from humble beginnings. Born in Sunderland, the third of eight children, he was described as 'a self-made man, that is to say, he does not owe a very large debt of obligation to educational training'.[1] Swan's reminiscence of his childhood is a potent reminder that the 'dark ages', as far as domestic lighting is concerned, extended well into the nineteenth century. Any improvements in domestic lighting were not usually enjoyed by the majority until many years after a new technology had been introduced. Until the 1920s, therefore, it would have been unusual to live in a house exclusively lit by electricity, as the costs involved with this luxurious form of lighting ensured its use was confined to a small minority.

In times past an abundance of light in the home signalled prosperity and well-being; the technology employed, the quantity of light and the use of sumptuous fittings provided a medium through which the householder could display their conspicuous consumption. Lighting as an expression of wealth was as significant as that indicated by furniture, paintings, textiles and other precious objects. Conversely, homes with a paucity of light generally revealed the lack of means of the inhabitants. Even in the homes of the very rich, a spectacular display of illumination was reserved for those visitors who needed to be impressed, otherwise light was used sparingly. The light-fittings used in poorer homes were cheaply bought and when eventually replaced could be scrapped without a second thought; consequently relatively few early light-fittings have survived. Fine and costly light-fittings were another matter; silver candelabra and candlesticks continued to have a use, and wall-sconces and chandeliers could be adapted to changing technologies, thus ensuring their survival.

LEFT: *Night*, one of the Four Times of the Day painted by William Hogarth *c.*1736. This London street is full of disorder, lit overall by the full moon, the time when lunatics were out of their wits. The Salisbury Flying Coach has been overturned, a link boy blows his torch into a flame, two figures stare lugubriously at a lantern unaware that the contents of a chamberpot are about to land on their heads, and the barber illuminates his customer and shop window with the help of many candles.

The custom of retaining the precious, discarding the cheap and replacing with the up-to-date is usual. As a result all manner of once commonplace household objects have, over time, been abandoned to the rubbish dump. This pattern of behaviour has its consequences, and it is possible when visiting houses to come away with a distorted picture of historic lighting. Although we can compare the spectacular fittings in the grandest rooms of great houses with the serviceable and modest ones in servants' quarters, and the interiors of moderately wealthy homes with those of impoverished cottage dwellers, representations of domestic lighting are not always accurate. This has as much to do with the scarcity of humble fittings as with an incomplete understanding of how our ancestors once lit their homes.

Social and Economic Perspective

Percentages, averages, and all the hocus-pocus of statistics are only mists, fogs, curtains, and sleeping-draughts, except to the official mind; and we, the public, require something more gross – more palpable. The deaths from 'privation', 'deaths from want of breast-milk', 'deaths from neglect', 'deaths from cold' – or, in plain unsavoury words, from utter starvation increase every year. They were two hundred and twenty two [in London] in 1848, they were five hundred and sixteen, within the same area, in 1857, and this without questioning how many of the returns under the head of 'fever', ought to be classed as starvation.

'A New Chamber of Horrors', *All Year Round*, 2 March 1861

All artificial lighting came at a price, even the rushlights, dipped candles and crude oil lamps that could be made at home. For many poor families trying to live on subsistence wages, the fats and oils required for these humble lights were either too precious to spare from their meagre diets or too costly to buy. At the other end of the social spectrum lighting was used extravagantly. For example, at a subscription ball organised by White's Club at Burlington House in Piccadilly in 1814, which was attended by the Prince Regent, lighting costs amounted to £473 and this was in addition to £800 for hiring chandeliers from Hancock's lighting emporium.[2]

As this book aims to provide a comprehensive social and technological history of lighting the home through the ages, it is as well to have some idea of the relative wealth of the various sections of the population at different periods. In the mid-seventeenth century, hearth tax records show that 80 per cent of houses had one fireplace, 14 per cent had two and only 6 per cent had three or more. At this period, when most households depended heavily on firelight as their means of illumination, the hearth returns reveal that four-fifths of the population only had one fireplace. The size of the population of England and Wales at this time was around 5 million.

Social structure and annual incomes were considered by Gregory King, a pioneer statistician, in 1688. He calculated the number of noble families to be 160 and their average income £2,800. Other substantial landowners, with average incomes of £380, he estimated at 16,400. His estimates of larger sections of the population included the yeomanry, farmers and freeholders, numbering 330,000 with an annual average of £45; families of labourers and outservants at 364,000 with £15; and the largest group, comprising 500,000 families of cottagers and paupers, had an annual average income of £6 10s. From his survey, Gregory King reckoned that at least half the population of England was living below subsistence level.[3]

In the following century wealth and property continued to remain in the possession of a very small minority, the greatest landowning aristocratic families amounting only to perhaps three or four hundred. However in the nineteenth century, with the gradual inclusion of wealthy merchants, bankers and industrialists into their ranks, these numbers swelled and by 1900 some 30,000 families were listed in the Court Guide.[4] In earlier centuries prodigiously wealthy families had spent extravagantly on building and furnishing their homes, like Bess of Hardwick at Hardwick Hall and Elizabeth Dysart, Duchess of Lauderdale at Ham House. By the nineteenth century others had joined the ranks of conspicuous consumers – plutocrats like the Rothschild family at Waddesdon Manor and industrialists like Lord Armstrong at Cragside.

At the time of the first census in 1801 the population of England and Wales stood at over 8·8 million and in the course of the nineteenth century increased dramatically, so that by 1901 it had risen to 32·5 million.[5] This period also saw the rise and expansion of the middle classes. Traditionally the 'middling class' had included members of the professions and clergy and some who were making a good living in trade and commerce, but those in newer occupations were joining their ranks, from public administration, engineering and education. It has been estimated that those who could be termed middle-class amounted to about 15 per cent of the population in 1851 and 20 per cent by 1909. Middle-class is a vague term as it encompassed people with a broad range of incomes. In 1909 those with annual incomes above £700 were considered 'upper' middle-class whilst those with incomes below this but above £160 were in the mid- to lower range of the class.[6] But even so, some families with incomes below £160 who could afford a low-ranking domestic servant would also have considered themselves as middle-class. It has been suggested that membership of the middle class was not only a matter of income and occupation, but also 'more a question of style of life, of habits, tastes, values and aspirations which were quite distinct from those of the classes above and below them'.[7]

In earlier centuries it was the aristocracy who were the consumers of the most expensive forms of lighting, but in the nineteenth century well-to-do middle-class families were amongst the first to avail themselves of the latest lighting technologies. Although cheaper and more efficient forms of lighting became available to the working classes after the mid-nineteenth century, it remained a luxury for those on very low wages. The pitiful conditions of the multitude of rural and urban poor were closely scrutinised and condemned by social commentators and philanthropists who attempted to raise the consciences of the affluent and seek legislative solutions to the problems caused by low wages and appalling living conditions. These conditions and wages continued to be of concern into the twentieth century. It was estimated that nearly 8 million people were 'underhoused, underfed and insufficiently clothed', and living on incomes of less than 25s a week.[8] In 1905 an article in *Country Life* observed:

> For centuries the problem of lighting poor people's cottages has been unsolved. Light, as distinguished from mere warmth, or fires for cooking by, is a luxury. Many old-fashioned villagers always went to bed directly they had had their supper in the winter-time, in order to save the cost of a candle, and as there are, unfortunately, many very poor people in our villages now, it is not uncommon to see houses in which the families sit in absolute darkness, except for the glimmer of the fire, even though paraffin oil is cheap.[9]

Street Lighting

> When you attend your lady in a dark night, if she useth her coach, do not walk by the coach side, so as to tire and dirt yourself, but get up into your proper place, behind it, and so hold the flambeau sloping forward over the coach roof, and when it wants snuffing, dash it against the corners.
>
> Jonathan Swift, *Directions to Servants*, 1745

The cheapest and most evil-smelling fats and oils were used for lighting the streets but as the costs were only reluctantly borne by citizens, such lighting was not plentiful. In theory well-lit streets were desirable but long after the curfew had ceased to be enforced many town councils considered it injudicious to encourage the populace to roam at night. Generally those wanting a social life after dark or who needed to travel, particularly in country areas, arranged to do so on the nights of the full moon. In Birmingham in the late eighteenth century, the Lunar Society, a debating society that included Matthew Boulton and Josiah Wedgwood amongst its members, held monthly meetings to coincide with the full moon. Others who had no option but to travel on dark nights had to find their way as best they could, with or without the aid of lanterns. Parson Wood-forde noted in his diary in 1787 that, 'So dark was the lane that I fell down in the mud three times before I reached my gate much discomforted'. In towns, for a small fee, link boys with rigid torches of rope soaked in fat, resin or tar would guide pedestrians, sedan-chairs or carriages home.[10] This could prove hazardous, however, as link boys were often in league with footpads and thieves. At the beginning of the nineteenth century robberies were commonplace: the Prince Regent and his brother the Duke of York were robbed on Hay Hill near

Berkeley Square, and in Kensington 'it was customary on Sunday evenings to ring a bell at intervals, in order that the pleasure seekers from London might assemble in sufficient numbers to return in safety.[11]

Over the centuries there had been few pressures to improve lighting radically as that available was adequate to meet needs. However, gradual industrialisation during the eighteenth century created a demand for lighting of an illuminating quality that would enable cottage industries and manufactories to carry on production into and through the hours of darkness. This lighting, moreover, had to be efficient and reliable, requiring the minimum of maintenance. Subsequent developments in domestic lighting were a direct consequence of a society making the transition from being agriculturally based to one that was principally urban and industrialised. Throughout the nineteenth century people left the countryside in ever-increasing numbers to search for employment in towns. In 1851 the census revealed that 54 per cent of the population of England and Wales were urban dwellers; by 1911 this had increased to 79 per cent.[12]

For many of the poor who migrated to towns and cities, street lighting gave them their first opportunity to see new advances in lighting technology. After 1812 this was gas lighting and where streets were gaslit, these became safer. It was generally considered that 'every gas lamp was as good as a policeman', and in 1866 Richards observed that, 'Highway robberies in London at night are now very rare… The greatly improved illumination of the streets has tended to

'The Nemesis of Neglect', a cartoon from Punch, 29 September 1888, vividly portraying the horror of the Jack the Ripper murders in the ill-lit streets of London's East End.

The Pluto Hot-Water gas lamp, which could provide hot water at halfpence, from the *Journal of Gas Lighting*, 1897.

prevent crime'.[13] However, in the poorer areas of towns and cities streets remained unlit and this was reflected in crime rates. The Jack the Ripper murders in 1888 took place in dingy and unlit streets, courts and alleyways of Spitalfields and Whitechapel in the East End of London. Queen Victoria sent a telegram to the Prime Minister, Lord Salisbury, urging, 'This new ghastly murder shows the absolute necessity for some decided action. All the courts must be lit and our detectives improved'.[14]

Gas was found to offer benefits for street life over and above lighting. In 1894 Joseph Webb erected his Patent Sewer Gas Lamp in Birmingham. This extracted and burned off the smells, and claimed to destroy germs arising from the sewers. Equally inventive was a lamp made by the Pluto Hot-Water Syndicate that utilised waste heat. One was displayed at the Victoria Exhibition at Crystal Palace in 1897, and examples were later sited around London so that the public could draw a gallon of hot water by placing a halfpenny in a slot meter. It was estimated by the manufacturers that if one-tenth of the gas lamp posts in London were fitted with their apparatus, 'a total of 120 million gallons of boiling water per annum' could be supplied. A subsequent report indicated that this lamp post had truly become a vending machine, as 'The greatest development has been made in the base of the lamp; for the one in Leicester Square not only supplies hot water, but purveys light refreshments in the shape of beef tea, coffee, cocoa, sweets, &c. The novelty of the thing attracts good custom; but it is to be feared that, after the novelty has worn off, the competition of the street lamp with the existing cheap refreshment establishments will be short-lived'.[15]

The novelty presumably did wear off, as these lamps are not mentioned in any standard works on the history of and developments within the gas industry. Although electricity was introduced for street lighting in the last quarter of the nineteenth century, gas continued to be popular as it was cheaper and proved more reliable.[16] In comparison with the older illuminants gas and electricity were manufactured by complex processes, and as usage became more widespread, this led to large-scale industrial development. In the nineteenth century gasworks became prominent features of towns and cities and in the early twentieth century power stations began to dominate townscapes.

Domestic Lighting

The Greeks and Romans knew nearly as much about the lighting of interiors of houses and buildings as was known at the beginning of the 18th century.

Tyne and Wear County Council Museums Service,
The History of Domestic Lighting, n.d.

It is perhaps surprising to realise that no significant inventions were made to improve artificial lighting until the last decades of the eighteenth century. As

BEAUTIFUL GASHOLDERS

Designed by WALLACE COOP

THE GRAECO-ROMAN MODEL

THE BRIDES-CAKE MODEL - BASED ON THE INCOMPARABLE ALBERT MEMORIAL

THE ST PAULS MODEL: FOR SPHERICAL HOLDERS

THE ALBERT HALL MODEL

'Beautiful Gasholders', facetious but ingenious ideas from *The Gas World*, 3 August 1929.

In the late nineteenth century a gasworks was built on the estate at Cliveden, Buckinghamshire. To camouflage the retort house chimney, it was made to look like a tree trunk.

Joseph Swan makes clear, the solitary blaze of the hearth remained the primary source of lighting for many poor people who supplemented their firelight by frugal use of homemade rushlights, tallow dips and oil lamps. Although it has been considered that all forms of pre-electric lighting were little more than 'illuminated smells', the minority who could afford superior beeswax and spermaceti candles and oil were paying not only for greater illumination but also benefiting from decreased stench.

Gas lighting in the home was slowly adopted, as it was very expensive and only available in larger towns; those who lived in the country and wanted gas lighting had to build their own gasworks. An ardent advocate was Sydney Smith, who wrote in a letter to Lady Mary Bennett in 1821, 'What folly to have a diamond necklace or a Correggio, and not light your house with gas! The splendour and glory of Lambton Hall makes all other houses look mean. How pitiful to submit to a farthing-candle existence, when science puts intense gratification within your reach! Dear lady, spend all your fortune in a gas apparatus. Better to eat dry bread by the splendour of gas, than to dine on wild beef with wax candles'.[17] From the 1840s gas lighting grew in popularity and it was adopted enthusiastically by the middle classes. In general, gas was not favoured by the aristocracy, who were concerned about the damage caused to furniture and fittings from the by-products of gas lighting and the fact that its use had associations with trade.

The upper classes did not have the same reservations about electric lighting and for a number of years its high cost ensured exclusivity. Convenience, cleanliness and safety were the advantages claimed by electricity, although there were dangers with all forms of lighting, as the ensuing chapters will show. Accidents with rushlights, candles and oil lamps caused many domestic fires – not only in humble cottages with their timber and thatch, but also in great country houses such as Lanhydrock. For the general public, the invisibility of gas and electricity was both a source of wonderment and a cause for concern. Initially, relatively few completely understood how to use these forms of lighting safely. The fear of gas explosions and fires was very real, particularly if the householder explored for a leak with a naked flame, and although the dangers of electrical fires and electrocution were well known, consumers did not necessarily know how these occurred or could be prevented. At Hatfield House the Cecil family had recourse to throwing cushions at the ceiling in the Long Gallery to extinguish an electrical fire (see p.167).

By the late 1920s, good-quality domestic lighting, whether by gas or electricity, had become the norm, and in this process artificial lighting lost its significance as an indicator of wealth. At a conference in 1934 the Electrical Association for Women passed a resolution 'That the time has now come when electricity should be available at an economic rate to the homes of the working people'. In the same year the first stage of the National Grid became operational and eventually its network of power supply brought electricity into the homes of virtually the whole population. In the late 1930s, when the Modernist architect Ernö Goldfinger designed his home at 2 Willow Road, Hampstead, state-of-the-art electric lighting was installed. In post-war Britain, when the McCartney family moved into 20 Forthlin Road, Allerton in Liverpool they enjoyed a form of lighting that fifty years earlier had been considered only within the means of a privileged few.

The National Trust Collections

I have not bought things because they were rare or valuable, there are many things of every day use in the past, of small value, but of interest as records of various vanished handicrafts…This collection, not a museum, will be a valuable record in days to come.

Charles Paget Wade, 1945

The National Trust has in its care a wide range of properties that include humble dwellings of the poor, the former homes of yeomanry and gentry families and many grand houses that were once occupied by some of the wealthiest in the land. As a consequence the National Trust has outstanding examples of period lighting in its collections and these have been used extensively to describe and illustrate this history of domestic lighting. At the back of the book is a Gazetteer, listing examples of different lighting technologies and where light-fittings can be seen. For those who want to reinstate or renovate their own light-fittings, a list of specialist suppliers and restoration firms is also provided.

In the grandest of the National Trust houses, like Hardwick, Knole and Petworth, the light-fittings are sumptuous and of exceptional quality. By contrast, lighting that was cheap, commonplace and ordinary is much harder to find. Fortunately, early in the twentieth century some far-sighted individuals made conscious efforts to collect and preserve these humble light-fittings and other vernacular domestic objects that were fast disappearing. A notable collector was the garden designer Gertrude Jekyll and part of her collection of domestic bygones can now be seen in Oakhurst Cottage. The donor of Snowshill Manor, Charles Paget Wade, who 'scorned' electric lighting, had become concerned that hand-crafted objects were rapidly being replaced by machine-made products and he set about collecting early examples of rushlight-holders, oil lamps and lanterns, candlesticks and candle moulds. Another impressive collection of early domestic lighting and household objects is on display at Rufford Old Hall. These were assembled by Philip Ashcroft and presented to the National Trust in 1946. Rosalie Chichester, who lived at Arlington Court, was also an inveterate collector. Arlington is home to a remarkable and diverse collection of lighting, amongst which is an unsurpassed display of early pewter light-fittings and many examples of different types of oil lamps.

Although relatively few National Trust properties had gas lighting, some have remains of their original gasworks; for example at Chirk Castle. A number of houses retain their gas fittings and although most have been converted to electricity, at A la Ronde near Exmouth, and Sunnycroft in Wellington, working gas lights can still be seen. Acetylene gas lighting enjoyed a period of popularity with country-house owners around the turn of the nineteenth century and a complete installation that is perhaps unique in the United Kingdom can be seen at The Argory. Dating from the same period is an air-gas machine at Rufford Old Hall.

The National Trust is proud to have in its care the first house in the world to have been lit by hydroelectricity, Cragside. Lord Armstrong, who lived at Cragside, was a friend of Joseph Swan and it was there that Swan first installed his newly developed incandescent electric lamps in 1880. Today on the estate the

FAR LEFT: Cragside, Northumberland, was the first house in the world to be lit by hydroelectricity, using power generated from the lakes on the estate. Originally the electric lamps on the staircase were unshaded and suspended from the poles supported by the lions.

LEFT: When Philip Yorke handed his home, Erddig in Wrexham, to the National Trust in 1973, the drawing room was lit by candles in silver candlesticks and lamps lit by Calor gas, behind which he had placed silver salvers to reflect the light. His television was battery powered.

visitor can see machinery in the Ram and Power Houses, and in the house early electric lamps, accessories and light-fittings. A number of other properties also have early electricity installations and at Standen and Wightwick Manor, furnished and decorated with the work of Arts and Crafts Movement designers, the visitor will find many W. A. S. Benson light-fittings.

In the developed world, at the beginning of the twenty-first century, we have become accustomed to our homes being well lit. Only with the occasional power cut, when a source of alternative lighting is not immediately on hand, can we begin to experience how it might have felt for our ancestors to be without instantaneous and comforting light. This book will give some idea of that experience, and will show how lighting has played a fundamental role in so many areas of our domestic lives: turning night into day.

CHAPTER ONE

Fire and Firelight

The Dark Ages

It is horrible to have a cold nose and a burning hand; it is more horrible to have a burning nose and cold hands. Fried toes alone are small comfort so is one hot ear, yet it is not possible to be equally warm all around beside a fire.

Mrs Haweis, *The Art of Decoration*, 1881

Since prehistoric times, the most rudimentary form of domestic lighting was that provided by the hearth fire, and in some societies today, when the sun has set, the fire is the only source of light. In the nineteenth century for some of the poorest families in Great Britain the fire continued to be their primary source of interior lighting. Moreover, until the invention of the electric lamp late in the century, all lighting technologies relied on the flame to provide light, and for householders the risk of fire represented a constant danger.

The Central Hearth

Warming and welcoming, the hearth fire has for thousands of years provided mankind with security and comfort. By the early Middle Ages the centrally placed hearth had become firmly established as the hub around which the life of the household revolved; the hearth was the home and the two became inextricably entwined. The fire was lit by anything that could be gathered locally, and where wood, furze or peat were not in plentiful supply, animal dung had to suffice for some. The wealthier, however, had their own supplies. For example, on the land above Braithwaite Hall in North Yorkshire there was once a forest that supplied firewood to Middleham Castle. The less affluent colleges of the University of Cambridge purchased large amounts of sedge, gathered at Wicken Fen and brought by river to be unloaded in bundles at the quay opposite Magdalene College. Prosperous householders also had the means to ensure that the wood for their fires was kept dry and seasoned, whereas the peasantry generally had to make do with green and poor-quality fuels that produced copious amounts of smoke.

LEFT: Detail of the Housekeeper's Parlour in the Apprentice House at Styal Mill, Cheshire. The fire forms the central focus of the room, with its fire-irons, bellows and the kettle on a trivet. Tapers on the mantelshelf were used to light candles and oil lamps.

The hearth fire would rarely be allowed to go out and, according to tradition, in some homes fires remained lit for generations. At Townend and Hill Top, both sixteenth-century yeoman farmers' houses in Cumbria, the main living-areas where the fires were always kept burning were called Fire Rooms. Refuelling, nurturing and tending a fire required careful management and a person careless enough to allow a fire to burn out might not only have a long walk to neighbours to 'borrow a fire' but also face the difficulty of keeping a flame going on the journey back.

A number of medieval properties in the care of the National Trust were lit by central hearth fires. Alfriston Clergy House is a mid-fourteenth-century thatched hall-house with a restored central hearth in the Hall. The soot-blackened roof timbers are still visible and show where the smoke escaped through the thatch. In addition, although now glazed, the original shuttered or cloth-covered windows would have provided ventilation and escape routes for the smoke. At Marker's Cottage, a mid-fifteenth-century house of thatch and cob at Broadclyst in Devon, although the central hearth was replaced by a wall fireplace c.1530, the blackened thatch and roof timbers remain. It was by no means uncommon for sparks from fires to set ablaze roof timbers and thatch, and in this respect Alfriston Clergy House and Marker's Cottage are rare survivors.

At Tatton Old Hall the fire in the central hearth continues to be lit. As the smoke makes its way out through the timbers and roof slates, the smell of woodsmoke and thick atmosphere are pungent reminders of the centuries when

The central hearth in the medieval Old Hall at Tatton Park, Cheshire.

homes without chimneys were perpetually smoke-filled. At Ightham Mote, where there is no longer a central hearth, evidence has been found in the roof of the Great Hall of smoke louvres operated by a peg-and-cord arrangement, a sophisticated device which aided ventilation and helped to dispel the smoke.

Although central hearths became rarer as the sixteenth century progressed, their use persisted in isolated places. In the 1820s James Loch, a Member of Parliament, noted the conditions of hovels in Sunderland:

> Their huts dipped down with the slope of the ground; they were built of turf dug from the most valuable parts of the mountain sides and roofed with turves supported on the branches of trees. The inhabitants shared a roof with pigs and poultry and used the same door. The fire was set in the middle of the earth floor and its smoke allowed to circulate throughout the hut for the purpose of conveying heat. The effect was to cover everything with a glossy black soot, and to produce the most evident injury to the appearance and eyesight of those most exposed to its influence.[1]

In 1904, Gertrude Jekyll wrote of homes that could even then be seen in the Orkney and Shetland Islands with central hearths. The years of accretion of soot had led to these dwellings being called 'black houses'.

In the sixteenth century concern was expressed about the serious depletion of forests, particularly as oak, ash and beech were needed for shipbuilding. As a consequence the populace was encouraged to use coal for fires, and in 1698 a foreign visitor noted, 'None but people of the first quality burn wood in London'. Although the burning of coal had to be accepted, then, as today, a blazing log fire was considered infinitely preferable.

The Development of the Fireplace

> Now we have many chimnies, and yet our tenderlings complaine of rheumes, catarrhs and poses... For as the smoke of those daies was supposed to be a sufficient hardening of the timber of the houses, so it was reputed to be far better medicine to keep the good man and his family.

> William Harrison, *Description of Britain*, in R. Holinshed, *Chronicles of England*, 1577

The wall fireplace was introduced after the Norman Conquest. Initially these fireplaces were constructed with rudimentary chimneys; chimneys rising clear of the roof were innovations of the Tudor period. Early wall fireplaces remain in a number of National Trust houses. The Tudor Merchant's House in Tenby, a late fifteenth-century town house with a massive external chimney stack, has a large open hearth. On a more modest scale is the open fireplace at Oakhurst Cottage at Hambledon, a humble home to countless generations of agricultural workers.

Many country houses have fireplaces emblazoned with ancestral coats of arms to proclaim the family's power and status. At Montacute the chimneypiece in

the Dining Room bears the motto *Pro aris et focis* (for homes and hearths). At Knole the great carved chimneypiece in the Ballroom, formerly the Great Chamber, is made of alabaster and white, grey and black marbles, and displays Thomas Sackville, 1st Earl of Dorset's Star and Garter together with exquisite and intricately sculpted garlands of flowers and musical instruments. It was

Inglenook fireplaces for the rich and poor.

FAR LEFT: Sir William Armstrong is depicted *c.*1880 by Henry Hetherington Emerson sitting in comfort in the dining-room inglenook at Cragside. The inscription over the fireplace reads 'East or West Hame's Best'.

LEFT: An illustration from Gertrude Jekyll's *Old English Household Life* published in 1925, showing how the inglenook in a late nineteenth-century Surrey cottage continued to provide a cosy refuge of warmth and light for the poor.

crafted by Cornelius Cure, Master Mason to the Crown, who in 1607 was paid £26 10s for his work. In homes of the yeomanry the shelf over the hearth opening provided a convenient place to show prized possessions, including gleaming brass candlesticks, like the superb collection of the Roberts family, tenant farmers at Ty'n-y-Coed Uchaf at Penmachno.

As domestic technology improved the fire was required less for heating, cooking and lighting and, with the growing use of coal, the hearth became enclosed and the fireplace reduced in size. Nevertheless, it remained the focal point in rooms, and presented an opportunity for designers to display further their talents. At Kedleston Hall, in the mid-eighteenth century, the fireplaces, grates and fenders were designed by Robert Adam to harmonise with and complement his overall interior design and decoration.

The inglenook fireplace, which provided a cosy refuge from draughts, was rediscovered towards the end of the nineteenth century, particularly by designers and architects associated with the Arts and Crafts Movement. Many inglenook fireplaces created in the period are romanticised evocations of a bygone age and some interpretations of this vernacular style are frankly architectural conceits. The Drawing Room at Cragside is dominated by a flamboyantly carved marble chimneypiece. Designed by W. R. Lethaby, an influential member of the Arts and Crafts Movement, it incorporates a luxurious and spacious inglenook. At Wightwick Manor Edward Ould likewise designed a capacious inglenook in the Great Parlour. During the same period for many poor country families the inglenook fireplace continued to provide a haven of warmth and light.

Firelight Fittings

I have seen the King suddenly come in thither in a mask, with a dozen of other maskers, all in garments like shepherds, made of fine cloth of gold and fine crimson satin paned, and caps of the same, with visors of good proportion of visnomy; their hairs and beards either of fine gold wire, or else of silver, and some being of black silk; having sixteen torch bearers, besides their drums, and other persons attending upon them, with visors, and all clothed in satin of the same colours.

From *The Life of Cardinal Wolsey by his Gentlemen Usher George Cavendish* 1500–c.1561 [2]

When in the 1520s Henry VIII and his courtiers made their dazzling entrance at the Cardinal's banquet at Hampton Court, they were accompanied by torch-bearers. Torches, hand-held or fixed to walls and supported in iron rings, would have been used in many castles and large houses from the Middle Ages onwards. Although no tangible evidence remains of torch rings in castles like Bodiam, Chirk or Tattershall, it is not hard to imagine flaming wall-torches being used to light the great halls and passageways. Likewise we can envisage torch-bearers in attendance at banquets at Hardwick Hall and Knole. Resinous pine which sparked and exuded pitch was unsuitable for hearth fires but proved ideal for torches. Other types of flambeaux were made from tow or rags dipped in any flammable substance. In the fireplace at Oakhurst Cottage is a wrought-iron floor standard that probably dates from the eighteenth century. It has a candle socket and an attachment with circular jaws which was used to hold a splint of

A sixteenth-century torchlight procession. In George Cavendish's *Life of Wolsey*, he described just such a scene at Hampton Court: '[some noblemen] were then brought in with an escort of twenty torches and drums and fifes, and marched towards Wolsey in his chair of state and gravely saluted him'.

Electric wall-lights, in the
form of torches, in the
Entrance Hall at Tatton Park.

resinous pine, also known as candle-fir(e). These fittings are called peermen or puirmen, a corruption of 'poor men', a reminder of the vagrant tramps who eked out a living by cutting and selling the wood splints.[3]

To give an impression of age to interiors, or to have fittings that harmonised with genuinely antique interiors, many country-house owners selected their new light-fittings in 'historical' styles. In Caesars' Hall at Kedleston 'medieval'-style, early twentieth-century wrought-iron electric torches are fixed to the walls. The torches are fitted with moulded glass shades shaped to look like flames, a feature of many electric light-fittings from *c.*1910 until the 1930s. Perhaps more contrived and ostentatious is the pair of large gilt metal electric wall-lights, each comprising a bundle of five torches, to be seen in the Entrance Hall at Tatton Park.

Kingston Lacy is the repository of a number of very unusual mid-nineteenth-century Biancone marble light-fixtures. In the Inner Hall, for example, is a pair of torches complete with carved torch rings and, although the torch ends are hollow, it is highly unlikely they were ever used to hold flaming torches or fire-brands. The torches are possibly the work of Salesio Pegrassi, who carved other marble fittings in the house based on designs of two forms of classical Roman candelabra. In affluent Roman homes small candelabra served as supports for oil lamps, but to illuminate civic buildings larger candelabra were used as torchères with flammable material filling their hollowed-out tops. On the newel post on the half-landing of the Marble Staircase at Kingston Lacy is an elaborately carved torchère, and on the balustrade above are copies of smaller Roman candelabra. As with the fittings in the Inner Hall, it is unlikely these were ever used to provide light. The candelabra were carved by Pegrassi from sketches by William Bankes, who inherited Kingston Lacy in 1834, but from 1841 until his death in 1855 spent his life in Italy where he had fled to escape prosecution. During this period Bankes commissioned many carved marble pieces and his patronage was such that he was spoken of as 'this liberal Englishman who instead of trafficking in the immortal old works of art of Italy trains and encourages and commissions rising young artists'.[4]

Torchères of an antique design that were used to provide light can still be seen on the *piano nobile* loggia flanking the main entrance to Basildon Park. The pair of huge bronze torchères are mounted on tripod pedestals decorated with classical bas reliefs, thought to have been placed there by James Morrison MP, shortly after he purchased the house in 1840.[5] The torchères were reputedly fuelled with colza oil (see pp.102 ff.) and would have appeared as welcoming beacons of light to visitors finding their way across the park to the house at night.

Nineteenth-century candelabra carved in the Roman style by Pegrassi on the balustrade of the Marble Staircase at Kingston Lacy, Dorset.

The iron basket-shaped cresset was another type of early firelight fitting. When used in the home, cressets were generally in a fixed position but another form, mainly used out doors, was carried aloft on poles and was probably the prototype of the enclosed lantern. Placed around the walls in the Entrance Hall at Castle Drogo are six iron cressets mounted on poles. These, however, are electric standard lamps, early twentieth-century interpretations of an historical fitting. Cressets were also fashioned from stone or made of earthenware, and could be fuelled by oil. In the Kitchen Courtyard at Cotehele are two hexagonal stone receptacles dating from the late medieval period. They may possibly be rare forms of local cressets, though their exact use continues to be the subject of academic debate.

ABOVE: Bronze torchères dating from the 1840s, standing on the entrance loggia at Basildon Park, Berkshire. Probably fuelled by colza oil, they would have welcomed visitors making their way across the park.

LEFT: The Entrance Hall at Castle Drogo, in Devon, where Edwin Lutyens placed a series of iron cressets that are in fact electric standard lamps. This photograph shows the two flanking the fireplace.

Firelight Accessories

From at least Norman times, when the curfew bell rang all citizens were expected to extinguish any lights and cover their fires. The device for doing this without causing the fire completely to extinguish was the aptly named *couvre-feu* and one of an early date is to be seen in the Dining Room fireplace at East Riddlesden Hall. Although careful fanning or blowing on the glowing embers did help to revive the flame in the morning, implements were invented to encourage life back into seemingly lifeless fires. At Snowshill Manor there is a fine collection of hand- and mechanical bellows and, in the great fireplace in 'Dragon', a rare blowing-tube. The fact that so many timber and leather hand-bellows survive is a testament to how useful they have proved in everyday life.

When a fire did go out or was required elsewhere, firepans could carry embers from hearth to hearth or to braziers. Different fuels required different fireside accessories; brand tongs and faggot forks were necessary implements for wood-burning fires, whereas shovels and pokers were essential for coal fires. In the

A copper *couvre-feu*, probably dating from the seventeenth century, amongst the fireplace furnishings at East Riddlesden Hall, Yorkshire.

Brown Drawing Room at Blickling Hall is a large and elaborately wrought iron Gentleman's Fireside Companion, from which accessories were hung. The Companion dates from the late seventeenth century and is believed to have been made in south Germany or Switzerland.

Some fire accessories are of such high quality and craftsmanship that it is hard to imagine they were ever used. At Ham House there are late seventeenth-century silver mounted bellows and a silver firepan bearing the cipher of the Duke and Duchess of Lauderdale. The Sackvilles of Knole also exhibited their conspicuous consumption with silver andirons. The pair in the Reynolds Room have large finials in the shape of putti with a bellows and ash shovel.[6] Andirons or firedogs were used for supporting logs, but when made of luxurious materials they generally remained decorative and for practical use smaller, plain andirons, known as creepers, were placed inside the hearth.

Striking a Light

I determined to sit up all night...about two o'clock in the morning I inadvertently snuffed out my candle, and as my fire...was long before black and cold, I was in a great dilemma how to proceed. Downstairs did I softly and silently step to the kitchen. But, alas, there was as little fire there as upon the icy mountains of Greenland. With a tinder box is a light struck every morning to kindle the fire, which is not put out at night. But this tinder box I could not see, nor knew where to find. I was now filled with gloomy ideas of the terrors of the night. I was also apprehensive that my landlord, who always keeps a pair of loaded pistols by him, might fire at me as a thief. I went up to my room, sat quietly until I heard a watchman calling out 'past three o'clock'. I then called out to him to knock at the door of the house where I lodged. He did so, and I opened up to him and got my candle relumed without danger.

James Boswell, *London Journey*, 1762–3

In the days before safety matches became cheap and plentiful, getting a light could be fraught with difficulties. For many the need to have a light readily available was enough to encourage them to have a fire always burning in the hearth, so that a brand could be pulled from the flames. In enclosed grates, where coal fires were used, spills and tapers were usually kept to hand on the mantel shelf. When a fire was required, particularly when travelling away from home, a tinderbox could provide a light, though skill, care and attention were needed to do this quickly and easily, as many found out to their cost: 'You cannot get blood out of a stone, but the stone can easily have blood out of you. On a cold, dark frosty morning when the hands are chapped, frozen and insensible, you may chance to strike the flint against your knuckles for some considerable time without discovering your mistake.' The anonymous author of this booklet, writing in

1832, goes on to say, 'there are very few house-men, or house-maids, who can succeed in striking a light in less than three minutes'.[7] Making a fire by striking together pyrites and flint was known in ancient times and the tinderbox, which was manufactured in increasing numbers during the eighteenth century, was a direct development from this early method. The popular and relatively inexpensive sheet-iron canister tinderbox, which usually had a candle socket fixed to the lid, held the tinder, a steel, a piece of flint and a damper. Examples of canister tinderboxes can be seen at various National Trust houses, including Cotehele, Townend, Oakhurst Cottage and Buckland Abbey. The tinder was usually made from charred cloth which could be produced at home; an expensive alternative was amadou prepared from fungus.

Sophisticated mechanised forms of tinderboxes that took the knuckle-scraping pain out of getting a light were the commensurately more expensive strike-a-lights. Many of these bear similarities in construction and appearance to flintlock pistols. Some strike-a-lights were fitted with small candle sockets like the one in a display case in the Morning Room at Arlington Court. This 'cottage' type of tinder lighter dates from the end of the eighteenth century and was reputed to have come from Nelson's flagship HMS *Victory*. Wealthier individuals could afford highly decorated strike-a-lights with superior mechanisms. An ornately engraved brass box which conceals a strike-a-light and also incorporates a clock is to be found in 'Occidens' at Snowshill Manor.

In the late eighteenth and early nineteenth centuries other devices for obtaining a light were being developed, for example fire pistons and brimstone matches. But it was the safety match that was finally to make tinderboxes and strike-a-lights redundant by the mid-nineteenth century. In *c.*1890 the *National Encyclopaedia* described safety matches in the following terms: 'These useful articles for obtaining instantaneous fire and light, and which seem such an indispensable adjunct of civilisation, are of very recent introduction.'

The first practical wooden friction match had been invented in 1826 by John Walker, a Stockton-on-Tees chemist. Seven years later the 'lucifer' phosphorous match was introduced, though the fumes given off in the production process caused a serious and painful industrial disease, 'phossy jaw', which could only be prevented by good ventilation and cleanliness. These matches also had other serious disadvantages: they easily ignited and were often thought to be the cause of dangerous and fatal fires. The first commercial production in England of the safety match began in 1855 by Bryant & May. Other types of matches, vestas, made of wax, also came into common use and in 1881 the firm of Messrs Bell & Black were producing at least 80 million wax vestas a day. The name derives from Vesta, the Roman goddess of the hearth, whose temple was lit by a perpetual flame. Therefore, by implication, these matches would not easily go out. A box of Palmer & Son wax vestas can be seen in the Yellow Bedroom at Felbrigg Hall, and in the Library at Wallington is a box of Royal Wax Vestas. In 1886 the match trade in the United Kingdom totalled £1,500,000, representing daily production of 300 million matches.

LEFT: Tin sheet canister tinderbox (right) and an iron wax-jack, in the Firehouse at Townend, Cumbria.

Fire-fighting and Prevention

1. Be cautious how you use matches and candles. On no account throw a
   match lighted or unlighted on the floor. See that they are quite extinguished before leaving a room.
2. Mind the wind does not blow a curtain over a candle, and that all fire
   guards are properly on the grate.
3. Do not leave any wood, paper, shavings, rags &c. where a fire, or candle
   can possibly set them alight.
4. Report any unusual smoke, or smell of fire to the Butler or Housekeeper.

Precautions against Fire,
late nineteenth-century instructions to staff at Lyme Park

National statistics in 1888 revealed that out of every 1,000 fires, 111 were caused
by the upsetting of an oil lamp or candle, 98 by candle flames, 70 by defective or
foul flues, 34 by children playing with fire or 'lucifers' and 26 by smouldering hot
ashes. A number of National Trust houses have been badly damaged by fire;
Cliveden has twice been completely rebuilt following fires. The first, in 1795, was
caused when 'a careless servant knocked over a candle when turning a bed down'.
On the second occasion, in 1849, Queen Victoria, who was staying at Windsor,
saw the smoke and sent fire engines from the castle. In the twentieth century
several properties suffered serious fires. The most recent broke out at Uppark in
1989, but now, after years of painstaking restoration work, the house has been
returned to its former glory.

The National Trust has a formidable range of fire engines and fire-fighting
equipment in its care. Very early fire appliances, dating from the eighteenth
century, are to be found at, for instance, Felbrigg Hall, where the hand-pump fire
engine was probably obtained after an explosion in the Firework Shop in 1755,
and at Calke Abbey, where the engine has its own transporting wagon fitted
with a windlass to haul it up ramps. Not surprisingly, fire protection was expensive: at Ham House, the 6th Earl of Dysart paid £12 for a hand-pump fire engine
in 1756.

When a fire went out of control in the homes of the poor they had only their
neighbours to help them, but the owners of substantial properties made their
own provisions which, for some, included establishing their own fire brigades.
At the end of the nineteenth century the London firm of Merryweather & Sons
Ltd did a brisk business in supplying country-house owners with fire-fighting
equipment and a number of their fire engines, hoses and other apparatus can be
seen in National Trust houses. In 1881 at Lanhydrock House, a fire that started
when a kitchen chimney caught alight raged through the seventeenth-century
house, destroying all but the North Wing, which was saved by the use of dyna-
mite to create a firebreak. When the house was rebuilt four years later, fireproof
materials were used in the construction. Throughout the house and outside are
Merryweather fire hydrants fed from a hill-top reservoir three miles distant. An

ingenious system was devised by Merryweather's to supply water to St Michael's Mount, a castle built on the top of a rocky island that can only be reached by a causeway at low tide. Merryweather's supplied an oil engine to drive a pump that raised water to feed four hydrants and large tanks placed on the castle roof which, in the event of fire, could discharge water at the rate of one ton a minute. The engine was also used to drive a lift to bring up baggage and stores from the castle's quay.

Visitors to country houses will have noticed rows of leather fire buckets, some painted with family crests, which can usually be found in the corridors leading from domestic offices. Some of the earliest are at Ham House, where in the West Passage hang rows of pitched leather fire buckets, possibly dating from the seventeenth century.[8] For the use of those caught in the upper stories of burning buildings, patent safety ropes and ladders were installed. In the Dressing Room at Gawthorpe Hall a Davy rope-and-pulley fire escape is fixed to the window. At Penrhyn Castle Davy equipment was kept in the upstairs rooms under the floor-boards, and a mechanism on the Tower for an escape ladder. Still ready and waiting to assist those trapped on the top floors of flaming buildings are large pairs of extending ladders on wagons at Calke Abbey and Lyme Park. Ladders similar to these were probably employed to rescue the elderly Lady Robartes from an upstairs window at Lanhydrock in 1881. Sadly, she never recovered, and died from shock a few days later.

Detail from *The Country Gentleman's Catalogue* of 1894, showing fire escapes for those trapped on upper floors.

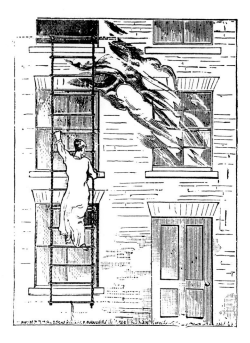

CHAPTER TWO

Rushlights and Tallows
The Light of the Poor

My grandmother, who lived to be pretty nearly ninety, never, I believe, burnt a candle in her life. I know that I never saw one there, and she, in a great measure, brought me up. . . . The rushes are carried about by hand; but to sit by, to work by or to go to bed by, they are fixed in stands made for that purpose. . . . These have an iron part something like a pair of pliers to hold the rush, which is shifted forward as it burns. These rushes give a better light than a common dip candle and they cost next to nothing. If reading be your taste you may read. . . as well by rushlight as you can by the light of taxed candles.

William Cobbett, *Cottage Economy*, 1822

Rushlights

Rushlights are an ancient form of domestic lighting, thought to have been in use in Britain before the Roman conquest. During the Middle Ages, while the wealthiest families made use of both rushlights and candles, in the homes of the yeomanry and peasantry it was rushlight that provided lighting additional to that of the hearth fire. Although rushlights would not have looked out of place even in the grandest homes in the seventeenth century, by the mid-eighteenth century their use was becoming confined to the servants' quarters. Rushlights had come to be regarded as the poor man's candle because they were easy to make and cheap to buy and, significantly, they were not taxed. According to Gilbert White, who described the preparation of rushlights in great detail in *The Natural History of Selborne*, published in 1788, 'a pound and a half of rushes will supply a family all year long'. White calculated that there were approximately 1,600 dry rushes to the pound and that 'a good rush, which measured in length two feet four inches and a half. . . burned only three minutes short of an hour'.

Rushlights remained in common use well into the nineteenth century and, in some isolated rural areas, into the twentieth century. In 1880 statistical information from records revealed that 'There is abundant evidence that the antiquated rushlight is still an article of domestic use. Messrs. Haynes supply between three and four tons annually, principally to the University towns.'[1]

LEFT: A rushlight holder and horn lantern, probably late eighteenth century, in the Firehouse at Townend, Cumbria.

Two types of rushes were suitable for making rushlights: the common rush, *Juncus conglomeratus*; and the soft rush, *Juncus effusus*, which grew almost everywhere in Britain. Rushes were gathered while still green in late summer by women, children and the elderly and would then be prepared for use during the long nights of winter. The freshly gathered rushes were soaked in water to prevent drying and shrinkage. With the exception of one strip of the outer skin, needed to support the exposed pith, the peeled rushes were left outside to bleach. They were then drawn through melted animal fat which, in poor country areas, was the scummings from the bacon pot, before finally being left out again to dry on pieces of bark.

Although Gilbert White was critical of poor families who bought 'expensive' candles in preference to making their own rushlights, William Cobbett, writing some years later, noted, 'Candles certainly were not much used in English Labourers' dwellings in the days when they had meat dinners and Sunday coats'. Bacon was a staple part of the diet for rural families, particularly as many kept a pig. However, in times of agricultural depression the diet consisted mainly of bread and vegetables, with any meat mostly being allocated to the working men of the household. In circumstances such as these there was no surplus fat to make rushlights and if extra light was required, beyond that provided by the fire, then a cheap tallow candle could be bought from travelling hawkers or the local chandler. Lighting was used not so much for reading, as many people were illiterate, as to help illuminate craftwork to supplement the family income and for the other household tasks that needed a close light.

Rushlights, held firmly at an angle in jaw-like holders, needed to be pulled forward as they burned down, causing a potential hazard from falling glowing pith-ends igniting the rushes strewn over floors. Although a rushlight only provided a small source of light it was, nonetheless, considered to be adequate, if not brilliant, with a clear and steady flame. Cobbett, who was mostly brought up by rushlight, did not find that he saw 'less clearly than other people'. If additional light was needed, the rushlight could be lit at both ends, and it is from this practice that the expression 'burning the candle at both ends' originated.

RUSHLIGHT FITTINGS

The rushlight-holder, or rushnip, bears similarities in design to the peerman described in Chapter One. Rushlight-holders stood on a table or floor, or could be suspended from beams. Most had a counterweight or a spring that kept the rushlight firmly in its jaws, while superior-quality holders were made with candle sockets. The holders that have survived are generally made of cast or wrought iron and the slight differences in the design of these plain and functional objects are accounted for by local, regional and national variations. Many were made by local blacksmiths and, although not expensive, were probably beyond the means of the very poor, who could easily split a stick to hold any rushlights they might want to use. Most of the examples of iron rushlight fittings in National Trust collections date from the late eighteenth and early nineteenth centuries.

Some of the most basic table rushlight-holders were spiked into crudely fashioned blocks of wood. Others, which were more expensive to buy, had turned wood bases. A good collection of both these types can be seen at Snowshill Manor.[2] Other types of holders were made complete with iron tripod bases, and where decoration was possible on such a lean and functional object, it is on the holder support and counterweight. Floor-standing rushlight-holders required more iron and were therefore an expensive item. These holders also generally had greater decorative refinements and, as befits a better-quality fitting, many were made with candle sockets and were height-adjustable. There is an example of this type in the Forge at Ardress House, and others can be seen at Snowshill Manor. Pendant holders that were suspended from beams are now very rare. However, one with a rushlight still held in its jaws and which is combined with a candle socket is hanging over the large open fireplace in the Hall at Moseley Old Hall, where visitors can also see a small display showing the stages of rushlight preparation.

The Entrance Hall, the main room at Moseley Old Hall, Staffordshire, which served as both kitchen and dining room. Hanging over the seventeenth-century fireplace is an iron rushlight pendant combined with a candle socket. On the table is a pair of open twist, brass candlesticks.

RUSHLIGHT ACCESSORIES

Long-handled iron grissets with large boat-shaped pans, placed over the hearth fire, were used for melting the fat through which the rushes were drawn. In the homes of all but the poorest, grissets were once common domestic objects, though now rare.[3] To have rushlights accessible and ready to hand, Cobbett suggested that the bark on which they had been dried could be hung from a wall with a couple of leather straps and used as a holder. Families could also buy or make their own long, coffin-shaped, timber rushlight boxes, like those at Oakhurst Cottage and Rufford Old Hall.

Tallow Candles

A tallow candle, to be good, must be half Sheep's Tallow and half Cow's; that of hoggs makes 'em gutter, give an ill smell, and a thick black smoak.

Anon, eighteenth century

Candles made from beeswax and tallow are thought to have been introduced into Britain by the Romans. Beeswax candles were a luxury and for centuries their use was confined to a very small and select segment of the population, who are considered in Chapter Three. Tallow is made from animal fat and throughout the Middle Ages and beyond, sheep and sheep products underpinned the English economy. In 1688 Gregory King estimated that there were 12 million sheep, 4·5 million cattle and 2 million pigs.[4] Theoretically at least, there was tallow aplenty to satisfy the growing demand for candles from the yeomanry, gentry and aristocracy. Nonetheless tallow was required by a number of trades, most notably the soapmakers, who maintained bitter disputes with the tallow chandlers over their control of the supply. From the mid-sixteenth century onwards tallow was imported in increasingly large quantities from Russia and the Baltic countries, and in the nineteenth century from Australia, where there was a large surplus of sheep and cattle.

The making of tallow candles was first mentioned as a craft in England in 1283 and by 1390 was ranked with the other great 'misteries', or crafts, in the City of London. The tallow chandlers were granted their Royal Charter in 1462 by Edward IV and their present Hall, which was rebuilt in 1672 following the Great Fire of London, stands on the same site in Dowgate Hill, now neighbouring Cannon Street Station, that it has occupied since 1476. The tallow chandlers satisfied the demands of a different market from that of the wax chandlers and the two Worshipful Companies kept a detached, if not always harmonious, distance from each other. The tallow chandlers acted as the regulator of the trade firstly within, and later outside, the boundaries of the City, and they determined the price at which tallow candles could be sold. The Company was empowered to exercise quality control and had the right to fine, search for and destroy underweight and adulterated candles. Over the centuries these powers were enforced vigorously. But a turning-point came in 1709 when candles were destroyed at a shop in 'Pick a Dilley' and the Company lost the subsequent court case brought by the aggrieved vendor. As the Company lost its authority and went into decline, another enforcer, the Customs and Excise man, was to step into the breach and his far-reaching powers were to affect everyone making, selling and buying candles.

In 1709 a tax was introduced on all English and imported candles, the rate on tallow being one halfpenny a pound and on wax fourpence a pound. These amounts were doubled two years later. Throughout the Georgian period the role of the Customs and Excise officers was strengthened; they were given extensive search powers and forfeiture and fines were imposed on all who had not paid duty. As the tax was frequently evaded, all candle-making premises, including private properties where candles were made for their own consumption, were registered and checked regularly. Despite taxation, in 1711 31·4 million lbs of tallow candles were subject to duty; by the end of the century this had doubled and in 1830 the amount had increased to 109·4 million lbs.[5] This unpopular tax ceased in 1831 and although, as a result, there was a considerable loss of revenue for the government, it also meant that more people could afford to use candles to light their homes.

CANDLE-MAKING

The scenery of a boiling down establishment is a dreadful sight, large herds of noble looking animals are driven into the slaughtering shed, there they are 'pithed' by the dozen, drawn up, skinned, and chopped into chunks ready for the boilers; and there may be seen little pyramids of quivering flesh.

Henry Melville, *Australia*, 1851

During the rendering process, the fat collected at the top was skimmed off and the leftover fibrous matter made into greaves or tallow cakes to be fed to animals, including 'the greater part of the ducks that are reared in the Vale of Aylesbury'.[6] Until the nineteenth century, the remaining grease was not only used for making candles but also represented an important ingredient in soap manufacture. The finest and whitest tallow came from the first skimming, subsequent skims produced tallow with a yellowish tinge and the coarsest was obtained by squeezing the remaining bones and flesh in presses.

Tallow candles were made either by hand-dipping or by pouring the molten fat into moulds. The most ancient method was repeatedly to dip a wick of peeled rush into melted fat to produce a rush candle. Others were made with wicks from cotton rovings, twisted hemp or flax which were suspended from broaches or rods. The most evil-smelling dip candles were made from pig fat, which produced copious amounts of thick black smoke. In 1833 at Penrhyn Castle the contents of the Housekeeper's Store included 2lbs of rush candles and 10lbs of dip candles and these would have been used by the household staff.[7]

To give schoolchildren an experience of one of the disgusting smells that were once part of everyday life, tallow candles are still lit occasionally at George Stephenson's Birthplace, Wylam. In 1781 Stephenson was born in the one room occupied by his parents and four brothers and sisters in a small, four-roomed tenement building. The room originally had unplastered walls, an earth floor, unglazed shuttered windows and outside the back door was the communal cesspit. In this situation, should the Stephensons ever have afforded a tallow dip its smell would hardly have been noticed. The local colliery, where Stephenson's father worked as a fireman, rented out the rooms to its workers and, in comparison to many, these families would have considered themselves well housed.

From at least 1360, better-quality tallow candles were made in moulds. This method had the advantage of uniform-sized candles that could more easily fit into candle sockets. Pewter was one of the earliest materials used for making candle moulds, but examples of these are now very rare. More frequently seen are moulds made from sheet iron that date from the eighteenth and nineteenth centuries. Candle moulds for domestic use generally comprised between two and six elements, and some were made with carrying-handles. A pewter six-element mould with a carrying-handle is in 'Dragon' at Snowshill Manor, a four-element tin sheet mould is in the Kitchen at Aberconwy House, and two single moulds can be seen at Arlington Court. Larger houses that used tallow rendered from the herds raised on their own estates probably used multi-element moulds which were contained in a timber frame, and one of these is shown in 'Mizzen', at Snowshill Manor.

Welsh ladies making candles by dipping broaches into melted fat. This photograph was taken in 1901 at Bank Farm, Abergorlech in Carmarthenshire.

At Castle Coole the Tallow House is the first building to be entered by visitors as it is now used as the ticket office and shop. Castle Coole, a Neo-classical house designed by James Wyatt in the last decade of the eighteenth century, has numerous and impressive outbuildings that are ranged around two large courtyards. At the back of one of the courtyards there were once pig, bullock and cow yards in close proximity to the slaughterhouse in the courtyard, and it was no doubt from here that the Tallow House was supplied with the raw material from which the household candles could be made. The Tallow House is in a range of buildings that also included two Turf Houses, where the turves for the household fires were stored.

CANDLE TENDING

The flame of a tallow candle will of course be yellow, smoky, and obscure, except for a short time after snuffing. When a candle with a thick wick is first lighted, and the wick snuffed short, the flame is perfect and luminous... on this account tallow candles require continual snuffing.

Abraham Rees, *The Cyclopedia* or *Universal Dictionary of Arts,*
Sciences and Literature, 1819–20

Tallow has a considerably lower melting-point than beeswax or spermaceti (see pp.62 ff.), and therefore to produce a good light the candle requires a thick wick that needs frequent snuffing to keep the flame in contact with the fat. Snuffing, or trimming the end of the charred wick, helped both to prevent the candle from guttering, whereby rivulets of molten fat ran to waste down the side of the candle, and from smoking, which added to the already unpleasant smell. Draughts, a common problem in many homes, caused candles to burn down more quickly, gutter and smoke and for the consumer any unburnt candle fat represented a waste of light and, more importantly, money. Snuffing, as opposed to extinguishing, was a skilful art which required careful attention and a practised hand and eye, as the heroine, Catherine Morland, in Jane Austen's *Northanger Abbey* (1818) discovered; '...she hastily snuffed it. Alas! It was snuffed and extinguished in one....Catherine, for a few moments, was motionless with horror. It was done completely; not a remnant of light in the wick could give hope to the rekindling breath. Darkness impenetrable and immovable filled the room.'

It has been estimated that the best-quality tallow candles could last for at least twenty minutes before snuffing, while the cheapest tallow candles, if a decent flame was to be kept and guttering avoided, needed snuffing every few minutes. The device for wick-trimming was the scissor snuffer, thought to have been developed in the sixteenth century. As it was important that the charred ends did not fall into the molten fat, where they could cause guttering, snuffers were made with a box attached to the blades in which the cut ends could be contained. Jonathan Swift in his satirical and subversive *Directions to Servants* (1745)

Silver chamberstick made
by Richard Sibley, London
1815. Attached are snuffers
for trimming the wick, and
a dousing cone.

advised, 'Snuff the candles at supper as they stand on the table, which is much
the securest way; because, if the burning stuff happens to get out of the snuffers,
you have a chance that it may fall into a dish of soup, sack-posset, rice-milk, or
the like, where it will immediately extinguish with very little stink.'

Snuffers were expensive, even those made of iron, and if such a luxury item
were owned by a poor family it would have been a prized possession. A large
number of silver and silver-plated snuffers are to be found in the grander
National Trust houses, their value having prevented them from being scrapped
in the nineteenth century, which was generally the fate that befell iron snuffers.
A pair of silver scissor snuffers dating from 1798 is to be found in the Dining
Room at Nunnington Hall. Examples of iron snuffers can be seen at Aberconwy
House. Chambersticks, where a candle socket is fixed to a pan with a carrying-
handle, were developed for use in bedrooms, and some very luxurious ones came
complete with snuffers and dousing cones (extinguishers). In these fittings the
snuffer slotted into an opening below the socket and the small conical extinguisher hung from the end of the handle over the pan. One of the most

impressive collections of early nineteenth-century silver chambersticks with snuffers and extinguishers is in the Silver Vault at Attingham Park.

Nineteenth-century Developments in Candle-making

… some means must be devised to enable the candle to snuff itself, as the wax candle does; or the tallow itself must be rendered less fusible by some chemical process.

Abraham Rees, *The Cyclopedia* or *Universal Dictionary of Arts, Sciences and Literature*, 1819–20

Before the ink was dry on Rees's multi-volume work, discoveries and inventions to overcome these and other difficulties were introduced. In 1820 Cambacérés found that a plaited wick resulted in a snuffless candle as the wick bent into the flame and was fully consumed. This discovery coincided with a candle made of stearine, a constituent of tallow, developed by a French chemist, Michel Chevreul, who separated fatty acids with a mixture of strong alkali into liquid and solid parts. This process, saponification, was known and used by soapmakers but it had never been applied to candle manufacture. Another Frenchman, de Milly, improved on this process in 1831 and is also credited with impregnating wicks with borax, which eliminated guttering. In the same year 'metallic' wicks were introduced that were made with one side of the wick coated with bismuth or a paste of borax, bismuth, flour and charcoal.

Tallow was a principal ingredient in the stearine candles that were introduced during the 1820s. Edward Price & Co., later Price's Patent Candle Company, further improved on them by using a composite of refined tallow and coconut oil, with the result that these 'composition' candles, which were hard and pure white, produced a bright flame without smell or smoke and furthermore were 'snuffless'. Price's later added palm oil to their repertoire of composition candles. A box of Price's Palmitine Chamber Candles can be seen in the Pantry at Sunnycroft. Candles made from tallow and vegetable products were edible and in hard times could provide sustenance, if not a gourmet meal. Lighthouse keepers are known to have eaten their candles when stormy seas prevented supplies being landed and it was for this reason that Captain Scott chose to take 2,300lbs of Price's Belmont stearine candles on his ill-fated Antarctic expedition in 1910–11.

Industrialisation in the nineteenth century led to demands for more efficient machinery that could produce articles in greater quantities. In 1801 Thomas Binns invented a water-cooled candle mould that was further improved in 1823 by Joseph Morgan, who used a movable piston to eject the finished candles. Subsequent improvements were advanced by two Americans, Humiston and Stainforth, who, working independently of each other, produced a candle-making machine in 1855 which endured well into the twentieth century.

The Dormition of the Virgin, painted by Peter Brueghel the Elder in the mid-sixteenth century. The sub-fusc colours demonstrate how candles could only provide local pools of light – the brightest lights in this painting come from the hearth fire and from Our Lady herself.

Lighting the Home

Emily was at Leinster House, entertaining Lady Leitrim, when the 'Groom of the Chamber' came in and announced that the new tutor, Mr. Ogilvie, was come. 'Show him to his room', said the Duchess. 'Please, your Grace, is he to have wax candles, or tallow?' the butler asked. Upon which Emily turned to Lady Leitrim and said in French, 'Que pensez-vous?' 'Oh, moulds will do, till we see a little!'

Brian Fitzgerald, *Emily, Duchess of Leinster*, 1949

The discussion between the Duchess of Leinster and Lady Leitrim in 1777 as to whether Mr Ogilvie should be given wax or tallow candles would have indicated immediately to both the new tutor and the rest of the staff his estimation and status within the household. At this period a mould was not the slight it might seem, as many grand families used these candles when not entertaining. However, what the conversation does imply is that the Duchess and her family were accustomed to using wax candles as a matter of course, as no doubt Mr Ogilvie was to become when he later married the Duchess.

RIGHT: Richard Morton Paye's self-portrait, painted in 1783, shows how the artist used light for his work on engravings. The mirror served a double purpose, to produce a reversed image so that he could copy directly on to his plate, and to enhance the light provided by the candle.

The gentry and aristocracy made use of the best grades of tallow candles that were considerably more expensive than tallow dips but substantially cheaper than wax. Until the nineteenth century artificial light was used sparingly, except in those homes where extravagance was the order of the day and where there was money to burn. Even in the greatest houses, when the family did not have company to impress, tallow candles were used in preference to wax and only when and where light was needed. Unless candles were used in great numbers, the darkness would be relieved by pools of light provided by individual candles, the brightest light still being that emanating from the hearth fire.

Most socialising took place in daylight hours and only on rare occasions would a lavish display of lighting be required. Then all light-fittings, and possibly some which were hired, would be lit with wax candles. In French, tallow candles are *chandelles* and the chandelier was originally their holder, as opposed to candles of wax, *bougies*. However, the term chandelier came to mean a multi-branched fitting of a type that was only seen in the wealthiest homes and used almost exclusively for wax candles. This was partly because a luxurious light required a suitably opulent fitting, but it was also due to the fact that tallow candles needed to be snuffed frequently. Although chandeliers could be raised and lowered, it would not have been *de rigueur* at a grand party to do this in order to keep snuffing the candles. Therefore tallow candles were generally used on fittings that were easily accessible and not placed above shoulder height.

All grades of tallow candles produced a smell of varying degrees of pungency and smoke that blackened decorations and furnishings. When tallow candles guttered and the fat spilled over drip-pans onto furniture and floors, this left grease marks which entailed more work for the servants in washing walls and ceilings and general cleaning-up. The candle sockets also had to be degreased and in some homes servants were allowed to keep the unburnt ends as a 'perk' for their own use or to sell. In other households unburnt ends had to be returned to the housekeeper to be used again. At Kedleston Hall in 1810 it was noted that John Doyle had not returned his candle ends, although by this period many domestic servants were allowed candles as part of their board wages.

Dipped or mould candles were usually sold by the pound; therefore the greater the number to the pound, the smaller the size. Although large candles were available, the candles most commonly bought were eights, tens and twelves, and purchasers, who knew how long each candle size would last, bought according to their personal and social needs. Most wax candles were bleached and the whiteness of a candle was an indicator of its composition (see p.64). Best-quality tallow was whiter than the cheaper grades, but whiteness could also be enhanced by bleaching or by being stored in a cool warehouse for several months to harden and whiten.

Few personal accounts have survived that provide everyday details of lighting in the home, and when lighting is mentioned it is usually in reference to a particularly spectacular display witnessed at a lavish party or great ball. However, eighteenth- and nineteenth-century novels do sometimes convey a picture of how lighting was used in homes in different strata of society. Charles Dickens created singularly atmospheric evocations of dark streets and courtyards and the gloomy, barely lit interiors of the homes of the poor, while in *Cranford* (1853) Mrs Gaskell gives an insight into impoverished gentility and the way in which light was managed to create an impression for visitors:

As we lived in constant preparation for a friend who might come in any evening (but who never did), it required some contrivance to keep our candles of the same length, ready to be lighted, and to look as if we burnt two always. The candles took it in turns; and, whatever we might be talking about or doing, Matty's eyes were habitually fixed upon the candle, ready to jump up and extinguish it and to light the other before they had become too uneven in length to be restored to equality in the course of the evening.

However, on occasions when visitors were definitely expected, 'The fire was made up: the neat maid-servant had received her last directions; and there we stood, dressed in our best, each with a candle-lighter in our hands, ready to dart at the candles as soon as the first knock came. Parties at Cranford were solemn festivities.'

Miss Matty Jenkyns economised by restricting the use of candles and she liked to keep 'blind man's holidays' and 'on winter's afternoons would sit knitting for two or three hours – she could do this in the dark, or by firelight'. The Victorian art critic John Ruskin, the son of a well-to-do wine merchant, wrote contemptuously of the strict economy of his parents, who 'kept only female servants... neither horse nor carriage, used only tallow candles in plated candlesticks'.

Candle Fittings

The servants' candlesticks are generally broken, for nothing can last forever: but, you may find out many expedients: you may conveniently stick your candle in a bottle, or with a lump of butter against the wainscot, in a powder-horn, or in an old shoe, or in a cleft stick, or in the barrel of a pistol, or upon its own grease on a table, in a coffee cup or a drinking glass, a horn can, a tea pot, a twisted napkin, a mustard pot, an ink-horn, a marrowbone, a piece of dough, or you may cut a hole in a loaf, and stick it there.

Jonathan Swift, *Directors to Servants*, 1745

Although in some homes tallow candles would have been used in fittings made of expensive materials, only the more humble fittings are described here; wax candle fittings are considered in Chapter Three. This is partly to underline how tallow candles were beginning to be viewed in the early years of the nineteenth century: as inferior and only worthy of being used in poorer homes.

A very early fitting was the candle beam, which, as its name implies, consisted of horizontal or crossed timber beams. Although few, if any, genuinely ancient candle beams have survived there are modern interpretations of this fitting to be seen. Following reconstruction and restoration work in the 1950s of the Hall at Compton Castle, which dates from the fourteenth century, electric fittings of this design were introduced.

An unusual twentieth-century fitting inspired by the candle beam was designed by T. E. Lawrence *c.*1930 for his retreat at Clouds Hill, where electricity was not supplied. Hung over the main beam that spans the Music Room are wrought-iron trays on which are placed candles, their light intensified by the use

of silvered metal reflectors cut into the shape of leaves that stand behind the candle sockets. The fitting was made for Lawrence by the blacksmith who worked in the forge at nearby Bovington Camp.

Before mechanisation in the nineteenth century brought forth cheap and plentiful factory-produced goods, many humble light-fittings were made by the local village blacksmith. For tallow dips rather than moulds, simply-shaped conical sockets would have been used. It was not with crudely forged fittings such as these that people ostentatiously displayed their wealth, although the fact that candles rather than rushlights were being used would be enough to impress poorer neighbours. Pendant fittings with one or two candle sockets could be considered the yeoman's chandelier, and examples of two-branched fittings that were suspended from low beams can be seen at Hill Top and the Elizabethan House Museum, Great Yarmouth.[8] An impressive collection of early domestic objects assembled by Philip Ashcroft, who wanted to preserve fast-disappearing relics of everyday life in south-west Lancashire, is on display at Rufford Old Hall. Many pieces are in the back tea-room, where there are two very rare pendant fittings of an elongated cage shape that still have yellowed tallow candles in their sockets.

Table and floor-standing candle fittings were perhaps more useful than suspension fittings as the light could be brought close to where it was needed, and when seen in a yeoman's home would have indicated some prosperity. Floor-standing fittings can be seen at Snowshill Manor, Moseley Old Hall and Rufford Old Hall. In the Ship Room at Lindisfarne Castle is an unusual ornate wrought-iron table candelabrum with three sockets, which is possibly German and dates from the late eighteenth century.

There is a large variety of wrought-, cast- and sheet-iron candlesticks still to be seen in National Trust collections. Many have slide ejectors; the tallow candle was held within the body of the candlestick, allowing the flame to be kept at a constant height by pushing the lever upwards as the candle burned down. Candlesticks with this mechanism commonly date from the mid-eighteenth century and are mostly seen on chambersticks (see p.46). A variant of this type of candlestick is the spiral ejector, where the stick is made from a coiled iron strip and the socket attached to the ejector tongue which, as the candle burns down, can be pushed upwards around the spiral. Some of these candlesticks were made from crudely fashioned flat metal strips, others from coils of rolled iron. Wrought-iron ejector candlesticks forged from flat metal strips are to be seen in the Great Kitchen at Cotehele and candlesticks with rolled iron spirals at East Riddlesden Hall. Dating from the same period are rare elongated iron or brass 'pulpit' candlesticks with slide ejectors which held unusually long candles. Despite the name, these were most likely to have been used by office clerks working in counting houses and law firms rather than vicars making it clear to parishioners that they were in for a long sermon. Examples of these candlesticks can be seen in the Family Room at Gawthorpe Hall, and in the Kitchen at Wallington.

LEFT: A detail of the Music Room at Clouds Hill, the tiny Dorset cottage that was a retreat from army life for T. E. Lawrence in the 1930s. He had no electricity, but rigged up an unusual light fitting on the main beam – iron trays on which were placed candles with silvered metal reflectors. In this and other rooms, Lawrence supplemented the candle lighting with oil lamps.

Although now rarely seen, iron wall fittings were once used to light cellars and work areas. Spiked into the wall of the brewhouse at Charlecote Park is an iron fitting with two candle sockets which is hinged to allow the light to be directed to where it was most needed. At Petworth House, because of the risks of fire, the domestic offices were kept separate from the house, and food, linen, coal and other essentials were carried under a courtyard through a dark tunnel that would have been a busy thoroughfare with servants going back and forth. Along the length of the tunnel the visitor can see niches in which candlesticks, and later oil lamps, were placed to light the way.

Wall-sconces and brackets designed for use with tallow candles were generally placed at a height that would allow the candle to be easily snuffed. Although few wall-sconces made from inexpensive materials appear to have survived, in a servant's bedroom at Townend there is a sheet-iron sconce complete with a tallow candle, and in another bedroom is a crudely fashioned timber candle bracket. In contrast, at the former home of a wealthy merchant, Benjamin Cowper, are ornately carved timber wall-brackets fixed to the wood-panelled walls in the Conspiracy Room at the Elizabethan House Museum that possibly date from about 1596, when the house was built.[9]

In moderately affluent homes, candle fittings were made of pewter. An alloy of tin and lead, pewter is thought to have been introduced into Britain by the Romans in the third century AD, and although not as durable as iron, was much cheaper than brass. The City of London Pewterers were granted a Royal Charter by Edward IV in the fifteenth century, giving them control of production throughout England. Pewter is not hard-wearing, and worn or antiquated pieces were often melted down to make new objects in more fashionable styles. As a

Pewter candlesticks from the collection at Arlington Court, in Devon. Left to right: a pricket candlestick, a nozzle candlestick; and a hollow-cylindrical stemmed candlestick with a wide 'flowered' base (not to scale). The nozzle candlestick has a bell base – in 1612 the records of the Pewterers' Company referred to this form as a 'great bell'. These candlesticks are very rare, the design is thought not to have endured beyond the first quarter of the seventeenth century.

result, comparatively few pewter candle fittings have survived. However, a very important collection of early pewter is on display at Arlington Court, including a number of seventeenth- and eighteenth-century candle fittings, such as a large pricket altar candlestick of Baroque design, socket candlesticks and a very rare pair of seven-branched candelabra. Other early pewter candlesticks can be seen in the Drake Chamber at Buckland Abbey, where there are pairs of trumpet-based candlesticks and pricket altar candlesticks of Baroque design. Another West Country house, Cotehele, has a pair of pewter candlesticks of Arts and Crafts design, and outstanding examples of seventeenth-century candlesticks. Pewter wall-sconces are also rare but some that are thought to be of Dutch origin, dating from the seventeenth century, are in the Oak Bedroom at The Greyfriars in Worcester.[10]

Candle Accessories

To augment the light given by tallow candles, many trades and crafts, particularly printers and engravers, made use of light-intensifiers. However, intensifiers were also used in the home and a large glass bowl, once used as a lens to magnify candlelight, is in the Down House at Townend. Women could supplement the family income by making lace, although the wages for such intricate and delicate work were pitifully low. To save on candle costs groups of women and girls would do this work together, sitting around a 'lace maker's condenser'. One such condenser used at a village lace school was described by Mrs Palliser:

> In the evening eighteen girls worked by one tallow candle, value one penny; the 'candle-stool' stood about as high as an ordinary table with four legs. In the middle of this was what was known as a 'pole-board', with six holes in a circle and one in the centre. In the centre hole was a long stick with a socket for the candle at one end and peg-holes through the sides, so that it could be raised and lowered at will. In the other six holes were placed pieces of wood hollowed-out like a cup, and into each of these was placed a bottle made of very thin glass and filled with water. These bottles acted as very strong condensers or lenses, and the eighteen girls sat round the table, three to each bottle, their stools being on different levels, the highest nearest the bottle, which threw the light down like a burning glass.[11]

In the Small Sitting Room at Paycocke's, where there is a permanent exhibition of Coggeshall lace, stands a mid-eighteenth-century candle stool that once held four water-filled flasks.

Tallow candles were an expensive household commodity and were treated with care. According to Abraham Rees, 'Good housewives are said to bury their candles in flour, or bran, which it is said, increases their durability, almost one half.' However, because tallow candles were made from animal products, they had to be kept out of the way of vermin. To keep candles safe and ready to hand,

A light intensifier with
candle from the Firehouse
at Townend, Cumbria.
Glass flasks filled with water
were used by lacemakers
to magnify candlelight,
as can be seen in this early
twentieth-century
photograph.

boxes were made from timber, brass and sheet iron. Candle boxes are to be found in a number of National Trust properties: for example, timber candle boxes can be see at Bateman's and at the Old Post Office, Tintagel; and cylindrical sheet-iron boxes at Erddig and Baddesley Clinton.

How much do our comforts, and how greatly does the extent of our powers, depend upon the production and supply of artificial light. The flame of a single candle animates a family, every one follows his occupation, and no dread is felt of the darkness of night.

Frederick Accum, *A Practical Treatise on Gas-Light*, 1815

In the following chapters it will be shown how discoveries and inventions of the late eighteenth and early nineteenth centuries significantly improved domestic lighting. Nonetheless, many of these advances were beyond the means of the poor, who continued to rely on firelight, rushlights and the cheapest oils and candles for their light. This situation was to change dramatically later in the nineteenth century when, following the discovery of vast quantities of mineral oil in North America, good-quality lighting became affordable to all but the very poorest.

Edward Hudson, founder of *Country Life*, commissioned the architect Edwin Lutyens to convert Lindisfarne, a Tudor fort off the Northumbrian coast, into a summer retreat. Even in the middle of summer, the castle could be cold and dark – here Lutyens sketches himself with his daughter Barbie and Hudson, making their way by candlelight to bed.

CHAPTER THREE

Wax Candles

The Age of Enlightenment

Instead of dirt and poison we have rather chosen to fill our lives with honey
and wax; thus furnishing mankind with two of the noblest things, which
are sweetness and light.

Jonathan Swift, *The Battle of the Books*, 1704

The golden age of lighting by wax candles began in the eighteenth century and
lasted until the first quarter of the nineteenth. During this period sumptuous
light-fittings of superb quality, design and craftsmanship were produced. To
proclaim their wealth and status, rich households lavished as much care and
expenditure on spectacular fittings and displays of lighting as on other individual
items of furniture and fixtures. As the beeswax candle was a manifestation of
Christ in an earlier age, so the spermaceti candle epitomised Mammon in the
Age of Enlightenment. The spirit of the age was captured by Jean Le Rond
d'Alembert in 1759: 'If one looks at all closely at the middle of our century, the
events that occupy us, our customs, our achievements and even our topics of
conversation, it is not difficult to see that a very remarkable change is taking
place, one of such rapidity that it seems to promise a greater change still to come.'[1]

Chapter Two was largely concerned with lighting the homes of the lower
ranks in society; this chapter will mostly concentrate on the lighting and fittings
of a very small, wealthy minority. Nonetheless, after 1860 the use of wax candles
came within the reach of the majority when paraffin wax candles became widely
available and industrialisation led to the manufacture of cheap light-fittings.

Beeswax Candles

Paris burns perhaps a thousand times more wax candles; for in London,
except in the Court quarter, nothing is burnt but tallow.

Voltaire, 1749[2]

For centuries the use of beeswax candles remained the prerogative of the
Church, the Crown and the nobility. Pre-Reformation English churches were lit

LEFT: Silver candlesticks at
Saltram, in Devon. Middle
row, right, candlestick in
the form of a Corinthian
column, made in London
in 1698 by Richard Syngin.
Back row, a pair of Georgian
pillar candlesticks of
inverted baluster form
with octagonal bases, made
in 1722 by David Willaume.
Front row, candlestick
in form of Corinthian pillar
with heavily embossed
base, made in 1763 by J H.
Both silver chambersticks
have dousing cones, but
the snuffers are missing.
Back row, centre, a plated
candelabrum with fluted
stem. Centre row, left,
Victorian plated candlestick
of plain columnar form.

with quantities of candles, largely supplied by monastic apiaries. The bee, its wax and candles were suffused with religious significance and the beeswax candle was looked upon as an embodiment of Christ as the 'Light of the World'. An important event in the Church calendar was 2 February, Candlemas Day, when candle-lit processions preceded the consecration of ecclesiastical candles required for the coming year. To celebrate Candlemas Day in 1247, Henry III gave 1,000lbs of beeswax to Westminster Abbey for the making of a giant taper. It was also customary at Easter for the rich to provide paschal candles for church altars. The royal household employed its own wax chandlers and although independent workers in this craft are thought to have emerged in the thirteenth century, it was not until 1484 that the Wax Chandlers of the City of London were granted a Royal Charter by Richard III.

Although their Charter was granted some years after the Tallow Chandlers', the Wax Chandlers were, and remain, twentieth in order of precedence of the one hundred City Livery Companies. This is one before the Tallow Chandlers, and this order precisely reflects their superiority in terms of the quality and illumination of their candles. In the mid-fifteenth century wax candles cost 2s or more a pound, whereas the humble tallow candle fetched about 6d a pound. Between 1479 and 1483 the total value of imports of beeswax through the Port of London exceeded £11,000. Much of this trade came through Venice, an important source of supply of both wax candles and untreated wax to all major ports of Europe. Large amounts were also imported through Antwerp, and beeswax formed an important part of the Baltic Trade.

The Wax Chandlers exercised the same quality control and regulatory role within their trade as the Tallow Chandlers and were thus empowered to ensure that only unadulterated beeswax candles were sold. Wrongdoing resulted in destruction of goods, fines and imprisonment. Other misdemeanours were also punished; thus c.1530 William Ormond was fined because 'he came to prosession in nawghty Rayment and for Ungodly wordes'. Wax chandlers enjoyed brisk business in supplying churches with candles but the trade decreased dramatically at the Reformation. Fortunes revived briefly in the reign of Queen Mary Tudor and in those of subsequent monarchs tolerant of Roman Catholicism.

Another substantial area of business for the Wax Chandlers was their supply to other Livery Companies and the bereaved for their ceremonies, masses and funerals. Wax candles were important in the rituals surrounding death; in 1422 at the funeral of Henry V the assembled clergy carried 1,400 lighted candles from Southwark to St Paul's Cathedral and 'every householder from London Bridge onwards had a servant holding a lighted torch at his door'.[3] When the bankrupt Henry Daubeney, Earl of Bridgwater, died at Barrington Court in 1548, however, there was 'no means to buy fire or candles or to bury him but what was done in charity by his sister'. Through this close association with funerals many wax chandlers diversified into embalming and supplying and hiring furnishings and hearses and, as life expectancy was short, this also proved to be a lucrative business for a time. Perhaps one of the most bizarre pieces of furniture in the

National Trust's collection is the seventeenth-century, four-poster bed in 'Ann's Room' at Snowshill Manor. It is possibly a corpse bed used for lying-in-state, with holes for five candles around the mattress frame. The antiques expert Arthur Negus suggested that these represented Death, Judgement, Heaven, Hell and Eternity.

Following a dispute over embalming with the Barber-Surgeons in 1612, wax chandlers were barred from carrying out this aspect of the funeral trade and by the eighteenth century upholsterers had taken over the supply and hiring of all that could be required for a lying-in-state.

Although not directly related to lighting, another significant part of the wax chandlers' business was in making sealing wax, which was used extensively on legal documents and to seal letters. They also supplied miniature tapers for tapersticks and lengths of thin tapers for wax jacks, which were used to melt sealing wax, once a common item to be found in commercial establishments and on desks in private homes. Ornately decorated silver wax jacks are to be found at Cotehele and Kingston Lacy. An iron wax jack of unusual design that may be German in origin is at Townend, and Attingham Park and Snowshill Manor have examples of sheet-iron canister wax jacks.

CANDLE-MAKING

Hence it appears, that the difficult fusibility of wax renders it practicable to burn a large quantity of fluid by means of a small wick; and that this small wick, by turning on one side in consequence of its flexibility, performs the operation of snuffing upon itself, in a much more accurate manner than it can ever be performed mechanically.

Abraham Rees, *The Cyclopedia* or *Universal Dictionary of Arts, Sciences and Literature*, 1819–20

In the Middle Ages the candle wick was made of flax, and later of twisted cotton. One of the skills of the wax chandler was getting the right dimension of wick in relation to the size of the candle. If this was done correctly the candle needed little attention and would not require snuffing.

After the wax was taken from the hive, it was rendered and refined to remove impurities. The best-quality beeswax candles were made from bleached wax; this process left the candle white, translucent and virtually odourless. All beeswax candles burned slow and bright and did not deteriorate if kept in cool, dark conditions such as candle boxes and chests.

Until the nineteenth century it was unusual for beeswax candles to be made in moulds because of their tendency to adhere. Therefore beeswax candles were made by hand, mostly by ladling the heated wax over suspended wicks to build up layers: a long and laborious process which added to the high cost. The candle was then formed into a cylindrical shape by rolling on a moistened hard wood surface and by this method could be kept to a fairly uniform size.

The large beeswax candles used on church altar candlesticks were made with hollowed-out ends that allowed the candle to be easily impaled onto pricket candlesticks. Tallow candles, which were of a softer composition and because of their low melting-point bent or melted in warm surroundings, fared better in sockets. Candle fittings with 'nozzels' – sockets – became more usual from the sixteenth century. Pricket candle fittings could be adapted, and very rare brass pricket-socket converters can be seen on a pair of large brass candlesticks of early seventeenth-century design at Shaw's Corner.

Spermaceti Candles

Once the whale had been stripped of its blubber, it was decapitated. A sperm whale's head accounts for close to a third of its length. The upper part contains the case, a cavity filled with up to five hundred gallons of spermaceti, a clear high quality oil that partially solidifies on exposure to air. . .the men cut a hole into the top of the case and used buckets to remove the oil. One or two men might then be ordered to climb into the case to make sure all the spermaceti had been retrieved.

Nathaniel Philbrick, *In the Heart of the Sea*, 2000

Philbrick was describing a scene based on the accounts of survivors from the whaling ship *Essex* that left Nantucket harbour in 1819 to hunt for sperm whales in the Pacific Ocean. The *Essex* was rammed and sunk by an enormous sperm whale and it was on this event that Herman Melville based his book *Moby-Dick*. In the eighteenth century whales were being hunted for their baleen (whale-bone) and oil when it was discovered that sperm whale oil was superior to that of other species for lighting. As sperm whale stocks became depleted in the Atlantic, whalers had to search further afield in the Pacific to satisfy consumer demand. Sperm whales yielded valuable cargo: candles were made from the headmatter, oil from the headmatter and blubber, and ambergris, retrieved from the intestinal tract – the most valuable part – was used in making perfume (see also Chapter Four).

CANDLE-MAKING

To be sold. . . by James Clemens, Sperma Ceti candles, exceeding all others for beauty, sweetness of scent when extinguished; Duration being more than double tallow candles of equal size; Dimension of the flame nearly four times more, emitting a soft, easy, expanding light, bringing the object close to sight, rather than causing the eye to trace after them, as all tallow candles do. One of these candles serves the use and purpose of 3 tallow ones, and upon the whole are much pleasanter and cheaper.

An advertisement, *Boston News Letter*, 30 March 1748

The wax used for making spermaceti candles was obtained by compressing the headmatter in bags to remove the oil, boiling once to get rid of impurities, then boiling again with a weak solution of potash. The resulting wax was hard and of a crystalline appearance; it had the advantage that the candles could be made in moulds and, because of a small wick, did not require snuffing. Spermaceti candles and oil were available in London from about 1750, mainly in exclusive West End shops that also sold beeswax candles. Initially slightly more expensive than beeswax, spermaceti candles produced a brighter flame. In the nineteenth century the standard unit of measurement, one candle power (c.p.), was the light given by one pure spermaceti candle weighing 2oz and burning 120 grains an hour.

Paraffin Wax Candles

Let us comfort ourselves by thinking that Louis Quatorze in all his glory held his revels in the dark, and bless Mr. Price and other Luciferous benefactors of mankind for banishing the abominable mutton of our youth.

William Thackeray, *The Virginians*, 1858

Thackeray may have considered the populace well blessed by Mr Price's candles, as indeed they were, but Louis XIV hardly sat in the dark. At one function at

Mid-nineteenth-century candle-making machine used by Price's Patent Candle Company.

Versailles, as reported in a letter in 1695, the Galerie des Glaces was lit by 7,000 wax candles, the light being enhanced by reflection from the mirror-panelled walls, creating endless vistas of light. Although Price's composition candles did oust the humble tallow in popularity, in the mid-nineteenth century a new candle, of paraffin wax, was to eclipse all others and provide the poor with lighting that offered both cheapness and quality. Even though paraffin was first described and named by Reichenbach in 1830 it was some time before the oil was found in sufficient quantities to become widely and cheaply available. In 1859 seemingly infinite quantities of mineral oil were discovered in Pennsylvania; from January to June 1862 more than 4,500,000 gallons were exported.

CANDLE-MAKING

This flood of American petroleum poured in upon us by millions of gallons, and giving a light at a fifth of the cost of the cheapest candle made by the company when it first started.

James Wilson of the Price's Patent Candle Company, 1879

Paraffin wax was extracted from crude oil and, after refining, it could be made into moulded candles. However it was not until 1870 that an improved hard white candle was developed. These candles were made with a glossy surface that rivalled other wax candles in appearance, offering all the advantages at a fraction of the cost.[4] By this time wax chandlers had become a thing of the past and consumers could get all their candle supplies from ironmongers, hardware shops and department stores. At the end of the nineteenth century 90 per cent of all candles were made of paraffin wax, available in different shapes and sizes and in a variety of colours.

Lighting the Home

... for the chimney pieces I would make them with mirrors... from top to bottom; that is the taste that prevails here and which is all the more justified since with two or four candles a room, on account of reflection, is lighter and more cheerful than another with twelve.

The advice of the Swedish architect Nicodemus Tessin to
Countess Piper on furnishing her house in Stockholm, 1697

Until the end of the eighteenth century, when significant advances were made in domestic lighting, interiors could only be well lit if candles were used in profusion. This was possible only in the wealthiest households, where they could be displayed to their best advantage in fittings made of the most expensive materials.

Bess of Hardwick, Countess of Shrewsbury, one of the richest women in sixteenth-century England, recorded the light-fittings at Hardwick Hall in her

The 'great glass Lanthorne'
from Bess of Hardwick's
inventory of 1601, shown
here on the half landing
of the main staircase at
Hardwick Hall, in
Derbyshire. It now hangs
on the landing of the
Chapel Stairs.

inventory of 1601. 'A great glass Lanthorne' was suspended over the Chapel
Landing, where it can be seen today. The fittings now in the Dining Room and
the Long Gallery provide the best examples of how grand rooms were lit at this
period. At a time when mirrors were rare and prohibitively expensive, wall-
sconces provided the best means of maximising light by reflection. In the Dining
Room are five brass sconces with repoussé wall-plates, to which are fixed additional reflectors canted forward to direct the candlelight downwards. In the
Long Gallery hangs a pair of two-tiered, sixteen-branched brass chandeliers,
described in the 1601 inventory as 'too great copper candlesticks with several
places to set lightes in hanging'. These chandeliers, probably German or Flemish in origin, have highly polished baluster-shaped bodies, which provided an
ideal reflecting surface.

   Chandeliers and sconces represent the most extravagant light-fittings. They
were not necessarily permanent fixtures, as they could be taken down and
moved, but their use was confined to state apartments and any room where

important visitors were to be received and entertained. Although they provided central and wall illumination, this was not always where light was most needed, and the fittings which could give out the most useful and economical light were candlesticks and candelabra. These sometimes came with their own pieces of furniture: candlestands in the seventeenth century, torchères in the eighteenth and early nineteenth centuries.

Many candlestands were relatively plain and functional, usually of walnut, with barley twist or turned wooden stems. The National Trust has many examples; for instance at Cotehele, Lyme Park, Ickworth and Beningbrough Hall. Other stands were made as decorative objects in their own right, and some are grim reminders of a dishonourable trade. These are the gilded and ebonised blackamoor candlestands where the carved support figures are invariably shown in positions of servitude. Many of these stands were made in Venice and proved popular until the slave trade was abolished in Europe in the nineteenth century.

Two Dutch, seventeenth-century brass chandeliers hanging in the Ship Room at Lindisfarne Castle, Northumberland.

Seventeenth-century blackamoor candlestands can be seen in the Balcony Room at Dyrham Park, where they flank a tea-table, just as recorded in an inventory taken in 1703. These stands were inherited by Dyrham's builder, William Blathwayt, from his uncle, Thomas Povey, whose wealth derived from administering Jamaican plantations.[5]

Candlestands often came *en suite* with other items of furniture. A particularly sumptuous ensemble stands in the Cartoon Gallery at Knole. The gilded, inlaid table and accompanying stands decorated with cherubs were presented in 1670 to Charles Sackville, 6th Earl of Dorset, by Louis xiv on the successful completion of the secret Treaty of Dover. This furniture provides a tantalising glimpse of the magnificence of the Sun King's court, and of the highly developed skills of his designers and craftsmen.

Also at Knole, in the King's Room, is a set of silver furniture, again influenced by the style of the French court. This set includes a table, a pair of candlestands,

One of a pair of blackamoor candlestands that flank an Oriental tea table, in the Balcony Room at Dyrham Park, Gloucestershire. Originally belonging to Thomas Povey, who owned plantations in Jamaica, the candlestands were inherited by his nephew, William Blathwayt, who had placed them in this room by 1700.

Table with flanking
candlestands and a wall
mirror, part of the
magnificent set of silver
furniture in the King's Room
at Knole in Kent. The table
was made in London in
1680 by the Anglo-Dutch
cabinetmaker, Gerrit Jensen,
the candlestands and
the mirror probably date
from 1676.

sconces and three silver-framed mirrors, two of which have candle-branches.
The light in the room would have been maximised by reflection from the silver
furniture and mirrors, further enhanced by the upholstery and bed-hangings
that are made of gold and silver tissue.

In the most affluent homes illumination would be enhanced by the light
reflected from mirrors and other burnished surfaces, like gilded furniture and

Detail of a sofa developed
from Robert Adam's design
by the great cabinetmaker,
John Linnel, 1762, in the
Drawing Room at
Kedleston Hall, Derbyshire.
This shows the wonderful
gilded decoration, here in
the form of a dolphin and
an ecstatic mermaid.

picture frames, which sparkled and shimmered in the half-light. It was not until
the eighteenth century, when interior decoration changed markedly, that rooms
increased in brightness, with light painted surfaces which acted as reflectors.
Interiors with dark wood panelling and tapestry-hung walls may have been
warmer but they were also light-absorbing and only served to increase the
gloom. At houses such as Cotehele and Chastleton it is not hard to imagine how
the interiors would have looked at night, when only illuminated by very few
candles, and with the flickering flames of the hearth fire animating the scenes
portrayed on their sumptuous tapestries.

Artificial light robbed colours of their vibrancy, and textural qualities of furniture and fabrics lost definition. In one of his *Essays*, Francis Bacon recommended
the colours for the costumes of actors and masques; 'The colours that show best
by candle-light are – white, carnation, and a kind of sea-water-green, and oes
and spangs, as they are no great cost, so they are of most glory. As for rich
embroidery it is lost and not discerned.' 'Spangs' can be seen to great effect in the
Spangle Bedroom at Knole, where the seventeenth-century bed-hangings were
sewn with thousands of silver sequins that shimmered in the candlelight.

Apart from being woven into textiles, threads of precious metals were used to make trimmings to produce eye-catching sparkles of light. Opulent trimmings and tassels were one of the great extravagances of Elizabeth Dysart, Duchess of Lauderdale whose home, Ham House on the banks of the Thames at Richmond, was noted by the diarist John Evelyn as 'furnished like a Great Prince's'. In two months in 1673 the Duchess bought 152 tassels made of gold and silver threads. Some were probably used to embellish further the 'Ten Sconces of brasse hung with gold and Silke strings with tassells' that were once in the Chapel and recorded in the 1683 inventory.

Shoppers had to beware when buying in artificial light, and a number of trades regulated by the City of London guilds were not allowed to sell their wares after dark, as it was believed that inferior merchandise could easily be foisted on a buyer unable to see goods clearly. A proverb probably dating back to the sixteenth century warned, 'Fine linnen, girls and gold so bright. Chuse not to take by candlelight'. And this was what Anne Robinson of Saltram found, as she complained in a letter after shopping in London in 1784; 'so I took a coach, and did your commissions as well as I could by candlelight, which is not the best time to chuse many things... I fear you will not like your china much'.

Eighteenth-century Interior Lighting

They dined in the hall which was lighted by 130 wax candles, and the saloon with 50, the whole expense in that article being computed at fifteen pounds a night.

The Prime Minister Sir Robert Walpole's reception for the
Duke of Lorraine in 1731 at Houghton Hall

During the eighteenth century, the lifestyle of the rich and fashionable became less formal. Taste and fashion dictated that the spaces occupied earlier by state apartments were given over to reception rooms, and towards the end of the century many grand houses dispensed with them entirely on the ground floor. The daily routine altered: the hour for dinner, which in earlier centuries was set at midday, became progressively later, and by the late 1700s had turned into an evening meal. The passion for parties, routs, balls and assemblies had made socialising at night the norm by the end of the century.

Nevertheless, without fundamental improvements in lighting, reflective surfaces remained a solution for boosting illumination. Technical advances had increased the possible size of mirror glass, and large pier-glasses, whose ornately gilded frames were often fitted with candle-branches, became a feature of many grand interiors.[6] But the cost of glass remained exorbitantly high and a glass tax, introduced in 1745 and only repealed finally one hundred years later, ensured that anyone in possession of large and plentiful windows, pier-glasses and cut-glass chandeliers was very rich indeed.[7] For instance, the pier-glasses supplied by John Belchier for Erddig in the 1720s, before the imposition of the tax, cost the

The silver pier-glass was made by John Belchier in 1723, commissioned by John Meller to complement his silvered furniture in the Withdrawing Room of his country house, Erddig, Wrexham. The mirror would have enhanced the light from the attached candle branch.

enormous sum of £107; and when Robert Adam was installing mirrors in the Drawing Room at Kedleston in the 1760s, he used old glass to save money. The pier-glasses installed in the Drawing Room at Osterley Park were so large – 8ft 3ins by 4ft 4ins – that they could not be made in England and had to be imported from France.

As the century progressed, lighter painted rooms, often highlighted with gilded decoration, helped to brighten interiors: the effect can be appreciated when looking at the Neo-classical interiors designed by Robert Adam at Kedleston and at Osterley Park. Gilding was expensive; when the Drawing Room at Osterley was decorated in 1777, the cost for painting the ceiling was £66 12s 11½d, while the gilding amounted to £262 3s 3d. In the same period at Wimpole Hall, where Lord and Lady Hardwicke were considered to lead a frugal life, a visitor,

William Cole, noted their discussion about painting a room. 'My Lord was for having it an ash or olive colour as being the cheaper and more durable. But my Lady objected that, although more expensive, the fashionable French white would be cheaper in the end.' The lighter colour allowed the room to be lit with two rather than four candles. The greatest designers and craftsmen of the age produced gilded furniture and fittings to complement richly decorated interiors, and door furniture, also brightly gilded, could help to signal the way out of a dimly lit room.

Francis Bacon's advice on using gilt thread and sequins on party clothes continued to be observed. By the mid-eighteenth century, the most formal dress worn by women was the court mantua, where the wide, panniered skirts were fastened up at the back in a precursor of the bustle. The star of the costume collection at Springhill is a magnificent court mantua of cream tabby silk brocade, woven in Spitalfields c.1760. Interwoven with the poppies, forget-me-nots and ears of corn are threads of silver gilt, seen at best advantage in the candlelit splendour of the reception rooms at St James's Palace. Likewise, a man's court coat c.1780 from the Snowshill collection has sumptuously embroidered pockets highlighted by sequins and spangles.[8]

Except when entertaining, light was used sparingly and only those who lived extravagantly would consider using wax or spermaceti candles in any great quantities when on their own. Even royalty could be thrifty, as the Duchess of Northumberland discovered when she went to visit Queen Charlotte in her dressing room in 1772; 'being very large and hung with crimson damask, [it] was very dark, there being only four candles on the Toilet and these being in Branches, and the King, wanting to shew us some improvement he had made in the stove, was obliged to carry one of them about in the nossell of the candlestick in his fingers'.[9]

The Duchess was clearly one of those who believed in plenty of light. Count Kielmansegge, who was one of 600 guests at an entertainment given by the Duke and Duchess in the 1760s, thought that the four glass chandeliers, each of 25 lights, in the Great Gallery 'light the room even more brilliantly than necessary'. It was estimated that one burning candle consumed the same amount of oxygen as two people; this, together with the heat produced from a multiplicity of candles and that generated by crowds of people, was stifling. When guests complained of the heat at a ball given by Sir Laurence and Lady Dundas in 1769, the servants were ordered to break panes of expensive crown glass in the windows. Although the heat was the cause of many complaints, guests would have been disappointed, if not insulted, to be entertained in a room that was not well lit.

Wax candles were used for show and their fabulous fittings were all part of that elaborate display. How worthwhile such a display was is indicated in a letter Frances Bankes sent to her mother-in-law in December 1791 describing a ball; 'We had twenty candles in each Supper Room, and indeed that whole floor was lighted up in the same proportion, and looked magnificent. I am persuaded that

RIGHT: Detail from a court mantua of silk brocade, woven in Spitalfields, c.1760 and worn for presentation at the court of St James. The formalised design of flowers and ears of corn, woven in coloured silks and silver gilt, would have glittered in the candlelight.

the money spent on Lamps and Candles at an Entertainment of this kind makes infinitely more show than if you spend the same sum in any other way.[10] The ball was to celebrate the completion of major alterations to her home, Kingston Hall, later Kingston Lacy, to which upwards of 130 people had been invited. What the guests could hardly have failed to notice was the 'noble lustre', the ten-branched chandelier which lit the Ball Room. Cut-glass chandeliers were the most admired of all light-fittings and their ownership was synonymous with wealth. Candlelight refracted from a multitude of faceted lustres, prisms, drops and beads intensified the light and produced glittering and dazzling rainbow effects.

Some of the finest cut-glass chandeliers were those made by William Parker for the Assembly Rooms at Bath. Assembly Rooms were springing up in towns all over England during the eighteenth century. The members of polite society who flocked to them and mingled with the 'quality' would have been impressed both by the company and the lighting. Charles Dickens conjured up the atmosphere of Assembly Rooms in *The Pickwick Papers* (1837):

> In the ball-room, the long card-room, the octagonal card-room, the stair-cases, and the passages, the hum of many voices, and the sound of many feet, were perfectly bewildering. Dresses rustled, feathers waved, lights shone, and jewels sparkled.... Brilliant eyes, lighted up with pleasurable expectation, gleamed from every side; and look where you would, some

BELOW: The Ballroom in the Assembly Rooms at Bath, dominated by William Parker's magnificent cut-glass chandeliers made in 1771.

RIGHT: William Parker's trade card.

exquisite form glided gracefully through the throng, and was no sooner lost than it was replaced by another, as dainty, and bewitching.

At Bath, where the season lasted from October to early June, the New Assembly Rooms opened in 1771, providing areas where subscribing patrons could dance, eat, drink tea and play cards. However, their enjoyment was not necessarily without risk. Shortly after opening, 'One of the arms of the chandeliers in the Ballroom fell down during the time the company were dancing', narrowly missing the painter Thomas Gainsborough.[11] The chandeliers had been supplied by Jonathan Collett and these were reassembled into one chandelier which now hangs in the Octagon. Collett's chandeliers were replaced by others made by William Parker, who had already supplied those in the Tea Room. In all, the cost for nine chandeliers amounted to £999 and the bill for candles and oil in the first season alone was the considerable sum of £556 3s 8d.[12]

During the eighteenth century chandeliers became permanent fixtures in rooms and were usually hung at a fairly low level. Apart from illumination advantages, this allowed for the cleaning, replacement and lighting of candles to be done without too much difficulty. For ease of management some chandeliers were suspended on cords and pulleys, like the pair of c.1740 giltwood chandeliers in the Saloon at Sudbury Hall, which typically have their counterweights concealed by elaborate tassels.[13] Other chandeliers were suspended from

Giltwood chandeliers, c.1740, in the Saloon at Sudbury Hall in Derbyshire. Their counterweights are concealed by red tassels.

Detail of the chandelier in the White Drawing Room at Arlington Court, Devon, showing the cut-glass socket prisms that could be used to relieve the plainness of empty candle sockets during the daytime, or as light intensifiers when not all the candle branches were in use in the evening.

winches; still operational is the winch that raises and lowers the huge brass chandelier that hangs above the Staircase Hall at Hatchlands Park. At Gawthorpe Hall, it was the footman's job to wind the ormolu and bronze chandelier up and down in the stairwell to illuminate whichever floor of the house the family was using. When chandeliers were not in use the candle sockets were usually empty. To improve their look, some had decorative cut-glass tapering prisms to fit into the sockets, where a few could usefully remain as light-intensifiers if occasion or economy dictated less light. An example of a chandelier with these decorative socket prisms is in the White Drawing Room at Arlington Court.

Possession of a chandelier did not necessarily mean it was lit frequently and, for some, a very grand occasion had to arise to justify the extravagance. In 1779, when King George III visited the Duchess of Portland, Mrs Delany noted that 'Her Grace had the house lighted up in a most magnificent manner; the chandelier in the great hall was not lighted up before for twenty years'. This may explain why so many chandeliers from this period have survived remarkably intact. Nonetheless some did get damaged; at Erddig the arms of a George III chandelier had to be replaced when 'the butler accidentally unscrewed the ceiling fitting by turning the chandelier as he was cleaning it'.[14] A badly damaged chandelier could be reconstructed using old or new parts, like the one in Princess Victoria's Room at the Treasurer's House, York. The result was not always successful or aesthetically pleasing when repaired with parts from different styles and periods. For those who wanted to keep abreast of changing fashion but did not want to invest in a new chandelier, their old one could be dismantled and reassembled with new cut-glass decorations.

Silver, gilded or mirrored wall-plates of sconces and girandoles reflected and enhanced candlelight and provided additional lighting for wall and side areas, although if any servant dared to follow Jonathan Swift's advice they would not have been used at all:

> Sconces are great wasters of candles, and you, who are always to consider the advantage of your master, should do your utmost to discourage them: therefore, your business must be to press the candle with both your hands into the socket, so as to make it lean in such a manner, that the grease may drop all upon the floor, if some lady's headdress or gentleman's perriwig be not ready to intercept it: you may likewise stick the candle so loose that it will fall upon the glass of the sconce and break it to shatters; this will save your master many a fair penny in the year, both in candles, and to the glassman, and your self much labour, for the sconces spoiled cannot be used.[15]

For everyday use, a candle in a candlestick was sufficient for many, although for dining a candelabrum might also be used. However, when guests were expected, candelabra on torchères were ideal for lighting dark corners of large rooms. By the mid-eighteenth century many torchères had become fabulous pieces of furniture. Those in the Drawing Room at Ardress House, for example, were made with their own detachable candle-branches. Although giltwood torchères

A pair of neo-classical giltwood torchères with detachable candle branches, c.1780-90, in the Drawing Room at Ardress House, Armagh. The torchères are decorated with sphinx heads.

were overwhelmingly popular, some were also made in other materials. In the Marble Hall at Kedleston, Robert Adam designed the twelve bronzed iron torchères that have candelabra with gilded branches. Thomas Chippendale the Younger supplied the four bronzed torchères in the entrance hall at Stourhead.

As close lighting was essential for work and leisure, some pieces of furniture, such as pianos, music stands and dressing-room mirrors, were designed to incorporate candle fittings. To help the servants in their duties in the Dining Room at Canons Ashby House, there is an Adam-style buffet with a two-branched candle fitting that is both height-adjustable and swivelled. In the Library at Lyme Park an architect's table, c.1790, has two candle-slides. Bureau bookcases were often fitted with candle-slides and on desks, tapersticks and small candlesticks were components of expensive desk sets. Some French desks were designed with candle-branches and perhaps the most exquisite examples, made in the 1770s by Riesener for the French royal family, are now at Waddesdon Manor. For those who liked to embroider and to read, their needs were catered for by small tables fitted with turned wood candle sockets. In Beatrix Potter's Room at Melford Hall there are two nineteenth-century tables, one with a socket that can be moved horizontally as well as vertically. Many card-tables were made to accommodate candlesticks at the corners. At Ickworth there is a

Silver-gilt inkstand made in Madrid in 1777 for Thomas Robinson, 2nd Lord Grantham when he was British Ambassador. Thomas's sister, Theresa, married John Parker of Saltram in Devon, and the inkstand is now in the house. The inkwell sits in the middle, surrounded by three candles.

pair of rare *c.*1715 laburnum wood tables and a walnut table of a similar age is at Montacute House. The expression 'the game's not worth the candle' derives from it not being worth the cost of the candles to the players.

Nineteenth- and Twentieth-century Interior Lighting

The London winter commenced; and the young Earl of Glenthorn, and his entertainments, and his equipages and extravagances, were the conversation of all the world, and the joy of the newspapers... the hundreds of waxlights, which burned nightly in his house, were numbered by the idle admirers of folly; and it was known by everybody that Lord Glenthorn suffered nothing but wax to be burned in his stables....

Maria Edgeworth, Tales of Fashionable Life, Vol.1, 1809

Few could compete in extravagance with the Prince Regent, whose profligate lifestyle was notorious and who spent 1,000 guineas on a fifty-six-light chandelier for the Crimson Drawing Room at Carlton House. Others maintained the customs of the previous century, content to put on a display only when occasion demanded. For a ball at Saltram in 1810 the Countess of Morley described the lighting arrangements: 'The Saloon was prepared for dancing and looked quite brilliant and beautiful – we lighted it by hanging lamps over the windows and putting a quantity of candles over the doors, the places in which they were fixed being concealed by large wreaths and festoons of leaves and flowers beautiful to behold…round the room we had two rows of seats affording comfortable anchorage for about 200 persons'. But in 1811 the Countess's brother, the Rev. Thomas Talbot, wrote to his wife that although he thought the Staircase Hall and Saloon 'equal to anything one can see in the first Houses in England', he also commented, 'As to the mode of existence here in the absence of Company it is the most remote from show or even elegance that can be conceived, the whole lower part of the house is abandoned, the library excepted…the living room is upstairs'.[16] This arrangement appears not to have been unusual and at Kedleston Hall, which Dr Johnson thought 'would do excellently for a town hall', the Curzon family lived in the north-east pavilion, the formal rooms in the central block being largely reserved for entertaining.[17]

In grand houses the ordering and issuing of candles were the responsibility of the housekeeper, who kept a watchful eye on stock. In 1810 at Kedleston Hall there were 326lbs of wax candles in store. During the following year the house was regularly supplied with copious amounts of tallow mould candles and rush-lights, and the housekeeper kept careful note of how many and to whom they had been given. Invoices of tradesmen's accounts at Dunham Massey in the period 1835 to 1842 reveal that in addition to deliveries of oil, quantities of wax candles were bought; the last invoice amounted to £80 15s. In the 1870s, there is a note of an invoice from a tallow chandler. During the day candle fittings were de-waxed and cleaned in the domestic offices and at night chambersticks, replenished with candles, were left at the bottom of the stairs for the family to take up to their rooms.

By the time paraffin wax candles became widely available, other lighting had come into the marketplace: gas was established and paraffin oil was cheap and plentiful. Nonetheless candles still had their place in the home, especially for those who wanted to look their best because, as one writer put it in 1881, 'candle-light is the only artificial light by which beauty shows all its beauty – it even makes the plain less plain'.[18] For others candles remained their primary source of lighting, either through economy or choice, and this included some who lived in grand houses. At Osterley Park, where electricity was not installed until 1925, Margaret, Lady Jersey continued to hold receptions in the Gallery lit 'with 400 candles, some being placed over the shuttered windows'.[19] Calke Abbey did not have electricity until 1962 and shortly before that date the Duchess of Devonshire recalled seeing the house on a wet and dark November evening, 'glowing with the light of hundreds of candles'.[20] The Church of All Saints, Little Claydon, which stands beside Claydon House and where there are ancient monuments to generations of the Gifford and Verney families, continues to be lit by candles for services. Here there are highly decorative Gothic Revival-style brass pew candlestands and smaller candelabra to light the pulpit and lectern.

Candle Fittings

The Two Waterford Glass Lustres that are now suspended in the Great Coffee Room of the Parliament House are justly esteemed the most superb of their kind ever publicly exhibited in this Kingdom. While their brightness throws every beautiful tinge of the most beautiful prismatic colours, the workmanship reflects credit on the ingenuity of the artist who made it [*sic*], and an honour upon those who encouraged and rewarded that ingenuity, in purchasing his production.

Faulkner's *Dublin Journal*, 29 January 1788

The nation's design repertory was influenced and enriched by a wealth of imported goods and by the craftsmen who came to work in Britain. The Dutch style, from gardens to blue-and-white china, was much admired in seventeenth-century England, all the more so when William of Orange and his consort Mary Stuart became joint monarchs in 1689. Italian wares were brought back in cartloads from the Grand Tour to adorn the homes of connoisseurs. The French court always provided a source of style as well as bitter rivalry. When the Edict of Nantes that protected French Protestants from persecution was revoked in 1685, thousands of Huguenot artisans fled: Louis XIV's loss was Britain's gain.

Technical advances in manufacturing processes in the late eighteenth century made an increasing range of products available to a growing market. In the past only a very few could afford to commission furniture and fittings from individual designers and craftsmen; now industry could more than satisfy the demand for these articles from an emerging 'middling' class of consumers.

As fashions changed and new technology was introduced, many light-fittings were scrapped. If a fitting was expensive it was more likely to be adapted, hence the large number of chandeliers that can still be seen in historic houses. On the other hand, smaller fittings like silver sconces and candlesticks could be melted down and remade into more fashionable styles. This is particularly true of fittings from before the eighteenth century; generally, the candlesticks that survived had been made for church altars. Early pricket candlesticks in brass, bronze, silver, and carved and gilded wood can often be found in family chapels, as at Belton House, Ightham Mote and Hardwick Hall. Some of the oldest were rescued by Charles Paget Wade, and form part of his Snowshill collection. In a number of other houses, for example Antony, early candlesticks have been converted into electric table lamps. Some very early candlesticks for secular use have, however, survived. At Montacute, for instance, are sixteenth-century Limoges enamel candlesticks bearing the monogram of Henry II of France, and of his mistress, Diane de Poitiers.

Early corona fittings that produced a circle of light are very rare and yet, according to the architect and designer A.W.N. Pugin, 'there was scarcely a church in ancient times which was not provided with a corona richer or plainer in design, according to the wealth of the foundation'.[21] An unusual wrought-iron corona with both prickets and sockets is in the Queen's Room at Sizergh Castle. A highly decorative wrought-iron corona, dating from the seventeenth century, and probably of Spanish origin, is in the Dining Room at Anglesey Abbey. In the mid-nineteenth century the corona design was resurrected, most notably by Pugin whose Reformed Gothic architecture, furniture and fittings became highly influential. Examples from this period in Gothic Revival style can be seen at Gawthorpe Hall and Knightshayes Court.[22]

Brass was not produced in England until 1565 when Queen Elizabeth I granted a patent for its manufacture. Before then, brass production was centred in Flanders and Germany and ingots and finished articles were imported. Although increased production by the end of the seventeenth century helped to

Brass corona in the Gothic Revival style, hanging in the Morning Room at Knightshayes Court, Devon.

lower costs, candlesticks, sconces and chandeliers continued to be imported from the Low Countries. The multi-branched brass chandelier with its bulbous baluster-shaped body, often referred to as 'Dutch' style, and familiar from Dutch paintings, became immensely popular for use in churches and homes. By the early eighteenth century this style had come to look distinctly old-fashioned, although the chandelier enjoyed a revival in the late nineteenth century, particularly amongst those who wanted to give their homes a 'period' appearance. In the Priory Church at St Michael's Mount is a brass chandelier that was made in 1788 as a replica of a fifteenth-century Flemish chandelier which hangs in Bristol Cathedral. However, Lord St Aubyn, who commissioned the replica, transformed the original figure of St George into St Michael by adding wings.[23]

Sconces and candlesticks of cast and sheet brass produced in the seventeenth century were often decorated with incised, punched or repoussé patterns, and candlesticks from this period are distinctive in having flared bases and large drip-pans that were necessary if tallow candles were used. Towards the end of

A multi-branched brass chandelier hangs over the doubting – or doubtful – lady in Gerard Ter Borch's seventeenth-century painting of *An Officer Making his Bow* (see illustration, page 66).

RIGHT: One of a set of
ornate six-branch candelabra
made by Matthew Boulton
in 1772 for Saltram.
Originally there were six
candelabra: this is one of
four that stand in the Saloon.
They are a version of a
design for George III, known
as the King's vases, now at
Windsor Castle. The bodies
are bluejohn mounted in
ormolu, and they stand on
gilded torchères, probably
based on a design by
Robert Adam.

FAR RIGHT: One of a pair
of Empire candelabra in
the style of Pierre-Philippe
Thomire in the Dining
Room at Hinton Ampner,
Hampshire. The candle
branches are supported by
a bronze Victory on a
circular gilt base.

the seventeenth century these features on candlesticks were reduced and in the next century had all but disappeared. At the beginning of the eighteenth century brass had fallen in price. Brass sconces were rapidly going out of fashion and these and brass candlesticks were being replaced by fittings made of more costly materials like silver, giltwood and ormolu. Gilded bronze chandeliers with chased decorative details looked considerably more opulent than those made of brass. At Ham House there is a much restored, seventeenth-century example. Elaborate gilt chandeliers that are nineteenth-century interpretations of the style can be seen at Tatton Park and Belton House.

In the last quarter of the eighteenth century ormolu fittings in Neo-classical styles became very fashionable, many made at Matthew Boulton's celebrated Soho Manufactory in Birmingham where highly skilled craftsmen produced pieces from the sketches of leading designers.[24] Considered amongst the finest of Boulton's light-fittings were candelabra with ormolu candle-branches and Derbyshire feldspar bodies. These candelabra were often shown to their best advantage when placed on giltwood torchères of Adam design, as in the Tapestry Room at Osterley Park.[25]

In France ormolu was used extensively; in the early nineteenth century it was

One of a pair of silver-gilt chandeliers hanging in the Library at Anglesey Abbey, Cambridgeshire. These chandeliers form part of a set of five designed by William Kent for George II, and made *c.*1737 by the King's goldsmith, Balthasar Friederich Behrens.

often combined with patinated bronze. Napoleon's Egyptian campaign inspired new designs, and candlesticks, candelabra and chandeliers made in this period are to be seen in many National Trust houses, including Attingham Park, Berrington Hall, Clandon and Petworth. Fittings from both the First and Second Empires are also represented amongst the many outstanding light-fittings in the Faringdon Collection at Buscot Park, where there is a pair of huge bronze and ormolu candelabra from a set of four that King Louis-Philippe presented to the 1st Duke of Wellington.

Some of the most expensive light-fittings were made of silver. In the Library at Anglesey Abbey hangs a pair of silver-gilt chandeliers designed by William Kent for George II, part of a series of five made between 1736 and 1737 by the court goldsmith, Balthasar Friederich Behrens for the king's summer palace at Herrenhausen in Hanover. An assortment of objects in the royal vault had been melted down towards making the chandeliers.[26]

In the seventeenth and early eighteenth centuries, the most luxurious sconces were made of silver. However, many were replaced by giltwood and ormolu, materials that complemented better the Rococo and Neo-classical designs of furniture and fittings that became fashionable as the eighteenth century progressed. Of the silver sconces set aside, a sizeable proportion were probably melted down to be made into candlesticks and candelabra that were often used to light dining-tables. Several National Trust houses have silver candlesticks and candelabra made by acclaimed Huguenot and English silversmiths. At Ickworth, for instance, there are four Rococo candelabra, c.1758, by Simon le Sage, and at Kedleston, of the same period and style, an epergne with candle-branches by Thomas Harrache. The work of the leading silversmith of the Regency period, Paul Storr, is to be seen in the vaults at Attingham Park, where there is a complete dinner service, candlesticks and candelabra.[27] Expensive silver candle fittings were made throughout the nineteenth century: at the centre of the dining-room table at Shugborough stands a large, elaborate candelabrum by Robert Garrard, dated 1855.

A good substitute for those who could not afford silver fittings was Old Sheffield plate. In 1765 Boulton's Silver Manufactory began to produce a wide range of silver-plated wares, of which he noted 'Our plated candlesticks are greatly approved'. In the 1840s, Elkington & Sons of Birmingham developed the process of electro-plating; as a consequence, silver-plated goods were cheaper than ever to produce and became sought-after by an increasing number of middle-class consumers.

Although silver candlesticks were eminently desirable objects as far as the Georgians were concerned, porcelain pieces were equally admired for their beauty. Connoisseur collections of English, European and Oriental porcelain that include candlesticks and candelabra are to be found in several National Trust houses. In the Bearsted Collection at Upton House there is a rare group of English Chelsea Gold Anchor candlesticks, c.1765, that depict various Aesop's fables. In the Gubbay Collection at Clandon Park are pairs of Japanese Arita carp and geese, with applied ormolu candelabra branches, dating from c.1700. For European porcelain, the Rothschild Collection at Waddesdon Manor is a treasure house, with outstanding examples from Sèvres and Meissen.

Carved wood chandeliers were probably never made in great numbers and very few early examples survive. However, in the Dining Room at Sizergh Castle hangs an eight-branched, ornately carved, silvered wood chandelier that reputedly dates from the early seventeenth century and whose design is based on the Dutch-style brass chandelier. Although giltwood chandeliers were illus-trated in Thomas Chippendale's *The Gentleman and the Cabinet Maker's Director* (1762), their fragility may explain why so few have survived. A late seventeenth-century giltwood chandelier that originally hung in Hamilton Palace is now in the Tapestry Room at Antony. A magnificent suite of three giltwood chandeliers dating from c.1750 can be found at Lyme Park.[28]

In contrast, giltwood sconces and girandoles were overwhelmingly popular, their designs providing the patterns for many electric sconces in 'historical' styles that were produced in the early twentieth century. Although quantities of gilt-wood girandoles and sconces are to be found in National Trust houses, few could compete in number and quality with the giltwood girandoles in the Long

One of a pair of rare
Meissen parrots mounted
on Louis xv ormolu bases
at Fenton House, London.

Gallery at Osterley Park. Here hang six large girandoles, each with four candle-branches that have unusual heart-shaped glasses, almost certainly the work of the celebrated cabinetmaker John Linnell. Equally splendid are the large *c.*1750 Rococo giltwood sconces, each with two candle-branches, in the Drawing Room at Sudbury Hall, which in terms of their size could be considered nothing short of ostentatious.

The mid-seventeenth century marks the appearance of chandeliers that were so costly, their acquisition would have been beyond the means of anyone but the very richest and most privileged. These chandeliers have frames hung with lustres of carved rock crystal. Although such chandeliers were rare in Britain, this was not the case in France, where their use in aristocratic households continued into the eighteenth century. In the Rothschild Collection at Waddesdon Manor there is a magnificent French fifteen-branch, steel-framed chandelier that has rock crystal and cut-glass decorations.

In the seventeenth century table candelabra were also decorated with lustres

of rock crystal. These were called girandoles, the term that was also later applied to cut-glass candelabra and sconces with mirrored wall-plates. Mirrored girandoles with candle-branches dating from the late seventeenth century are extremely rare, but there is a pair made of engraved Venetian glass with coloured glass insets in the state bedroom at Clandon. Unusual, too, is the pair of giltwood girandoles with ribbed mirror wall-plates in the Lower Ante Room at Blickling Hall. Cut-glass table candelabra with their light-intensifying decorations were easily transportable, and usually found in pairs on mantelpieces as well as on tables. Although probably not uncommon in wealthy homes in the late eighteenth and early nineteenth centuries, their delicacy perhaps accounts for why relatively few have survived. Amongst the finest that have endured is a pair decorated with amber-coloured glass, made by William Parker *c*.1780, now at Blickling Hall.

Glass to rival the luxuriousness of rock crystal began to be developed in 1671 when George Ravenscroft obtained a patent to produce 'a particular sort of Chrystalline Glasse'. His work eventually resulted in the production of a robust

LEFT: Giltwood sconce, bearing the coronet and Garter of Lionel Sackville, 1st Duke of Dorset, and dating from *c*.1720, in the Ballroom at Knole, Kent.

Ormolu Rococo wall sconces and candelabrum (both one of pairs) in the Drawing Room at Felbrigg Hall, Norfolk.

glass with enhanced brilliance that was variously termed flint, lead or crystal glass. This lead 'crystal' glass enabled British chandelier-makers to create fittings that by the 1770s were unrivalled in terms of the quality of the glass-cutting and unsurpassed in beauty. The delicate designs of the late eighteenth century were superseded in the Regency period by large tent-and-waterfall, and tent-and-bag chandeliers, where the body of the fitting was enveloped by cut-glass drops. Throughout the nineteenth century cut-glass chandeliers were made for all lighting technologies and their continuing popularity has ensured that they have never gone out of production.[29]

Cut-glass chandeliers of superb quality and of different periods and styles are to be found in many National Trust houses. Rivalling Parker's chandeliers in beauty were those made by Christopher Haedy, the son of a Bohemian glass-maker. Chandeliers dating from the 1770s attributed to Haedy can be seen at Clandon, and two at Uppark have been restored to their former magnificence after the 1989 fire. Regency tent-and-waterfall chandeliers are also well represented; a good example is in the Dining Room at West Wycombe Park, and another with candle vase shades is in the Saloon at Oxburgh Hall. Two superb examples of tent-and-bag chandeliers are at Castle Coole. A mid-Victorian chandelier, where the glass has a red flush overlay, is at Buscot Park, along with a large Venetian Murano glass chandelier that was shown at the Great Exhibition of 1851. A number of French eighteenth-century cut-glass chandeliers of the finest quality can be seen at Waddesdon Manor.[30]

Candlesticks were the most useful of all candle fittings but could pose fire risks if the candle became dislodged; candle flames igniting curtains and bed-hangings was an all too familiar cause of fires in eighteenth- and nineteenth-century homes. To reduce this hazard, candlesticks with hand-operated slide ejectors were developed (see Chapter Two), and at the beginning of the nineteenth century, a simple and efficient mechanism was introduced to keep the candle in a fixed position and the flame at a constant height. This new candle fitting, where the candle was not exposed to view, used a mechanism by which the upward pressure of a coiled spring pressed the candle against a partially enclosed top opening. In 1832 William Palmer introduced his patent spring-loaded candlestick, and a pair of rare large bronze candlesticks from this period, marked 'Palmer & Co. Patent', is at The Argory. Initially Palmer's candlesticks were designed for use with newly introduced metallic wicks and later, very successfully, with paraffin wax candles. Not unsurprisingly, spring-loaded candlesticks became instantly popular for use in carriage lamps and in the home, and were sold in great numbers. Some types with polished metal cowled shades that focused light downwards remained in production into the twentieth century. At Arlington Court, where electricity was not introduced until 1951, Jan Newman, who went to work there in 1927 as house parlourman, recalls how Miss Chichester and her companion Miss Peters used these lamps for reading. A pair of cowled nickel-plated lamps can still be seen in Miss Chichester's Bedroom. Spring-loaded candle lamps of different sizes and patterns are to be found in the

RIGHT: Regency tent-and-waterfall chandeliers hanging in the Saloon at Saltram.

study and kitchen at Carlyle's House in Chelsea, and one with a glass shade decorated with pierced brass is in Spenser's Room at Canons Ashby.

By the end of the nineteenth century improved manufacturing processes were producing candle fittings to suit most tastes and virtually all pockets. However, the writings of John Ruskin and the work of William Morris and other members of the Arts and Crafts Movement were influential in creating a market for those with artistic sensibilities who were wealthy enough to reject mass-produced goods in favour of hand-crafted work. It is paradoxical, therefore, that the Movement's foremost designer of light-fittings, W. A. S. Benson, designed his fittings to be produced entirely by machine. At Wightwick Manor there are numerous Benson light-fittings, including a pair of brass and copper chandeliers that were originally made for the Pre-Raphaelite artist Holman Hunt. In contrast is the hand-crafted work of Sir Edmund Harry Elton, who inherited Clevedon Court from his uncle in 1883. Both an inventor and a potter, Sir Edmund established the 'Sunflower Pottery' and his art-pottery, Elton Ware, won international awards and was sold through Tiffany & Co., New York. A collection of Sir Edmund's pottery is exhibited at Clevedon Court and a large Elton Ware paschal candlestick is in the family chapel.

The majority of the fittings so far described were predominantly used in state apartments and grand reception rooms; many would only have been lit when entertaining important guests. However, other fittings were essential, particularly to light halls, staircases and passageways. Lighting in these areas posed difficulties as they were notoriously draughty, particularly if windows and doorways were ill-fitting. Therefore many of the fittings were glazed to protect the vulnerable candle flame. When exposed to draughts candles were liable to gutter and extinguish; in both instances smoke would be produced, and to protect decorations some lanterns were fitted with smoke shades. The hall lantern was usually the first fitting visitors saw on arrival, and for this reason these lanterns were generally very handsome, many being made of gilt metal. Few homes could boast the quantity of hall and staircase lighting of Petworth House, where in 1764 the Grand Staircase was lit by 'Nine guilt Square Lanthorns' and 'Two Hexigon Lanthorns hung with gilt Iron Chains under the Landing'.[31] Nonetheless a large number of National Trust houses do retain impressive hall and staircase lanterns. Of particular interest are two lanterns at Uppark that, despite being severely damaged in the 1989 fire, have now been restored. In the Stone Hall is a splendid c.1785 Louis XVI ormolu lantern, and in the Staircase Hall a c.1760 English gilt lantern in Gothick style. Both lanterns have smoke shades. Flat-backed, wall-mounted lanterns were also used to light stairways and passages and the most luxurious, like a pair at Wallington which date from c.1725, have mirrored backs to reflect the light.

An elegant form of lantern, the candle vase lamp, came into use in the eighteenth century. Here the candle was placed in a socket at the base of a large glass vase which could then be suspended from chains, mounted on wall-brackets or placed on torchères. When used for staircase lighting, some lamps were fixed to banister rails or newel posts. A number of early or rare forms of these lamps are in National Trust houses. At Antony the two staircase lamps date from the Queen Anne period. In the Lower Hall at Nostell Priory there are eight bracket lamps that incorporate smoke shades which cost £20 when they were supplied by Thomas Chippendale in 1771. Examples of suspension lanterns are to be found at Gawthorpe Hall and Dyrham. The four painted timber torchères with large glass vase lamps in the Grand Entrance Hall at Castle Coole were made with covers that replaced the lamps when they were not in use.

Perhaps one of the most unusual and aesthetically pleasing solutions to staircase lighting is at Sudbury Hall. In 1676 the superlative woodcarver Edward Pierce was paid £112 15s 5d for making the Great Staircase. He incorporated carved baskets of flowers on the newel posts and along the top of the panelling on the staircase wall. At night the baskets could be replaced by candelabra or lanterns. An innovative approach to lighting a dark passageway was adopted at Rufford Old Hall, where candelabra or candlesticks were placed in a glazed space above a doorhead. The space has a lead lining to protect against fire and is ventilated by a small flue through the external wall.

Although some state bedrooms were lit by chandeliers, generally bedroom lighting was provided by a candle in a chamberstick. For those who wanted the security of a light at night and one that also afforded protection from fire, a 'hundred-eye' lantern or candle-guard was used. These candle-guards were made of iron pierced with holes and fitted with wide shallow sockets that held

BELOW LEFT: One of a pair of nickel-plated spring-loaded candlesticks in Miss Chichester's Bedroom at Arlington Court, Devon. The candlesticks have cowled shades which intensified and focused the light downwards.

BELOW: A gilt-bronze wall lantern in the Chinese style on the South Staircase at Nostell Priory, Yorkshire. It is attributed to Thomas Chippendale as it corresponds closely to one of his designs in the 1762 edition of *The Gentleman & Cabinet Maker's Director*.

The very theatrical seventeenth-century staircase at Sudbury Hall, with its elaborate carving by Edward Pierce. The baskets of flowers and fruit on the newel posts and wall banister rails can be unscrewed, and it is thought that they would be replaced by candelabra or lanterns for evening entertainments.

short stubby candles called mortars, the name deriving from the time when these candles were left burning during a lying-in-state. A number of 'hundred-eye' lanterns can be found on fireplace hearths in the bedrooms at Knole.

Enormously popular in the mid-nineteenth century were 'Fairy' nightlights with decorative faceted glass covers that were manufactured by Samuel Clarke. These could be bought in many colours and cost from 1s to 2s each. The night-lights developed by Clarke were descendants of 'Vauxhall lights', floating-wick oil lamps used in the eighteenth century in great numbers to illuminate Vauxhall Pleasure Gardens, where they were hung from tree branches (see Chapter Four). In the nineteenth century these open-top nightlights were also used with paraffin wax candles, mainly to light gardens. A number of 'Vauxhall lights' can be seen in the Lamp Room at Penrhyn Castle (see p.114).

Candle Accessories

In affluent homes scissor-like douters with flat circular blades or, more usually, extinguishing cones were used to put out candle flames. Long-handled varieties of the latter were indispensable for putting out candles on chandeliers. Ever contrary, Jonathan Swift in *Directions to Servants* advised a variety of ways that a candle flame might be quenched without the aid of an extinguisher:

> …you may run the candle against the wainscot, which puts the snuff out immediately: you may lay it on the floor, and tread the snuff out with your foot: you may hold it upside down until it is choked with its own grease; or cram it into the socket of the candlestick: you may whirl it round your head till it goes out: when you go to bed, after you have made water, you may dip your candle in the chamber-pot: you may spit on your finger and thumb, and pinch the snuff until it goes out: the cook may run the candle's nose into the meal tub, or the groom into a vessel of oats, or a lock of hay, or a heap of litter: the housemaid may put out her candle by running it against a looking-glass, which nothing cleans so well as candle snuff: but the quickest and best of all methods, is to blow it out with your breath, which leaves the candle clear and ready to be lighted.

A candle extinguisher of unusual design is to be found in a display cabinet at Berrington Hall. The small Worcester extinguisher has a woman's body and the head of a singing nightingale, representing the nineteenth-century singer Jenny Lind, who was known as the 'Swedish nightingale'. In the eighteenth century shields and shades were used to protect the eyes from the 'glare' of the candle-light. In a poorly lit room the light from one or two candles would have appeared very bright, so for reading the reflective inner surface of the shade concentrated light downwards. By the late nineteenth century candle shades had become highly decorative, but as these posed fire risks, many were used in conjunction with patent candle-holders that fitted into candle sockets and worked on the same principle as spring-loaded candlesticks. For these fittings the candle sleeves were invariably finished to look like wax candles.

Wax candles remained the prerogative of the wealthy until the general intro-duction of paraffin wax candles in the late nineteenth century. Nonetheless it was possible at the beginning of the twentieth century for those who still wanted spermaceti candles to buy them through department stores like Harrods. Whales are now an endangered species and spermaceti candles are no longer available, although beeswax candles continue to be made. Keeping up a centuries-old tradition, the Worshipful Company of Wax Chandlers even now supplies beeswax candles for the High Altar at St Paul's Cathedral and to other churches.

CHAPTER FOUR

Lighting by Oil
Light for All

Many old forms of oil lamps,... such as were in common use everywhere in the British Isles before the introduction of paraffin and petroleum, have disappeared so completely that there are only a few specimens, in various museums and private collections, still in existence.

J. W. Johnson, 'Light from the Earliest Times',
Illuminating Engineer, 1912

Grease and oil lamps have been used to light homes since prehistoric times and numerous examples have been excavated at sites across the world. Crudely fashioned, hollowed-out stones were used to burn animal fat and as time progressed sea shells were adapted for hanging oil lamps. These were the prototypes of floating-wick oil lamps and spout lamps, whose simple and functional designs remained unchanged over centuries. The oil lamps made by the ancient Greeks and Romans were not only of a form still recognisable in lamps being produced in the late eighteenth century, but also gave the same amount of illumination which, for a single-spout oil lamp, was about equal to one tallow candle.

Oils from animals, vegetables and minerals were used for lamp fuel and were generally sourced from whatever was available locally. In Mediterranean regions olive oil was abundant and readily obtainable, but for the poor cottager in Britain, if there was oil to be spared from food it was likely to have come from fish. The wealthy could afford superior imported oils. Until paraffin became widely available, the difference in quality of oils was akin to that between tallow and wax candles, with the price being commensurate to increased luminosity and decreased smell and smoke. In 1709 the tax imposed on candles was also levied on oils except that from fish which, like rushlights, was exempted in recognition that this was a fuel of the poor.

Animal and Fish Oils

...once the boiling process had begun, the crispy pieces of blubber floating on the surface of the pot... were skimmed off and tossed in the fire for

LEFT: One of a pair of massive stone pedestals in the Grand Hall at Penrhyn Castle, Gwynedd. As befits this neo-Norman castle built by Thomas Hopper from 1820, the pedestal is decorated with sea-serpents and dragons, from whose mouths are suspended double-burner Argand lamps.

fuel.... While this was a highly efficient use of materials, it produced a thick pall of black smoke with an unforgettable stench.

Nathaniel Philbrick, *In the Heart of the Sea*, 2000

For centuries malodorous fish, whale and seal oils had been used for lighting, particularly by people living in coastal areas and near ports. They provided a light for all those who were fussy neither about the smell nor the smoke, which left greasy black deposits. Whaling was a harsh and uncompromising life; once the whale had been captured it was stripped of its blubber, which was cut into chunks and boiled in try-pots on the ship's deck. In Britain the whaling industry was important not only for the cargo but also because whaling ships provided both the training and recruits for the British Navy in times of war. Chandler and Lacey summed up the arguments made in the early nineteenth century by the whaling lobby against the introduction of gas lighting:

> 'What would become of our Navy, if this pernicious invention were allowed to develop?' The argument advanced was that light is obtained from oil; oil is obtained from whales; the whales live in Greenland; we send out ships to catch the whales; the ships are a training school for the British Navy – therefore, if we burned gas instead of oil the Greenland fisheries would decay, and the British Navy would go to the dogs.[1]

The finest and most expensive illuminating whale oil, from the sperm whale, first became available in Britain in about 1750 (see pp.62–3). The oil produced a good light with little smell and was considered only slightly inferior to colza. In England in 1784 the lamp inventor Ami Argand wrote, 'I have bought for 4s 6d a gallon of that fine American spermaceti oil which they call liquid spermaceti,

A crusie lamp, producing a copious amount of smoke, illuminates the wine cellar in this caricature by Thomas Rowlandson, published in 1800.

which indeed has not the least smell and is very clear and pure'. By 1788 the growing demand for spermaceti oil had created a shortage and prices rose to 7s 6d a gallon.

Vegetable Oils

The value of our vegetable oil produced annually is 250 million francs; twenty-five years ago we imported 20 million francs of vegetable oil; today we export 6 million worth. This difference is due to the introduction of large scale production of Colza.

Report to the French Legislature, 1813

Argand found that spermaceti and olive oils had to be at different levels in the lamp reservoir for it to operate efficiently, and it seems that after experimentation spermaceti was declared the better alternative. However, demand for spermaceti oil was soon outstripping supply and a more economical solution was to find an oil that could be produced in quantities at home or was cheap to import. Colza oil was extracted from rape seed, *Brassica campestris*, by grinding and pressure, with the leftover, highly nutritious matter made into cakes to fatten sheep and cattle. Colza oil was slow to deteriorate and produced a clear, bright, smokeless flame. Its one disadvantage was its viscosity. Like many oils with a thicker consistency, it was difficult to produce the capillary action to take the oil to the top of the wick.

A vegetable oil that did not have this viscosity was camphene, which enjoyed some popularity between 1830 and 1850. Camphene was rectified from oil of turpentine and when mixed with alcohol gave a bright white light, which some thought equal to 'six mould candles and the smoke of three kitchen chimneys'. With a low flashpoint, camphene was highly volatile and lamps were known to explode. Its inflammability was the cause of many serious accidents and fires; in America *Godey's Lady's Book* of 1857 commented, 'We consider it suicidal to have camphene lamps in the house'.

Mineral Oil

Kerosene, coal and carbon oils, have already, in a very short time, worked their way into public favour, to an extent scarcely credited.... At first imperfect, and exceedingly disagreeable in smell, the oil has at length been DEODORIZED and brought to a state of perfection hardly anticipated by the most sanguine. It may now be obtained in any desired quantity and of superior quality. The material for its manufacture is absolutely inexhaustible. That it will eventually come into universal use, with all such as desire to avoid danger, and at the same time possess themselves of the very best and MOST ECONOMICAL artificial Light within their reach, there cannot be a doubt.

S. E. Southland, a Philadelphia dealer, 1859

The process of refining mineral oil had been discovered by a Glasgow chemist, James Young, in 1847 and patented three years later.[2] Although mineral oil was considered a superior means of lighting, it was not found in sufficient quantities in England or Scotland to satisfy the home market and only small and expensive amounts were imported from Russia and Burma. The situation changed dramatically after 1859 when massive oil deposits were found in Pennsylvania that were soon to flood the world's markets with cheap and plentiful supplies of paraffin (kerosene). Unadulterated paraffin lamp oil was stable, it produced a flame of good colour, was practically smokeless and had only a slight smell. Moreover, as the oil was thinner, it travelled by capillary action in sufficient quantity to the wick.

Nevertheless, by the end of the century fires and fatalities caused by accidents and explosions of paraffin lamps were a cause of great concern. Blame was partly laid on the low flashpoint of adulterated or unsuitable oils that were being sold to the poor by unscrupulous vendors, but it was also apportioned both to manufacturers who produced cheap oil lamps of flimsy construction and to the ignorance of some consumers who did not handle or manage their lamps safely. Despite these dangers, the cheap price of paraffin oil put it within the reach of almost everybody but the very poorest and by the early 1890s paraffin lamps had become the most widely used form of domestic lighting.

Oil Lamp Inventions and Developments

THE ARGAND LAMP

This invention embraces so many improvements on the common lamp, and has become so general throughout Europe, that it may justly be ranked amongst the greatest discoveries of the age. As a substitute for the candle, it has the advantage of great economy and convenience, with much greater brilliance...

Abraham Rees, *The Cyclopedia* or *Universal Dictionary of Arts, Sciences and Literature*, 1819–20

A development of *c.*1773 that advanced oil lamp technology was the introduction by Leger of a flat wick of woven cotton that improved combustion and produced a larger flame. The flat wick was subsequently used to good effect with the 'air burner' lamp that was first patented in France in 1783 by Ami Argand.[3] When he applied for his English patent the following year, he described his lamp as 'so

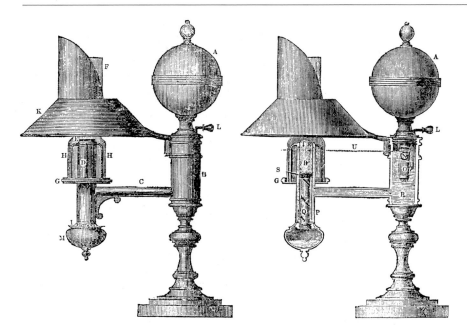

Cross sections of Argand lamps from *The Penny Cyclopaedia*, 1838.

constructed to produce neither smoke nor smell and to give considerably more light than any lamp hitherto known'. The burner comprised a wide, cylindrical woven wick held between two concentric metal tubes. This increased air supply to the wick which was drawn up the central tube and, together with the airflow on the outside of the wick, allowed for full aeration of the flame. Combustion and efficiency were further increased by the addition of a glass chimney. In terms of light-output the lamp had no rivals as it claimed to produce illumination equal to that of ten wax candles, 10 c.p., and if used with a quality oil and properly maintained it produced a bright light.

Towards the end of 1783 Argand had come to England looking for partners to make and sell his lamps and in the following year went into partnership with William Parker, the celebrated chandelier-maker, and Matthew Boulton. The metal parts of the lamps were to be made at Boulton's Soho Manufactory, with Parker responsible for the glassware and retailing the finished product. The partnership, however, was dogged by considerable difficulties.[4] Meanwhile in England and France Argand's lamps were copied and cheaper lamps appeared on the market, causing lengthy patent disputes on both sides of the Channel. Argand's invention was pirated and exploited in France by Lange and Quinquet, and Argand lamps are known there as *quinquets*. At the end of a third court case in England in 1786 Argand's original patent was rescinded and the partnership with Parker and Boulton ended. Over the years various component parts were improved, thus making the lamp more reliable and efficient, and it was favoured by all those who could afford the luxury of an expensive fitting together with the high cost of large quantities of oil.

A reservoir placed above the height of the wick was found to be the best solution in getting the thick and viscous oils to the burner, and a piston at the base of the reservoir helped to control the oil flow. However, there were disadvantages to this arrangement on table lamps: the reservoir obstructed a portion of the light and it also made the lamp top-heavy. To counteract instability some Argand lamps had ballast in their bases. A number of lamps invented in the first half of the nineteenth century attempted to solve these problems and a few of the most significant are described below.

One solution to light-obstruction was to place the reservoir below the wick, but this required other means to get the oil to the burner. A lamp developed by Carcel in 1800 had a clockwork mechanism in the base but it had its problems: 'Properly managed, this lamp gave a steady and bright light for seven or eight hours; but it was costly and easily disarranged, and though it is still retained by Parisians as the standard for photometric investigation, it never became very common'.[5]

Colza oil, which was largely used in these lamps, was called Carcel oil in France, the birthplace of several inventors of improved oil lamps. A more popular lamp was introduced by Franchot c.1830; his Moderator lamp combined a wound spring and piston to push the oil to the wick and a tube device which moderated the flow. Both Carcel's and Franchot's lamps were susceptible to problems with their mechanisms and unless cleaned regularly became easily clogged, particularly when fuelled with sticky colza oil. In 1860 Cassell's *Household Guide* informed 'these lamps are liable to get out of order soon and for constant work are not to be compared with the old Argand burners'. A number of well-used Carcel and Moderator lamps can be seen in the Lamp Room at Calke Abbey. In the Bachelors' Wing at Waddesdon Manor, Moderator lamps have been converted into electric table lamps. A Moderator lamp in the Drawing Room at Killerton shows how it was first converted to paraffin, then became an electric lamp.

Another ingenious idea to reduce the shadow cast by Argand lamps, and one which did not rely on susceptible clockwork mechanisms, was the annular model. In annular lamps the oil was contained in a hollow ring from where it was gravity-fed to the burner through tubes; the ring reservoir also served as a shade support. The Astral (star-like) lamp, dating from the early years of the nineteenth century, involved Count Rumford[6] and Bordier-Marcet, Argand's successor, in a bitter dispute over the patent. The Sinumbra (without shadow) lamp was introduced c.1820 and although this lamp enjoyed a period of popularity, the need for gravity- and force-fed lamps diminished once paraffin oil became widely available. Sinumbra lamps are very rare and those that survive have generally been converted to electricity. There is a pair of bronze and ormolu lamps in the Dining Room at Uppark, and a pair of bronze lamps in the Gothic Revival style in the Dining Room at Killerton.

By 1900 *The Book of the Home* was commenting, 'The colza-oil lamp is now so little used; it is expensive, and inferior to the best petroleum lamps'. But for those who persisted in using their old lamps, spermaceti and colza oils were still obtainable in the early years of the twentieth century.

THE PARAFFIN LAMP

Paraffine Lamps are now the chief illuminators of the whole civilised world.

'The Duplex Burner, a Fashionable Illuminator',
Birmingham Magazine of Arts and Industries, 1897–8

Benjamin Franklin is credited with having observed that two flames impinging upon each other increased light-output. However, this revelation does not appear to have been put to effective use in Britain until the development of the fishtail or Union Jet gas burner in 1820. It may have been this gas burner that inspired James Hinks, a Birmingham lamp manufacturer, to develop the Duplex oil burner in 1865. Paraffin lamps were initially fitted with single-wick burners, but illumination was increased significantly to 30 c.p. by the Duplex burner, which comprised two parallel flat wicks separated by about an eighth of an inch. The burner produced a brighter flame with greater economy and from the time of its introduction has continued to be used extensively on all but the cheapest paraffin lamps.

Throughout the last decades of the nineteenth century numerous lamp patents were taken out to improve the illumination, economy and safety of paraffin lamps. Many developments concentrated on improving airflow to increase combustion and therefore illuminating capability. It was the central draught lamp, whose technology derived from the Argand lamp, that succeeded. These lamps were fitted with air diffusers or spreaders, and although some claimed illumination output of up to 200 c.p., those mostly used in the home provided up to 50 c.p. In the late 1890s Welsbach's incandescent mantle, originally developed for gas lighting, was used with oil lamps; illumination output rose to 80-100 c.p. and it was possible to convert Duplex lamps by changing the burner. The final advance in the early twentieth century was in pressure lamps like the Tilley lamp which are still in use.

The thinness of paraffin oil led to a change in lamp design as the reservoir could be placed below the wick, although this did not necessarily give stability to

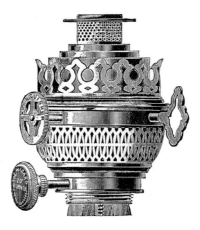

Illustrations from Falk Stadelmann catalogue, 1899.

FAR LEFT: A 'Superior Quality' Duplex oil burner.

LEFT: A 20-line (50 c.p.) 'Wizard' Patent burner.

all lamps. Lamp accidents continued to be commonplace and many domestic fires were caused by oil lamps being dropped or knocked over, so better-quality lamps were fitted with extinguishers. A pair of very high-quality paraffin lamps in the White Drawing Room at Arlington Court were fitted with Thomas Messenger's clockwork mechanism that could be set to extinguish the lamps at a certain time. However, by the end of the century it was possible for those with cheaper lamps to buy penny extinguishers that were adaptable to any lamp.

LEFT: One of a pair of cast brass paraffin lamps in the White Drawing Room at Arlington Court, Devon. The lamp was originally fitted with a Thomas Messenger clockwork mechanism.

Lighting the Home

The evil arising from the smoke and smell of lamps was formerly so great, as to prevent their introduction into domestic life, notwithstanding the strong inducement to convenience and economy.

Abraham Rees, *The Cyclopedia* or *Universal Dictionary of Arts, Sciences and Literature*, 1819–20

A number of writers have suggested that oil lamps were little used in homes from medieval times to the mid-eighteenth century. Certainly very few are shown in drawings and paintings. The reason for this may be that oil lighting faced strong competition from hearth fires, rushlights, tallow and beeswax candles, whose illumination could not be outshone by spouted or floating-wick oil lamps. Therefore it is all but impossible to estimate to what extent oil lamps were used in the home before the importation of spermaceti oil and the introduction of Argand lamps. What is clear is that candles were not given up when Argand lamps became available but for a long time were used in conjunction with them. This was probably because the two forms of lighting fulfilled different requirements in the daily and social lives of families. It should also be remembered that many wealthy households had already made considerable financial investment in buying very expensive candle fittings that could not necessarily be adapted for use with the new lamp even if desired.

The immediate difference between the Argand lamp and all other forms of oil and candle lighting was its brilliance, each burner producing light equal to approximately 10 c.p. or less than 20 watts. To eyes generally accustomed to rooms lit by two to four candles, this level of illumination appeared glaring. When several were lit, overall illumination was increased significantly, and the lamp was thus taken up enthusiastically for practical reasons by industry and commerce. The benefits of the new lamp included not only brightness but also, ostensibly, safety as the flame was encased in a glass chimney. When oil costs and light-output of the lamp were compared to equivalent numbers of candles, the economy of the lamp was confirmed.[7]

Concerns about damage to eyesight from glare were overcome by the introduction of shades. Count Rumford advised 'screens composed of such substances as disperse the light without destroying it. Ground glass, thin white

Catalogue illustration of a table lamp fitted with an incandescent mantle, *c*.1900.

silk stuffs... and various other substances, may be used for that purpose, and have been used very often'.[8] Subsequently frosted glass shades were used to diffuse light without substantial loss of illumination and these were introduced on expensive fittings. For some there was another imperative in using shades. In 1811 Count Rumford observed that, 'no decayed beauty ought ever to expose her face to the direct rays of the Argand lamp'. As the nineteenth century progressed the shaded lamp became the norm in the domestic interior, even if this meant that precious light was sacrificed to fashion and vanity. Only the vulgar and the poor, who had to make the most of their lighting, were not concerned with the niceties of its presentation.

In 1810 when Humphry Repton redecorated Uppark and made alterations for Sir Harry Fetherstonhaugh he devised a novel method of screening and diffusing light when he lit the Servery with Argand lamps. As the Servery was to be seen from the Dining Room 'by day and candlelight', a stained-glass panel was installed where 'the effect will be magic as all the light may proceed from this Window with Argand Lamps properly adjusted behind'.[9] When the double doors at either end of the Dining Room were left open, the effects of the illuminated panel were increased by reflection from the overmantel mirror in the Stone Hall and this light, together with that of the candlelight in the Dining Room, was further reflected by four alcove mirrors.

For use in the home Argand lamps with single or double burners were usually bought in pairs as table, mantle or torchère fittings. Chandeliers, made of bronze or ormolu, or a combination of both, generally had oil reservoirs placed at the centre of the fitting, the exception being chandeliers fitted with annular lamps. Some chandeliers were designed to give the consumer choice of both technology and level of illumination by having alternate lamp arms and candle-branches.[10] A gilt metal chandelier with combined lighting at Gawthorpe Hall is mentioned in Chapter Three as being the one raised and lowered by the footman.

Other types of chandeliers that became fashionable in the early years of the nineteenth century incorporated a large cut-glass dish at the base of the fitting. The dish not only performed the function of a shade, helping to cut out glare, but also to obscure the light-source of one or more Argand lamps. A number of these chandeliers had combination fittings, with candle-branches fixed to the outer banding on the rim of the dished shade. A combination fitting of this type can be seen in the Boudoir at Attingham Park. Humphry Repton, however, was not impressed by these chandeliers, as he made clear in a letter to Sir Harry Fetherstonhaugh in 1812:

RIGHT: Two-branched Argand pedestal lamps on the 'Charlecote Buffet' in the dining room at Charlecote Park, Warwickshire. These would have illuminated the work of the butler as he prepared to serve food from this extraordinarily elaborate piece of oak furniture.

> I went first to Hancock's, where I saw nothing but the old dish pendant... and these are all from 12 to 16 gns each – then I went to (I forget his name) in Bond Street, the grand Luminary... of the Nation – He supplies Uppark with oil – the same kind of lamps I found for from 8 to 12 gns. Why the difference between tradesmen – I believe 'em all rogues alike and only differing in the more or less...[11]

For those who wanted a display of light for a special occasion but did not want the expense of buying either Argand fittings or cut-glass chandeliers, these could be hired from large lighting emporia. Specialist lighting shops also hired out staff to tend the lamps, although they did not always come up to expectations, as the Douglas-Pennant family of Penrhyn Castle discovered to their great embarrassment in 1859:

> A man was specially had down from Miller's the great lamp shop in London, to see after the lighting of the house during the Royal visit [of Queen Victoria and Prince Albert], instead of trusting to the services of the ordinary 'lamp-man' of the House. This man deserted his duties, to see the arrival of the Royal guests and omitted to light the corkscrew staircase up to the keep, so that when my Mother took the Queen to her room, she found the stairs in complete darkness. My Mother begged the Queen to wait while she ran upstairs for a light, but on returning to the head of the steps, she found the Queen had laughingly groped her way up behind her in the dark.[12]

Whilst the affluent were shading their lamps, the poor were doing as they always did, improvising and getting the best light from any oils or fat they could spare from their meagre diets. Grease and oil lamps of the type first used in ancient times, hollowed-out stones and sea shells, were recorded as still being used in the late nineteenth century in the homes of cottagers in remote parts of England and Scotland. A form of oil light that was free but required some skill to obtain was used in the Shetland Islands, where going out and a grabbing a bird had a different connotation to what it has come to mean in the late twentieth century. Here the islanders looked forward to the arrival of the stormy petrel, an oily seabird that was collected to make lamps. When required, the bird's feet were planted in a lump of clay and a wick threaded down its throat. According to O'Dea, writing in the 1950s, these lamps were in use 'up to quite recent times'.[13]

Top of an invoice dated 1825 to Lord Willoughby de Broke from James Smethurst, lamp manufacturer and supplier of spermaceti oil. The illustrations on the bill head show, on the left, a double-burner Argand pedestal lamp of a design very similar to eight lamps made by Smethurst in the Saloon in Calke Abbey (p.113); and, on the right, an annular lamp where the oil is contained in the ring reservoir which supports the shade (p.102).

109

Lighting by Paraffin Lamps

There are tens of thousands of homes to-day, even on a higher level than those of the cottager and the artisan, where lamps have taken the place of candles. Many homes where artificial light was almost unknown, nowadays boast a best lamp in addition to that of everyday use.... And even in the case of those who use either gas or electricity there is still a call for oil as an illuminant for reading, writing, needlework, and study.

'The Latest Progress in Artificial Lighting',
Birmingham Magazine of Arts and Industries, 1903–5

It proved somewhat premature of *The Times* to state in 1854 that 'Filthy tallow candles and stinking oil lamps have been rendered nearly obsolete by the introduction of gas'. After 1860, cheap, reliable paraffin lamps were not only an attractive alternative for householders considering the expensive option of gas lighting, but also gave the opportunity to poorer consumers, previously denied a quality illuminant. Unlike the majority of gas and electric fittings, they did not have to be permanent fixtures in all rooms, enabling the poor to invest in a few lamps. It was also possible cheaply to convert candle and oil fittings into paraffin lamps by using the simple expedient of peg lamps. As the name suggests, these lamps had a short tapered peg fixed below the oil reservoir that fitted neatly into sockets which had once held candles or oil burners. Peg lamps were a boon for

Peg paraffin lamp fitted on an ornate gas bracket in the dining room at Erddig, Wrexham.

the wealthy who had invested in Argand lamps at the beginning of the century but who wanted a cheaper and more easily maintained light. Very few fittings appear to have survived with their peg lamps intact. In Northern Ireland, at The Argory and Castle Ward, the visitor can see small peg paraffin lamps fitted into candlesticks. At Arlington Court a bronze and ormolu chandelier, c.1820, originally fuelled by colza or spermaceti oil, was adapted for paraffin. These lamps have cut-glass fonts and are now converted to electricity; it was probably during this last refurbishment that the central oil reservoir was removed. Peg lamps have been used extensively at Erddig, for example on an ormolu chandelier in the Entrance Hall. Other lamps with decorative pink frosted glass shades and matching reservoirs were fitted into elegant Arts and Crafts-style wrought-iron bases made by the estate blacksmith.

Even in homes with gas lighting, paraffin lamps would have provided supplementary and, sometimes, essential lighting when the gas supply was erratic. In households where oil lighting was the principal source of light, those with money and pretensions kept their utilitarian paraffin lamps out of sight of guests. In servants' bedrooms and domestic offices, these lamps could be left unshaded, although those suspended over kitchen tables generally had large shades with reflective inner surfaces. At Erddig, suspension lamps of different qualities can be seen in upstairs and downstairs corridors. In the kitchen, two wall-lamps with back reflectors were fixed to wooden doors on either side of the kitchen range, so that their light could be directed where required.

In rooms where visitors were received, they could expect to be greeted by costly, substantial paraffin lamps with glass reservoirs and shades with etched patterns and in colours that harmonised with furnishings and decorations. By the use of shades and adjusting the light, an atmosphere of mellow restfulness, romance or gaiety could be easily created. Although Alice Taylor was writing about life in rural Ireland in the 1950s, her account of how a 'best' lamp looked in use is evocative of earlier times:

> A second oil lamp was kept in the parlour, and this was a rich relation of the kitchen model. It had a heavy cream-coloured glass bowl embossed with green and pink flowers, and an elegant brass stand. The pink colour of the lampshade matched the base and was delicately fluted round the top.... When the lamp was lit it bathed our parlour in a muted pink light.... The dark marble fireplace shone in the lamp-light, which was reflected in the mirror above the mantelpiece.[14]

Until the end of the eighteenth century a good level of illumination in the domestic interior had been at a premium. It is paradoxical, therefore, that in many mid-Victorian reception rooms the lighting advantages gained earlier were lost when light-diminishing shaded lamps were used in areas filled with overstuffed furniture, cluttered by knick-knacks, papered and carpeted with busy floral patterns and curtained with light-absorbing, dark velvets. Fashion and taste seemed to be dictating that well-lit interiors were no longer desirable and that illumination in terms of light-output was no longer considered a luxury. In the last years of the century consumers were offered an enormous choice of highly decorative lamps and coloured glass shades, made in large quantities by factories. Now industrial processes could provide middle-class consumers with luxurious-looking and affordable fittings.

To protect eyes from the bright white light produced by the incandescent mantles now being used on paraffin lamps, shades were necessary. In the early 1890s a new fashion in shade design was described in withering terms by Aymer Vallance in the *Art Journal*: 'Unhappily it is the fashion to use elaborate shades of silk or lace and ribbons, or of crimped paper ruched like a lady's skirt. Such things savour too much of Parisian millinery, and moreover are liable, if left for any length of time unwatched, to become scorched and catch fire.'[15] Oil, gas and electric standard lamps were 'dressed' with these large frilled shades and candles too had smaller but equally exotic shades. The demand became so great that in 1901 the firm of James Hinks & Son was reported to have 'a large factory solely devoted to turning out these shades'. At Arlington Court Mr Newman recalled 'wonderful Edwardian lamp shades like big hats in pink silk with lace fringes, kept in boxes, and used on standard lamps'. Large frilled lacy shades can still be seen in the Morning Room at Cragside and the Chintz Bedroom at Dunham Massey.

It was rare for the poor to waste light, although in the homes of the 'respectable' working classes a shaded lamp may have been amongst the prized possessions in the parlour or 'front' room. For very poor city or country dwellers, abundant light was still beyond the means of many, even at the end of the nineteenth century. Rural labourers like the fenmen of Wicken, living in the cottages of the village of Lode, were no doubt glad of the light provided by their humble oil lamps and candlesticks. When money was tight, there was always the light from the turves burning in large open fireplaces. Others, through choice or financial considerations, continued with candle and oil lighting into the twentieth century and a number of properties were lit principally by oil lamps when they were handed to the National Trust.

The comfort and ease of use of oil lamps made them appealing and many liked to read or write by lamplight. Although Henry James had a telephone at Lamb House in Rye, electricity was not installed, and James worked by lamplight. For many years George Bernard Shaw did likewise at Shaw's Corner at

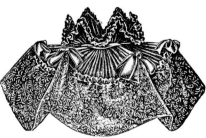

Frilled lamp shades in lace and silk from Falk Stadelmann catalogue, 1899.

George Bernard Shaw playing the piano by oil lamp and candles at Shaw's Corner, Ayot St Lawrence, Hertfordshire. It was his custom after dinner to play Beethoven and Mozart, and sing excerpts from operas and Irish songs to his wife Charlotte as she lay upstairs in bed.

Ayot St Lawrence. Estate workers at Felbrigg had electricity before the Hall, which was not connected until 1954 because Mr Ketton-Cremer liked the restful light of oil lamps and was concerned that electric lighting would spoil the look of rooms. A visitor to the house, Sir Brinsley Ford, recalled, 'one read by oil lamps and went to bed by candlelight'.[16]

The Lamp Room

…the lamp room at Arlington Court had a stone floor with shelves all around the walls, where extra lamps were stored, and also lamp chimneys of all sizes and shapes. There were lamp scissors for trimming the wicks and rolls of large and small wicks, six glass hand lamps, spare lamp shades and extra fittings for all types of lamp. There were bracket lamps in the passageways… a hanging lamp in the kitchen and two tall table lamps in the Servants' Hall. Filling the lamps, trimming the wicks and cleaning the soot off the shades was a daily chore, and the housemaids brought them down to the Lamp Room every morning. The paraffin was delivered from Barnstaple in large drums and kept outside.

Mr Jan Newman, who worked at Arlington Court from 1927 until 1978

The introduction of Argand lamps meant more work for servants. In large houses a designated room where the cleaning, filling and maintenance of lamps could be undertaken safely became a necessity. The lamp room was therefore an important centre of activity and in the grandest homes, where lamps and candles were used in profusion, light-tending could be a full-time job for more than one man. Lady Diana Cooper vividly recalled the tasks of the lampmen at her ancestral home, Belvoir Castle, in 1906:

> Then there were the lamp-and-candle men, at least three of them, for there was no other form of lighting. . . . They polished and scraped the wax off the candelabra, cut wicks, poured paraffin oil and unblackened glass chimneys all day long. After dark they were busy turning wicks up or down, snuffing candles, and de-waxing extinguishers. It was not a department we much liked to visit. It smelt disgusting and the lamp-men were too busy.[17]

After cleaning and replenishing, lamps, candelabra and candlesticks were returned to their places at dusk ready for use in the evening. For hygiene and safety reasons lamp rooms were generally sited on the periphery of domestic offices, close to oil stores. In large households, oil would be delivered in 68-gallon casks; between 1834 and 1843 casks of sperm oil arrived regularly at Dunham Massey and invoices show that the oil was at its cheapest in 1843, when a cask cost £22 19s 3d, and at a peak in 1840, when it rose to £38 7s 6d. The average price for a cask of oil during this period was approximately £25, or a little over 7s a gallon.

When the wick was too high or unevenly cut, smoke from lamps caused damage to ceilings and decorations. Some fittings, like suspension lamps, were made with smoke shades, but others had clear glass shades that could be suspended from hooks over the lamps. Oil leaks and spillages, due to overfilled lamps which seeped oil when the air in the reservoir became heated, damaged furniture and carpets. The results of seepage from Argand reservoirs can be clearly seen on some of the eight yellow scagliola columns in the Saloon at Calke Abbey, on which are placed large bronze pedestal lamps with double burners. These lamps, made by James Smethurst, one of the most celebrated lampmakers of the period, were bought in 1806-7 from the fashionable firm of Marsh & Tatham

The lamp room was traditionally a male preserve, but as by the beginning of the twentieth century households were keeping less staff, women became responsible for lamp duties. In the 1920s at Erddig there were, 'only maids to clean the forty-odd oil lamps needed when the Yorkes were entertaining and no footmen to resent this intrusion into their territory'.[18]

As soon as most homes were supplied throughout with electricity the lamp room became, like the oil lamp, surplus to requirements. There are now very few houses where lamp rooms can be seen, although at Florence Court both the oil stores and lamp room remain. Lamp rooms have been recreated at Uppark, and at Penrhyn Castle where, c.1900, 194 oil lamps were regularly cleaned, filled

and trimmed. In terms of the number and variety of lamps the lamp room at Calke Abbey is an Aladdin's cave, though as it is on the first floor the room was more likely used as a holding and distribution point than for the filling and cleaning of lamps.

LEFT: The Lamp Room at Penrhyn Castle. On the left are some coloured glass Vauxhall lights, which were suspended from wires to provide outdoor lighting at parties.

Design of Oil Fittings

SPOUT LAMPS

As an illuminant the crusie was anything but ideal. It frequently gave rise to an unpleasant acrid smell, owing to lack of proper access of air to flame and incomplete combustion. It required constant trimming and attention, and the light was of a feeble and flickering character.

J. W. Johnston, 'Light from the Earliest Times', *Illuminating Engineer*, 1912

In the days before the introduction of the Argand lamp and good-quality oils, few would probably have traded their candles for lamps. The fibrous home-made wicks in spouted lamps needed adjustment, and oil levels had to be checked regularly to get a flame with minimal smoke. But in poorer homes, if oil or grease were readily or cheaply available, lamps would be used in preference to rushlights or tallow dips. The crusie lamp, a simple open-top iron lamp, whose design derives from Greek and Roman terracotta spout lamps, was in use for centuries and in particular in Scotland until the nineteenth century. Fuelled by fish oil, the ones mostly used in the home were single-wicked with single or double bowls attached to a suspension hook. The purpose of the double-bowl

Metal crusie lamps – or sluts as they were known in America. The double crusie, or Phoebe lamp, has a second pan for catching the drips of oil. The 'Betty' lamp, from the Old English for 'bete', to kindle, had a wick holder in the spout of the lamp to support the wick above the pan, thus returning the spillage. The covered 'Betty' and the spout lamp resembled teapots.

RIGHT: The Great Stair at Osterley Park, Middlesex, a *Country Life* photograph taken in 1926. Three glass lanterns containing spouted oil lamps in the antique style were designed *c.*1770 by Robert Adam.

Whale-oil time-lamp in pewter, with a glass reservoir, from the collection of pewter objects at Arlington Court.

variety was for the underbowl to catch any spillages or drips from the wick. Many had a toothed arrangement by which the top bowl could be canted forward to keep the oil in contact with the wick. Crusie lamps are thought to have been in common use in Europe, and were taken by early settlers to America, where the 'Betty' lamp was used extensively. The 'Betty' looked like a substantial single-bowl crusie lamp with a closed top which burned grease. These lamps were generally of wrought iron and made by the village blacksmith; a small collection, which includes a 'Betty' lamp, is at Snowshill Manor.[19]

Whale-oil spout lamps were also used; in more affluent homes these were made of sheet brass or pewter. A lamp popular in Holland and in use throughout northern Europe had a small covered container with a long spout that fitted on a stand with a corresponding slightly longer trough to catch any overflow. This could be used either as a wall or table lamp. Dutch-style brass whale-oil lamps can be seen in the collection at Snowshill Manor, and a rare pewter whale-oil lamp is to be found at East Riddlesden Hall.

Lamps were also used for time-keeping, although any accuracy was dependent on consistent use of the same size wick and quality of oil. A rare whale-oil time-lamp in pewter with a glass reservoir can be seen at Arlington Court. More elaborate and costly were multi-spouted lucerna lamps of silver or brass which burned olive oil and better-quality whale oils. The lucerna was thought to have originated in southern Europe, its design inspired by classical bronze lamps. The lamps were generally height-adjustable and had wick-tending accessories hung from small chains. Some lamps also had adjustable polished metal screens to help to protect the eyes from glare and to reflect the light downward. Wick-tending accessories might include prickers, tweezers or scissors for wick adjustment and snuffing, buckets for the snuff and extinguishers. There are several brass lucerna lamps at Snowshill Manor and a pair in the Great Parlour at Wightwick Manor, although none has retained all their wick-tending accessories or has eye screens.

The introduction of the brightly burning and considerably less offensive spermaceti oil encouraged some suitably opulent designs that harmonised with furniture and fittings in Neo-classical interiors. At Osterley Park there are oil fittings described in an inventory of 1782: 'Three elegant Lamps mounted in Or Molee with brass ballance weights, lines Tassells and double pullies Antique burners hung with Chains compleat. . . . A Tripod term painted green and white with an elegant glass Lamp Vase mounted with Or Molee ornaments An Antique lamp with two burners'.[20]

These lanterns and lamps were designed *c.*1770 by Robert Adam, whose Neo-classical architecture and designs had earned him the nickname 'Bob the Roman', and were thought to have been made at Matthew Boulton's Manufactory. The Great Stair lanterns and the vase lamps in the North Passage and Staircase have green glass smoke shades, with four supporting dolphins that were derived from an illustration in James 'Athenian' Stuart's *Antiquities of Athens* (1762). Designs and motifs from the classical world were used extensively

by Josiah Wedgwood for his celebrated pottery wares. His 'Michaelangelo' lamp, for example, has a reservoir copied from a third-century BC Hellenistic bronze lamp, and the supporting slave figures are adaptations of figures from a Renaissance crucifix, possibly copied from models made by Michelangelo.[21] A pair of these lamps, each with six burners, is in the Morning Room at Saltram, bought from Wedgwood by John Parker in 1772 for 14 guineas.[22] In the Mirror Room is another smaller pair of Wedgwood and Bentley 'pebble' lamps *c.*1770 that have dolphins supporting the oil reservoirs.

LEFT: Black basalt 'Michaelangelo' lamp by Wedgwood. This is one of a pair bought by John Parker in 1772, in the Morning Room at Saltram, Devon.

FLOATING WICK LAMPS

God is the light of the heavens and the earth; his light is like a niche in which is a lamp, the lamp in the glass and the glass like a brilliant star.

The Koran

This text was often inscribed on floating-wick oil lamps used to illuminate mosques.[23] For centuries churches in England had sanctuary oil lamps kept perpetually alight by the simple but effective method of using a wick threaded through a metal-covered piece of cork or wood that floated on the oil and provided a small, glimmering light. Perhaps the most spectacular displays of these lamps were found in pleasure gardens that flourished during the eighteenth century. At the most famous, Vauxhall Gardens, there was an 'interminable blaze of radiance... impressed upon the bedazzled beholder' (see pp.94 and 114). In poor homes practically anything hollow would serve to hold oil, but for the wealthy small glass lamps, virtually shadowless, were sometimes used as nightlights. An elegant pair of these lamps, dating from the late eighteenth or early nineteenth century, can be seen in the Parnell Room at Castle Ward.

ARGAND LAMPS

Hanging lamps were equally of a strange design. Imitations of the Warwick vase formed the receptacle for the oil; the arms to which were attached the burners concealed below heavy cast 'boats', or bodies; bearded philosophers or ivy crowned satyr masks grinned down on the possessor of the lamp who stood below...

W. C. Aitken, 'Brass and Brass Manufacture', in
Timmins, The Resources, Products, and Industrial History of Birmingham..., 1866

Even though Argand lamps looked substantially different from earlier oil lamps, classical motifs were still used on better-quality fittings for Neo-classical interiors. Some of the earliest Argand lamps were made at Boulton's Soho works and designers such as Robert Adam, James Wyatt and John Flaxman were commissioned to provide sketches for wares produced at the factory. Boulton's silver-plated lamps were elegant and expensive and included peg lamps in designs that harmonised with the patterns of candlesticks into which they could be fitted. A pair of Boulton silver-plated mantel lamps with double burners, *c*.1785, is in the Italian Room at Stourhead. In the State Bedroom at Castle Coole there is a pair of ormolu single-burner table lamps, also of late eighteenth-century design, and in the Saloon single-burner Argand lamps are placed on four towering giltwood and porphyry torchères that were made by Preston's of Dublin in 1816, for the huge sum of £944. The Argand lamps at Stourhead and Castle Coole have been adapted to electricity and have lost their burners.

The earliest Argand lamps appear mostly to be smaller fittings, wall- and table lamps. This may be because initial technological difficulties had to be overcome before manufacturers could confidently produce chandeliers with multiple burners. By the beginning of the nineteenth century, however, chandeliers were being offered for sale. Chandeliers with cut-glass dish shades obscuring the light source that Repton scathingly referred to as the 'old dish pendant' in 1812 (see p.106) were of a design that broke with historical precedent. Although by the end of the Regency period these fittings were going out of fashion, the design in its simplest form was the prototype of semi-indirect light fittings that were radically to change how interiors were lit in the early years of the twentieth century (see Chapter Six).[24] Classical motifs continued to be influential and the chandeliers with 'bearded philosophers' and 'satyr masks' referred to by Aitken were, judging by the numbers in National Trust houses, a very popular design from the 1820s.[25]

A lamp produced *c*.1835 adopted a design taken directly from the antique. These were small table Argand lamps with reservoirs in the form of rhytons, drinking horns, inspired by a Piranesi illustration of an ancient Roman burial monument on the Appian Way. A noted Birmingham manufacturer, Thomas Messenger, is thought to have been largely responsible for producing these lamps, which were made in bronze or ormolu.[26] Pairs in bronze with a reservoir terminating in a boar's head at the burner can be seen at Uppark, Springhill and Kingston Lacy. Lamps with a dolphin's head decoration are more rare, but a pair can be found at Kingston Lacy, and two pairs at The Vyne.

Pedestal lamps with double burners were favoured for lighting halls and wall areas in large rooms. Some of the most unusual and impressive are at Penrhyn Castle, which was built in a neo-Norman style between 1820 and 1845 by Thomas Hopper. He is thought to have designed a number of the pedestal and suspension Argand lamps, which have mythological and antique references as befit a fantasy medieval castle. For example, in the Grand Hall is a pair of huge composition stone pedestals decorated with sea serpents and dragons from whose mouths are suspended double-burner Argand lamps. In the Entrance Gallery four pedestal lamps have reservoir covers decorated with wolf heads, possibly inspired by the Capitoline Wolf bronze in Rome. The expression 'not worthy to hold a candle to' is thought to have derived from the times when kings and courtiers had human torch- and candle-bearers. In an allusion to this, on the Grand Stairs there are two massive wall-brackets in the shape of

RIGHT: Chandelier decorated with gilded philosopher's masks, *c*.1820, hanging in the Staircase Hall at Arlington Court. Originally made for Argand lamps, the chandelier was converted for use with paraffin. The central oil reservoir is missing.

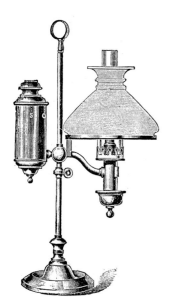

Catalogue illustration,
c.1900 of a Queen's pattern
reading lamp, a height-
adjustable Argand-style
lamp for colza and paraffin.

human arms from which are suspended chandeliers, each with four burners. The human arm is featured on many early Venetian bracket fittings. A pair of large, ornate, Venetian-style gilded lanterns of eighteenth-century design, supported by human arm brackets, can be seen in the Marble Hall at Clandon Park. Smaller versions hang in the Smoking Room in the Bachelors' Wing at Waddesdon Manor.

Despite the danger of being top-heavy, the most popular design of all Argand lamps was the height-adjustable 'Queen' pattern reading lamp, now often referred to as a 'student' lamp, which was made with one or two burners. Silver-plated 'Queen' lamps, made by Pillischers of New Bond Street, are in the collections at Speke Hall and Hughenden Manor. Although it was possible to convert this lamp to paraffin, because of the lamp's abiding appeal many manufacturers made it specifically for paraffin. These could still be bought in the early years of the twentieth century; versions for electricity have also recently become popular.

PARAFFIN LAMPS

The prices at which these articles are sold are surprisingly moderate, having regard to their manufacture… at the Viaduct show-rooms may be seen the humble paraffin lamp of the cottage, priced at a few shillings per dozen, and the most beautifully cast and chased duplex lamps… in all imaginable degrees of richly decorative ornament on porcelain, or in magnificent and massive combinations of artistic metal work.

Evered & Co. Ltd, *The Art-Trades Review*, January 1889

By the 1880s mechanisation had made it possible for manufacturers to produce large quantities of lamps to suit all pockets and for use in any location. Trade catalogues from the period reveal that the choice of paraffin fittings was truly immense. Designs of lamps ranging from the plain and functional to the large and ornate could be bought from ironmongers, lighting emporia and department stores. Late Victorian designs were eclectic but many manufacturers appear to have believed that classical designs could give lamps class and respectability, with superior brass- and silver-plated lamps often sporting support pillars in the Corinthian style. Although suspension lamps with large glass shades feature strongly in trade catalogues, chandeliers rarely do so, possibly because existing fittings could be converted by peg lamps. In the reception rooms of many middle-class homes, gasoliers would have provided the central illumination. The ormolu three-light chandelier in the Velvet Drawing Room at Saltram is a rarity. However the design is pre-1850 and this may be an example of a fitting in an 'historical' style, or one that originally contained small annular lamps. The paraffin lamps, which remain unconverted, have Hinks Duplex burners.

Wall-lamps to light passageways were usually of a plain design, with polished metal back-reflectors. When wall fittings were used in best rooms fancy lamps

RIGHT: Ormolu, three-light chandelier, hanging in the Velvet Drawing Room at Saltram.

were held in wall-brackets of ornate cast metal. Tall pillar lamps with decorative glass shades and reservoirs were hugely popular for reception rooms, but easily knocked over. A safer alternative, but not as aesthetically desirable, was a very cheap utilitarian lamp with a broad, square iron base. Glass reservoirs allowed the level of oil to be clearly seen but were easily broken; metal reservoirs were more robust but retained heat and were generally considered less attractive. However, in the early years of the twentieth century, as paraffin lamps were used less in best rooms, more serviceable and safer lamps with metal reservoirs began to win the day. Those made by Aladdin are still in production.

Much criticism was levelled against manufacturers either for producing dangerous cheap lamps or for using excessive and inappropriate decoration on expensive models. Paraffin lamps designed by leading Arts and Crafts Movement designers were admired by the style pundits; perhaps none more so than those made by W. A. S. Benson. Some Benson lamps used polished metal reflectors to focus light downward. For example, a brass paraffin lamp with an adjustable flanged copper reflector in the Morning Room at Standen was illustrated in a Benson catalogue in 1899 at a cost of £4 15s. A pair of Benson table lamps that have been converted to electricity can be seen in Lady Trevelyan's Parlour at Wallington. There are also a number of other late-Victorian paraffin lamps in the house, including a harp suspension lamp in the Writing Room.

Paraffin lamps and candles became the most widely used domestic lighting during the last decades of the nineteenth century. This situation changed only when gas suppliers realised that a large profit was to be made in supplying gas to working-class consumers by providing pre-payment meters (see pp.140 ff.). As increasing numbers of homes were supplied first with gas and later electricity, many oil lamps were abandoned and scrapped, whereas there still remained a place for a candlestick.

LEFT: One of several bracket paraffin lamps in the dining room at Kingston Lacy, Dorset.

CHAPTER FIVE

Lighting by Gas
Illuminated Air

Of the artificial lights now in use for domestic purposes candles are the most elementary and insignificant, oil-lamps the most general and economical, coal-gas the most convenient and trustworthy, electric lights the most healthy, safe, brilliant, and luxurious. Assuming that all methods are equally available, the average householder will choose gas, and the result will justify the preference.

H.C. Davidson (ed.), *The Book of the Home*, 1900

The Argand burner represented a significant leap forward in terms of lighting technology, but there were drawbacks. The lamps required regular attention, used large quantities of oil and proved insufficient to meet the demands of emerging industries, who ideally wanted maintenance-free and economical lighting that offered greater illumination. In the early nineteenth century the first large-scale application of gas was in factory, shop and street lighting and it made only slow progress into the home. By the beginning of the twentieth century, however, gas had overtaken paraffin and candles in popularity to establish itself as the most widely used form of domestic lighting, a position it maintained until the National Grid became operational in the mid-1930s.

A Brief History of Gas Lighting

The methods of procuring and distributing light, during the absence of the sun, have not hitherto attained their possible extent of perfection: there is yet a wide field for improvement in the construction of the instruments of illuminations, and the subject is highly deserving of every individual.

Frederick Accum, *A Practical Treatise on Gas-Light*, 1815

Natural gas was known to ancient civilisations; it is thought to have been the source of perpetual flames in Greek and Roman temples. Centuries later, in 1272, Marco Polo observed the burning of natural gas in Baku. In Britain attempts to manufacture gas from coal appear to have begun in the late seventeenth century.

LEFT: Gasolier designed by A.W.N. Pugin in the Reformed Gothic style, hanging in the Cromwell Hall in Chirk Castle, Wrexham.

'The Good Effects of
Carbonic Gas !!!', by Isaac
Cruikshank, published in
December 1807. Earlier in
the year, Frederick Winsor,
shown on the tight rope,
had demonstrated lighting
by gas in London when he
illuminated a length of
garden wall at the Prince
Regent's Carlton House
for the birthday celebrations
of George III.

In 1779 George Dixon used gas to illuminate a room of his house in County Durham and eight years later Lord Dundonald lit some rooms at his home, Culross Abbey near Edinburgh, with gas made from distilling coal tar, a process he had patented in 1781. Despite claims by others, it is a Scottish engineer, William Murdoch, who is generally recognised as the pioneer of the gas lighting industry.[1] Whilst working for Boulton and Watt supervising the erection of steam engines in Cornish mines, Murdoch experimented in gas-making and in 1792 he used gas distilled from coal to light his office in Redruth. After his return to Birmingham Murdoch organised a display of gas lighting and lit the exterior of Boulton and Watt's Soho works to celebrate the Peace of Amiens in 1802. A year later the interior of the Soho foundry was lit by gas, and shortly afterwards the cotton mills of Phillips and Lee in Manchester. It was unfortunate that Murdoch was dissuaded from patenting his gas-manufacturing process; nonetheless his achievement was eventually recognised when he was awarded the Rumford Gold Medal by the Royal Society in 1808.

A rival claimant was Frederick Winsor, an entrepreneur and opportunist who is important in the history of gas lighting as it was through his efforts that the

first public gas supply company was formed.[2] Rather than individual installations, Winsor envisaged supply from a central gasworks that would provide both
lighting and heating; but in his efforts to raise capital to fund a 'National Light
and Heat Company' he made ridiculous claims for gas, for example in a
pamphlet, *Plain Questions and Answers Refuting Every Possible Objection against
the Beneficial Introduction of Coke and Gas Lights*:

Q. Then suppose a room full of gas and you enter it with a candle?
A. It will never inflame because it is intermixed with the air of the room
Q. But is it not hurtful to respiration?
A. Not in the least! On the contrary it is more congenial to our lungs than
vital air. . .

Winsor's first demonstration of public lighting was in 1807 when, for the birthday celebrations of George III, he lit a length of the garden wall at the Prince
Regent's London home, Carlton House. Later in the same year he erected gas
street lights in Pall Mall, where he had set up business premises. The invisibility
of gas was part of its mystery and the public came to gawp and marvel at 'illuminated air'. Consequently gas lighting became the subject of numerous cartoons
that were inclined to portray its suffocating and explosive propensities. Many
were nevertheless persuaded to invest in his new venture by Winsor's publicity
and promises of huge dividends. Lady Bessborough wrote to Lord Granville
Leveson Gower in 1807 describing the escalating mania for buying shares,

Is it the seizure of Zealand? No! The investing of Copenhagen! No! The
Invasion? Oh no! War with Russia? Nothing like it. America? Still less.
What can occasion such a ferment in every house, in every street, in every
shop, in every Garret about London? It is the Light and Heat Company. It
is Mr Winsor and his lecture, and his gas, and his patent, and his shares –
these famous shares which are to make the fortunes of all who hold them,
and probably will involve half of England in ruin, me amongst the rest, and
prove a second South Sea Scheme. . . . Seventeen thousand shares have
been sold within these ten days. They were first a guinea, then three, five,
seven, they will be twenty, fifty, a hundred; there is scarcely any means of
passing thro' Pall Mall for the crowds of carriages and people on foot and
horseback. . . . I went last night to a very large party; I never saw so odd a
looking place – something like a cellar with crucibles and strange looking
instruments, resembling an Alchymist's shop in a Teniers picture, and
there, mix'd and squeezed together, were fine Ladies, a few Rabbi's,
Merchants, Peers, blue Ribbons and tallow Chandlers – all raving for
shares and entreating to sign their name first, lest none should be left.[3]

Winsor succeeded in raising capital for his renamed Gas Light and Coke
Company and, despite vigorous opposition from Murdoch , was granted a Royal
Charter in 1812 to light the Cities of London and Westminster and the Borough
of Southwark, the most populous areas of London.[4] Within a very few years

other private gas companies were set up in London and other cities and large towns, although investment by town councils in gasworks was generally more cautious.[5]

Gas became popular for street lighting, with shops, theatres, pubs and factories as the largest groups of consumers. Many large factories installed their own gasworks, and typical of these was the cotton mill at Quarry Bank, Styal, that had been founded in 1784. The factory was a comparative latecomer to gas lighting as the gasworks building was not completed until 1865, despite it being noted that maintenance of oil lamps was labour-intensive, and the use of tallow candles and Argand lamps in the factory the cause of eye inflammations. The total cost of installation was £1,453 4s and gas was supplied to the whole factory site including residential buildings. Although the factory was not in continuous production through day and night, employees and the 'apprenticed' pauper children were expected to work long hours, which were reduced from 60 per week to 56½ following the Factory Act of 1875. For some years the lighting was very unsatisfactory, with problems of purification. A new improved purifier was installed in 1874, leading to a reduction in the amount of gas used and increased brilliancy of light. From 1904 gas was supplied by the local gas company as it was more economical. Gas lighting continued in use at the mill until the 1920s and 1930s, and some fittings can still be seen in the manager's and clerks' offices.

The use of gas lighting in the home only began to grow in popularity after 1840. This was due in part to availability and fears about safety, and in part to cost. According to the original terms of their charter, the Gas Light and Coke Company agreed to supply street lighting for less than the cost of oil. As this was at a loss, private consumers paid a premium. Gas began as an expensive commodity; for example in London in 1823 the average price per thousand cubic feet was 15s, ten years later it was 11s 3d. From then onwards, prices gradually decreased, so that in 1905 it was sold in London at its lowest price of 2s.

For some years gas was only supplied after sunset to consumers who contracted to burn a specified numbers of lights for a limited number of hours. Those who wanted a supply for longer were expected to pay by volume, but as early gas meters were problematical and rarely accurate they were not in common use until after 1830. In response to demands for a day supply, arising through the use of gas stoves, a 'day' main was laid in Piccadilly in 1838. The gas supply system was open to abuses on both sides and fierce competition between companies led to undercutting and unprofitability. In a deteriorating situation some companies sabotaged the mains of rivals, causing leakages and even explosions. In London 'The quality of the gas was reduced by all the companies in an attempt to reduce costs. Consumers were lost, regained and lost again. Services were run from the mains of rival companies. Consumers received bills from companies which did not supply them, while the more unscrupulous among them ran an account with one undertaking until cut off for failure to pay, and then transferred to another'.[6]

Government intervention was necessary but legislation proved tardy. It was not until the Gasworks Causes Act (1847) that the rights and obligations of undertakings were codified and dividends and prices regulated. Nonetheless, the responsibilities of gas companies ended at the meter and only a few wanted to become involved beyond that point. Consumers were therefore generally left to the mercy of untrained gas fitters, many of whom were plumbers who, through their familiarity with pipework, were trying their hand at a new trade. Many of the terms to explain and describe gas and electricity were taken from those used with water supply; for example, mains, meters, taps, flow, pressure and current. For the most part, they remain in the technical language of both industries.

In c.1875 George King, a writer of consumer advice books, noted, 'I have been witness to hundreds of cases where homes have been badly fitted in the first laying of the pipes by inexperienced, clumsy, bungling workmen, and my experience compels me to say that there is a very great number of such workmen in the Gas-fitting line of business, perhaps more than in any other branch of industry'.[7] There was therefore a pressing need on the one hand for the training of fitters and engineers and on the other for the education of the consumer in how to use their gas fittings and appliances safely and economically. Although there were a number of advice books written by independent gas engineers who usually had their own products to promote, no formal response to these needs came from the industry until the turn of the century. The threat of electricity luring away richer customers, the introduction of pre-payment meters and the hiring-out of gas appliances to the working classes forced gas companies not only to ensure their hired property was being used properly, but also to promote and educate consumers in the use of newly introduced burners and appliances. Nevertheless in 1905 the *Journal of Gas Lighting* was still pleading with the industry, 'Let us advertise, and above all, let us educate our consumers'.

Gas Manufacture and Supply

COAL-GAS

The gas holder was described as 'an old rusty article', so unsafe that in windy weather it had to be held down by force, and so full of holes that it was no uncommon thing to see the manager on a fine morning lying down on top of it, stopping up the cracks with white lead. The manager, Mr Bliss, declared on oath, that the smell from the works was good as it made people sick, and so cleansed their systems. He described how he has cured five of his children of whooping cough by putting them in the boiler. Cross-examined, he admitted that they had developed scarlet fever immediately afterwards, but, he said 'I popped them in the purifier again and the fever disappeared'. In any case added Mr Bliss, New Malden deserved all it got because the people would not pay their bills.

A court report in the *The Surrey Comet*, 27 February 1868[8]

Coal-gas was manufactured by heating coal at high temperature in retorts. The gas released from the coal then passed through several stages of purification on its way to being stored in large gasholders. These are also referred to as gasometers. Early in the history of gas manufacture, a gasometer was so named because it had measurements marked on its side to indicate the volume being held. Exposing children with whooping cough to gasworks' fumes was thought to be a cure, and this practice continued into the twentieth century.

Initially some residuals from coal-gas manufacture were treated as waste and products like 'blue billy' from wet lime purifiers were discharged into rivers. However, it was soon realised that the by-products of coke, ammoniacal liquor and coal-tar were valuable commodities that became as important to the industry as the gas itself.[9]

In 1813 the Gas Light and Coke Company appointed Samuel Clegg as engineer to its gasworks in Peter Street, Westminster and shortly afterwards he was slightly injured when a gasholder exploded.[10] Fears of holders and pipes exploding and leaking were genuine causes for concern and despite reassurances from gas suppliers, poor maintenance together with bad practice and ignorance led to all-too-frequent disasters. From early on cast iron was used for the mains but service pipes were less substantial, and some early examples were described by Everard: 'Gun barrels, surplus from the demands of war, were introduced, first as pipes for public lamps mounted on walls. Subsequently, throughout 1814, they were bought in large quantities... for use as service pipes to private houses, being laid from the main to the point of entry into the premises'.[11]

Leakages from pipes with multiple joints and fractures of mains caused by decay, accident or sabotage were commonplace and proved to be one of the major causes of low pressure frequently complained of by customers. In 1860 Dr Letheby, Medical Officer of Health for the City of London, estimated that 386,000,000 cubic feet of gas escaped into the earth of the metropolis every year. This calculation was refuted by another authority, who estimated the loss to be 630,000,000 cubic feet, with the result that it 'darkens the soil, and makes it so offensive that the emanations from it can hardly be endured, renders the basement rooms of houses uninhabitable from the poisonous action of the gas, and even dangerous from explosions, and taints the water with filthy odour'.[12]

Conditions for gasworks' labourers were generally considered appalling; 'A more fatiguing, dirty and uncongenial occupation scarce exists in the whole round of manual labour, nor one that soon makes old men out of young ones'.[13] In 1859 London gasworkers went on strike to protest against working twelve-hour shifts seven days a week with one rest day a month when changing from day to night shifts. Although the strike was broken, working hours were gradually reduced for gasworkers in different parts of the country. In London, however, eight-hour shifts were not achieved until 1889.[14]

Until legislation forced the industry literally to clean up its act, manufactured gas contained varying degrees of impurities. This, coupled with fluctuating gas pressure, resulted in poor-quality light that was a major source of grievance for

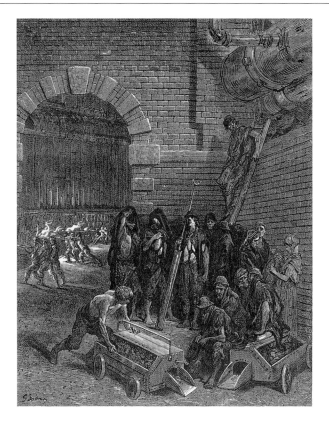

Gustave Doré's nightmare depiction of the gasworks at Lambeth, 1872, showing the terrible conditions under which gasworkers were expected to labour.

many consumers. The illuminating quality of gas was dependent on the coal used in its manufacture; common coal produced between 12 c.p. to 16 c.p. per standard burner and higher-quality cannel coal, found in Scotland and in some parts of England, produced 22 c.p. to 25 c.p. Legislation enacted from 1851 onwards compelled companies to produce gas to a specified illumination and purity that was subject to regular inspection and testing. Nonetheless when gas of good illuminating quality was produced, ignorance often prevented consumers from obtaining the best possible light from their burners.

OIL-GAS

The gas from oil would also be free from sulphuretted hydrogen and other impurities which cause considerable expense in the purification of coal gas... and the large supply of oil required would afford employment to thousands of fishermen, who would be engaged in the capture of fish suitable for yielding oil in sufficient quantity.

Michael Faraday, evidence to a Parliamentary Select Committee on the use of Oil-gas, 1824–5

Gas produced from oil had been mooted early in the nineteenth century and in 1815 John Taylor patented apparatus for the manufacture of oil-gas. In 1819

Taylor, in partnership with Martineau, installed a gas-making plant at the Apothecaries' Hall in the City of London and subsequently oil-gas companies were established in a number of cities and large towns. Several celebrated scientists were supporters of oil-gas lighting, including Michael Faraday, who discovered benzene from it. Sir Walter Scott, who had originally been scathing about gas lighting, had his home, Abbotsford, lit by oil-gas in 1823 and became chairman of the Edinburgh oil-gas company. However, oil-gas was found to be more expensive than coal-gas and there were problems in production. Following a number of accidents and fires, like the one at Covent Garden Theatre in 1828 where two men were killed, the use of oil-gas rapidly went into decline.

ACETYLENE

The pioneers of acetylene lighting can claim the credit of being the first to relieve the small country householder from the comparative gloom and discomfort of oil lamps and candles.

Maurice Hird in Weaver, *The House and its Equipment, c.*1910

It was discovered that calcium oxide, quicklime, produced a bright light when heated by an oxy-hydrogen flame and in the 1830s 'limelight' was used for spot-light effects in theatres. A gas considered to give a similar quality of bright light was acetylene. Although first produced experimentally in the same period, a commercial process for manufacturing calcium carbide was not developed until 1892, and within a very few years acetylene gas generating plant appeared on the market. Lighting by acetylene was considered ideal for country-house owners as it provided a cheap and relatively trouble-free system of illumination if installed by specialist firms and if certain precautions were taken. Acetylene was more explosive than coal-gas and the plant needed to be located away from the property in an enclosed, dry space; as the system needed little maintenance, it could be left to the charge of 'the most unskilled of attendants'. Acetylene light proved popular because the light was brilliant white and there were no harmful by-products of combustion to vitiate the atmosphere, or soots to dirty furnishings and decorations. Most of the burners used with acetylene lighting were based on the Union Jet principle and produced about 25 c.p., but it was also possible to use incandescent mantles of higher candle power.

The Bankes family of Kingston Lacy had another home, Studland Manor, that was lit by acetylene gas and Viola Bankes vividly recalled its generation: 'In a trough of vile smelling calcium carbide, in a long low shed, Savage produced acetylene gas, which gave a brighter light than came from ordinary gas. We would retch horribly as we peered in at him on our way to the kitchen. Savage did not mind the smell at all'.[15] A complete installation can be seen in one of the estate buildings at The Argory, where acetylene lighting was in daily use until 1983. In the house is a large range of acetylene fittings, including some adapted earlier fittings.[16]

RIGHT: Acetylene gas installation in one of the estate buildings at The Argory, County Armagh.

AIR-GAS

Its products of combustion do not contain either sulphur or ammonia, and are therefore far less injurious than those of ordinary coal-gas; furthermore, it is non-explosive. It has, unquestionably, a great future in country-house lighting.

Maurice Hird in Weaver, *The House and its Equipment c.*1910

In 1872 the Air Gas Light Co. Ltd announced their patented lighting system which used 'Gasogen' and which could be installed by 'any plumber'. It is difficult to ascertain whether or not the system was successful as it was rarely mentioned in gas journals until the first decade of the twentieth century. The machinery to manufacture air-gas, a mixture of petrol vapour and air, was considered to require 'no skilled attendance and can be worked with complete success by a housemaid' and it was claimed to give a light closer to daylight than any other form of illumination. Air-gas fittings were used with incandescent mantles which gave up to 60 c.p. and, although air-gas was safe, consumers were recommended to seek professional advice and warned against buying cheap plant. When Maurice Hird compared different lighting systems, he found the complete installation costs of a property with fifty lights to be: electricity £130, air-gas £105, acetylene £83, although air-gas was the cheapest to run. Both acetylene and air-gas lighting were considerably cheaper than coal-gas in terms of annual costs. Air-gas lighting was installed at Rufford Old Hall *c.*1915; light-fittings can be seen in the house and an 'Aerogen' generator in the Stable Block.

Inventions and Developments

GAS BURNERS

Through a strange variety of gas burners, of the 'rat-tail', 'batswing', 'fish-tail' and 'cockspur' patterns, the gas burned in varying degrees of smokiness and wastefulness. The gas itself was heavy with carbon dioxide, sulphretted hydrogen and ammonia...

South Metropolitan Gas Company, *A Century of Gas in South London,* 1924

The first gas burners were rudimentary, with names determined by their flame shapes. In his first gas-making experiments Murdoch devised a burner based on the principle of the Argand oil lamp and in 1809 Clegg constructed gas Argand burners that had a ring of small holes, to be used with glass chimneys. The burner produced a column of bright light but it was not popular for use in the home as the flame smoked if the burner was not frequently adjusted when pressure fluctuated. Although not equal in brightness to the Argand gas burner, two other improved burners were introduced: the batswing burner in 1816 that had a slit opening which produced a broad flat flame, and, from 1820, the fishtail or Union Jet. This burner had two small holes that allowed the gas jets to impinge on each other with the effect of producing a brighter flame. However, if gas burners were not properly adjusted they made a variety of hissing, roaring, singing or whistling noises that caused great irritation to consumers.

Good illumination from gas burners was subject to different variables: the quality and pressure of the gas from the gasworks and the care consumers or their servants took in cleaning and changing their burners regularly. Some of the problems were solved by William Sugg's introduction in 1858 of incorrodible burner tips. He also produced pressure-regulating governors.[17] Despite these improvements, consumers continued to complain about 'bad gas' but as Chandler notes, it was clear from a report of London Gas Referees *c*.1871 what lay at the heart of the problem; 'Fishtail burners purchased at random were found to give respectively only 27, 24, and 23 per cent. of light compared to the standard burner. They estimated that in London alone a sum of £500,000 might be saved by the use of good burners instead of bad ones.'

In 1874 Sugg produced the 'Christiania' burner that Chandler considered to be, 'probably the best flat flame burner ever made. It was pronounced by many eminent gas engineers of the day to be the perfection of flat flame burners, and when used with the beautiful white "Albatrine" shades it gave a most pleasing and delightful effect.'[18]

An invention that staved off competition from the electric lamp for many years and that superseded all other gas burners in terms of light-output and economy was the incandescent mantle invented by Carl Auer, Baron von

Advertisement, *c*.1870, showing different types of gas burners made by Bray's.

How the Sugg's Patent
Christiana burner could
transform the middle-class
home, 1886. Even the life of
the family cat is improved.

Catalogue illustration
c.1900, showing how to fit
an incandescent mantle on
a gas burner.

Welsbach, who was granted a master patent in 1885.[19] The cotton or ramie fibre mantle was impregnated with chemicals from rare earths and when heated by a Bunsen flame glowed to white incandescence that was infinitely brighter than the reddish-yellow light of flat flame burners.[20] A number of technical and production difficulties had to be overcome before the mantle was commercially successful, but by 1891 the company was able to claim that it gave up to 60 c.p. for 3,000 hours and the advantages were described in his company's promotional literature: 'the Welsbach burner can be screwed on to any existing gas-fittings in less than two minutes... the saving of gas amounts to from 50 to 70 per cent as compared with other gas burners... the combustion being perfect, no free carbon is thrown off, the atmosphere is kept pure, the ceilings are not blackened, and decorations are not tarnished'.[21]

Before the introduction of the electric lamp a problem for all lighting technologies was that light shone upwards. Attempts had been made to invert the gas flame with recuperative or regenerative lamps. The first was developed in 1865 and was used to light Galley Head lighthouse in Ireland. In 1879 Frederick Siemens, of the electrical engineering family, patented a lamp that was rapidly improved upon by others. Recuperative lamps were fully enclosed and produced a very bright flame by heating air and gas with some of the products from combustion. In the 1880s, Sugg described his 'Cromartie' recuperative lamp as 'A Special Patented form of Steatite Burner... used INVERTED... producing an intense white flame in the form of a camellia. It diffuses a perfectly steady, white, shadowless light, with great illuminating power'.

It is difficult to know how popular these lamps were as few survive. At Cragside, which is famous for being the first house in the world to be lit by electricity,
there is a pair of Wenham recuperative lamps with decoratively painted enam-
elled casings in the Bee Room. The gas came from the local gasworks at
Rothbury, founded by Sir William Armstrong in 1895 to supply a gas engine
used to drive a generator for his extended electrical installation. Gas was used to
light the domestic offices at Cragside, and some single and double swing wall-
brackets remain.

However, an inverted burner more suitable for domestic use was not invented
until the closing years of the nineteenth century. This burner offered all the
advantages of electric lighting at a fraction of the cost and was an immediate
success when it was finally launched in the early years of the twentieth century.
Moreover it was possible to convert upright gas fittings through the use of an
adaptor. At Sunnycroft a number of wall-brackets that were originally used with
flat flame-burners have inverted burner adaptors.[22] The inverted burner was not
widely advertised in the press until 1905, probably an indication that initial difficulties had to be overcome. At the Crown Liquor Saloon, Belfast, the gas lamps
with inverted burners are still in use. At A la Ronde, which is thought to have
been supplied by the local gasworks at Exmouth, a working inverted gas burner
is in the Entrance Hall.

BELOW LEFT: Recuperative
(regenerative) gas lamps
with Doulton pottery
casings, c.1880.

BELOW: A gas bracket
c.1910 at Sunnycroft,
Wellington, Shropshire,
that was originally fitted
with a flat flame burner.
New technology at the end
of the century enabled the
gas flame to be inverted, and
it became possible to convert
fittings with an adaptor.

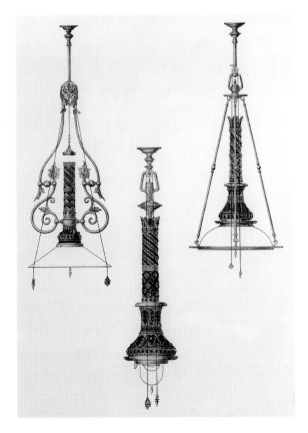

The pneumatic gas switch
was so easy that even a child
could work it, as shown in
this advertisement, *c*.1903.

AUTOMATIC IGNITION AND SWITCHES

What has the poor lamplighter done that he is threatened with banish-
ment from our highways and byeways…? Yet it is designed to exterminate
him and to supersede his office by a clockwork attachment to the taps of
our street lamps, which will turn them on at stated times every night, and
shut them off every morning…

Once a Week, June 1868

Safe and reliable automatic ignition became essential for inaccessible lamps.
Although primitive devices were developed as early as 1814, it took many years
before any system could claim complete success.[23] Automatic igniters were used
extensively for street and theatre lighting but were rarely needed in the home.
However, for those with gas lamps suspended in lofty halls automatic ignition
did prove useful; for example, at Wimpole Hall a control panel lit and extinguished the huge ventilating lamps in the Yellow Drawing Room and Great
Staircase. At the end of the century gas suppliers, faced with competition
from electric lighting, were happy to promote a product that matched the
convenience of electric wall switches. Gas switches were first developed in 1899
and subsequent improvements resulted in the pneumatic gas switch of 1906,
although the invention came rather late in the day as the consumers who
could most afford the luxury of its convenience were already turning towards
electric lighting.

METERS

Thus, with the electric light taking the richer consumer, and the cheap oil
holding the smaller ones, in 1892 the South Metropolitan Gas Co. began to

turn their attention to new ground... gas was practically unknown in the dwellings of the working classes. They would never... incur the cost of putting in gas-fittings and pipes.

W. J. Liberty, 'A Centenary of Gas Lighting and its Historical Development',
Illuminating Engineer, 1913

By the 1840s virtually all gas was being sold by volume. Domestic consumers were expected to pay the costs of connection, buy their own meters and settle their accounts quarterly. The accuracy of meters was still being questioned, many people believing they paid for more gas than they actually consumed. Finally in 1859 legislation decreed that gas was to be sold by the cubic foot and all meters were to be inspected for accuracy by Board of Trade officials. The high costs of connection and fittings together with quarterly payments put gas lighting beyond the means of many lower middle-class and working-class families. Although a pre-payment meter, operated by pushing a coin through a slot, had been invented in 1870 gas companies were not prepared at that time to take the 'risk' of supplying gas to working-class homes. It was the threat of electricity that stimulated companies to broaden their customer base.

From the mid 1890s, the offer of pre-payment 'automatic' meters to working-class consumers proved an immediate and resounding success. Gas companies bore all the costs of installation, with the consumer paying a hire charge for

Advertisement for penny-in-the-slot collection carts, from the *Journal of Gas Lighting*, September 1902.

fittings and appliances as a surcharge on the price at which gas was sold to account customers. So popular was this venture that in 1897 the Chancellor of the Exchequer reported to Parliament that the Mint had struck three times the amount of copper coins as in the preceding twelve months. George Livesey, the Chairman of the South Metropolitan Company, reported that, 'as much as ten tons of coppers had been removed in one collection'. As feared by the gas companies, temptation proved too much for some and breaking into meters was a common offence for petty thieves and needy families, often punished by imprisonment with hard labour or a birching. In 1899 the *Journal of Gas Lighting* reported a case of a chimney sweep who blamed pre-payment meters for his inability to pay a fine:

JUDGE BACON: 'Why don't you pay?'
DEFENDANT: 'I ain't got it. Business is blooming awful'
JUDGE BACON: 'I suppose people want their chimneys swept?'
DEFENDANT: 'Not as they used; I'm nearly ruined, all through automatics. They has the penny-in-the-slot gas stoves, and all the blessed summer they never lights a fire. What is a poor sweep to do?[24]

In 1882 there were 500 gasworks supplying less than 2 million consumers. By 1920 there were 827 gasworks supplying 8 million consumers, and of these 4.5 million had pre-payment meters.

Lighting the Home

Gas was always a middle class luxury. It never invaded the marble halls of the West End; and, of course, the poor could not get it. It was admitted to the rich man's kitchens and domestic offices, and its attractions beckoned the workman to his only club, the corner pub. As a domestic light in the fullest sense of the word, it was almost the sure sign of respectability as the keeping of a gig.

W. H. Y. Webber, 'Private House Lighting by Gas', *Illuminating Engineer*, 1912

At first the supply of gas for lighting was concentrated in densely populated areas where those risking financial investment could be fairly confident of recruiting customers. It was not until the 1840s that towns with populations of less than 2,500 could reasonably expect a gas supply, and it continued to be uneconomic to lay mains to very small rural communities and isolated properties. For wealthy householders determined to have gas lighting but whose estates were in secluded positions, their only option was to build a gasworks or, later in the century, invest in considerably cheaper acetylene or air-gas plants. Until the end of the century the overwhelming majority of consumers were the urban-dwelling middle classes.

Although the initial costs of gas and the fitting-up of houses was expensive, the light given per burner was, theoretically at least, more than could be obtained from an Argand oil lamp. For reasons already stated, consumers rarely got the full illumination benefits from their burners until later in the nineteenth century, and a good level of light could only be achieved if a number of burners were used. From the 1860s paraffin lamps and candles more than adequately met the lighting needs of most and it was only after a number of further improvements, like the incandescent mantle, that an increasing number of consumers gave up their lamps and candles in favour of gas lighting. This was despite arguments that 'A saving of time is effected, and the labour of servants is lessened, where gas is used; there being no candlesticks nor snuffers to keep clean, nor lamps to trim; whilst the furniture being no longer soiled by the droppings of tallow and oil, requires to be cleaned and renewed less frequently than before'.[25]

What gas lighting could offer prosperous middle-class consumers was an opportunity to flaunt their well-being to the world. As with the wealthy in the eighteenth century, it was in the rooms seen by visitors where the most expensive light-fittings were displayed.

The awe and wonderment many people experienced when first seeing 'lamps without wicks' was quickly replaced by fear as soon as fires and explosions began to be reported. It was not unknown even late in the nineteenth century for gas leaks to be investigated by the light of a candle or a match. Suffocation was of equal concern and for a long period householders were advised to turn off their gas supply at night. Deaths from carbon monoxide poisoning were caused by leaks from fittings and pipes. Consumers were therefore cautioned, 'But there is this objection to soft-metal pipes being used – in driving of nails, fitting of screws, or any alterations, you are liable to pierce the lead or composition pipes, or where rats or mice abound they very frequently cut the soft-metal Gas pipes, to the danger of life and property, saying nothing about the loss of Gas in such cases'.[26] It was argued that the noxious smell of gas was beneficial as it warned of leaks and for this reason a smell had to be added to natural gas in the late twentieth century.

Despite these very real dangers, gas lighting grew in popularity during the century with the consequence that most people had to have their rooms frequently redecorated to remove the blackening caused by soots: 'When you needed your ceiling whitewashed once a year, now you have to have it done three or four times. The filth from the impurities of the gas is something so extraordinary.'[27] Consumers were advised to use either glass smoke 'consumers' above their shades or mica screens within the shade; the consensus of opinion being that although the whole ceiling would become begrimed, the effect would not be so noticeable.

Initially gas jets were a novelty and fittings without shades were illustrated in Frederick Accum's *A Practical Treatise on Gas-Light*, published in 1815.[28] Rather like the first reactions to the Argand oil burner, there were complaints about the 'brilliance' of the light and suggestions that it was injurious to eyesight. Furthermore gas lighting was considered to be unflattering. A description of an evening

Early illustration for gas fittings with rat-tail burners from Frederick Accum's *A Practical Treatise on Gas-Light*, 1815 edition.

at Abbotsford by Sir Walter Scott's biographer J. G. Lockhart noted: 'In sitting down to table... no-one observed that in the chandeliers there lurked a tiny bead of red light.... Suddenly at the turning of a screw the room was filled with a gush of splendour worthy of a palace of Aladdin.... Jewellery sparkled, but cheeks and lips looked pale and wan in this fierce illumination; and the eye was wearied and the brow ached if the sitting was at all protracted.'[29]

The use of shades was necessary not just for reasons of vanity and aesthetics. Cross-currents of air cooled the flame and prevented complete combustion, while the shades had to be open at the top and bottom, otherwise insufficient air would cause the light to flicker and smoke.

Shades used with flat flame burners were generally globe-shaped – 'moons' – or bowl-shaped half-hemispheres – 'half moons'. These were not recommended for use with batswing burners as fluctuating gas pressure caused the flame to broaden and risked cracking the glass. Until incandescent mantles were introduced, fishtail burners were generally used in the home. Expert opinion about shade colour was that blue produced the closest to natural light, green gave a milder light than white but, 'any of these are better than the red, hot, glaring light of unshaded burners'.[30] The use of any shade reduced light and it was calculated that clear glass diminished light by 10-12 per cent, ground glass by 40-50 per cent and thick opal by 60-70 per cent. When light-absorbing shades were used in rooms fashionably decorated in rich colours and replete with mahogany furniture, any illumination advantages were dramatically reduced, if not lost entirely. With light shining upward from flat flame burners the most illuminated area was the ceiling; corners continued to be dark and gloomy.

Gasoliers and wall-brackets were fixed at a low height for accessibility when lighting, dimming and extinguishing, and to get the light closer to where it was needed. The recommended height for gasoliers was between 6ft and 7ft from the floor and for wall brackets the *Sanitary Plumber* in 1899 advised, 'Ordinary bracket dresser lights should be about 4ft 9in. from the floor; hall brackets 6ft.; mantel brackets, 5ft.; bathroom brackets 6ft.; alcove lights 4ft. 9in.... Care should be taken not to locate bracket lights where doors can be opened against them.... Many fires have been started in this manner.' Some gas engineers felt that wall-brackets should not be used at all, believing that the best lighting could only be achieved by diffusion from overhead lights and reflected from light ceilings and walls. This was precisely how lighting was to develop in the early twentieth century.

Middle-class homes were invariably connected to a mains supply and some country houses were near enough to a town supply to be connected. For example, Penrhyn Castle was supplied by the local town gasworks, and the stables continued to be lit by gas until the 1960s.[31] Some very wealthy families paid or largely contributed towards the funding for their local town gasworks so that there would be a supply available for their own use and for the local community. Furthermore, this spared the eyesore of a gasworks on the estate. An early initiative took place in 1836 when Lord Egremont had the Petworth town gasworks built. Subsequently the North Gallery in Petworth House was lit by gas.

Other country-house owners had no option but to build their own gasworks and on some estates there are remains of former works, for example at Chirk Castle.[32] An early installation that provided both lighting and heating was designed by Charles Babbage, the inventor of the Difference and Analytical Engines. In 1814 Babbage married Georgiana Whitmore, whose family lived at Dudmaston, and the system he designed for the house is reputed to have remained in operation until 1936. In 1859 Colonel Ridehalgh moved into a mansion that once stood in Fell Foot Park on the shore of Lake Windermere, where he had built a gasworks to light the house, boathouses, jetties and grounds. The Colonel was a keen sailor and in 1879 he replaced his old steam yacht with the *Britannia*, which cost £12,000 and had its own gas generating plant to supply the lights on board.[33]

Gas lighting in aristocratic homes was fairly uncommon and where gas was supplied it did not usually penetrate beyond the green baize door. Gertrude Pole, head housemaid at Sudbury Hall from 1919-1962, recalled her early days in service; 'it was all candle-light and oil-lamps, except for some gas brackets in the corridors'.[34] One reason for the reluctance to have gas lighting in formal rooms was snobbery; gas had associations with the middle classes and, perhaps even worse, with trade and theatres. Lady Diana Cooper, writing about the lighting at Belvoir Castle in 1906, summed up the attitude: 'Gas was despised, I forget why – vulgar I think'. This concurred with what Molly Hughes had heard in the 1870s, 'how magical it seemed to her when she first came to London to see someone turn a tap and produce light at once from gas. She had heard how the "best" people in London had stood out against gas as being vulgar, and that Grosvenor Square was the last place to adopt it.'[35]

But there were also far more practical reasons why gas should not be used in luxurious and expensively furnished and decorated rooms. These were described

146

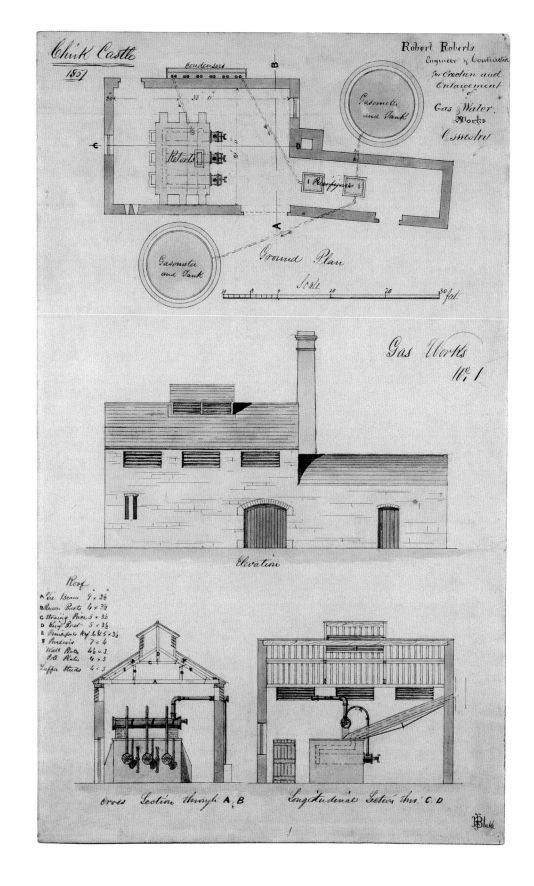

Chirk Castle
1857

Robert Roberts
Engineer & Contractor
for Erection and
Enlargement
Gas & Water
Works
Oswestry

Ground Plan

Scale

Gas Works
No 1

Elevation

Cross Section through A.B

Longitudinal Section thro' C.D

by King in 1875; 'But when Gas is very impure, it creates a disagreeable odour when burning; it also tarnishes gold and silver plate, gilt mouldings, and picture frames; it quickly blackens white ceilings, and turns the colour of the best wall papers, and the atmosphere where such Gas is consumed becomes very unwholesome'.[36] In a test at the Literary and Philosophical Society at Newcastle-upon-Tyne it was found that, 'as much as half-a-gallon of water is collected of a night from the gas burnt there – this water being so corrosive from the presence of sulphuric acid, that it attacks all metal fittings with which it comes into contact'.[37]

A solution to this was good ventilation, but few wanted the draughts from open windows and doors. A costly alternative came in the form of ventilating lamps that required the installation of ducts and flues to take the vitiated air outside the building. The first ventilating lamp was invented in 1817, but it took many years and a number of improvements before the lamp was perfected. At Wimpole Hall there are two large ventilating lamps, probably installed in the 1880s, with inner reflective surfaces to focus light downwards from their clusters of upright burners. The property had its own gasworks, some remains of which are still on the estate. The usual customers for ventilating lamps were those with large areas to light, for example theatres, pubs and churches. An impressive row of ventilating lamps, of similar design to those at Wimpole Hall, can be seen at the Birmingham City Museum and Art Gallery.

Another option was to use gas lighting externally and illuminate internal spaces through glazed windows. This was done with spectacular effects at the Prince Regent's Royal Pavilion, Brighton, where, according to the *Brighton*

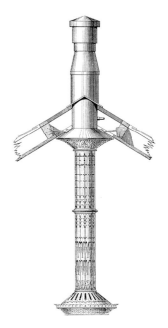

Catalogue illustration of Sugg's Patent Ventilating light, showing the flue above the fitting which discharged the by-products of combustion to the external atmosphere, rather than into the room, *c*.1880.

Gazette in January 1822, 'in no single instance has gas been used within the walls of the palace; exteriorly it is so illuminated, and most brilliantly, when needed, and the stained glass of the Music and Banqueting Rooms, together with that of the hall etc. are made to display their rich variety of tints inwards by the blaze of gas with out'.[38] It has been suggested that the Prince Regent may have got this idea after having seen Sir Harry Fetherstonhaugh's illuminated glass panel in the Servery at Uppark (see p.106).

New and substantial housing, built on the outskirts of towns for prosperous middle-class families, offered the luxury of gas lighting already installed. If not, the gas companies would have mains laid in the streets in the certain hope that requests for connection would sooner or later be made. A typical villa where gas was supplied from the outset is Sunnycroft, built on the outskirts of Wellington in 1880 for a brewery owner. In 1899 the property was enlarged and the gas lighting extended, and in 1912 Mr Lander, a local solicitor, moved in with his family. With the exception of the room shared by two housemaids, all rooms were gaslit, the cook having a wall-bracket in her room. It was not unusual for lighting to be introduced incrementally, and although domestic offices may have been amongst the first areas of the home to be lit, servants' bedrooms were generally the last, if indeed they were ever lit by gas at all.

Although the pre-payment scheme remained beyond the means of the very poorest, 'respectable' working-class people in regular employment with settled lifestyles became within a very few years the largest group of gas consumers. Even homes in fairly inaccessible places had pre-payment meters. A gasworker who lived in one of the Holy Austin Rock Houses carved into the soft sandstone at Kinver Edge arranged a supply for residents for both gas lighting and cooking-stoves. One of the Rock Houses at Kinver is open to visitors, and the remains of a gas supply pipe can still be seen.

Initially many gas companies believed the working classes incapable of using the incandescent mantle, with the consequence that poorer consumers were not only paying more for their gas but were also getting less light into the bargain. Nonetheless the additional benefits still outweighed the drawbacks of this discrimination, as outlined in the *Journal of Gas Lighting* in 1897, 'It will light his room, and on raw early mornings and late evenings will take the chill off also – thus saving a good many fire-lightings. Moreover the convenience of a simple boiling ring, or a neat little gas cooker, is in many instances a greater inducement to the cottager than even lighting.'

At the end of the nineteenth century incandescent mantles and burners helped extend the life of gas lighting. Shades used with upright incandescent mantles were longer and slimmer to take into account the shape of the mantle. Considerably smaller but equally powerful mantles were developed for the inverted burner and these were used with correspondingly smaller shades. By the outbreak of the First World War gas fittings had become unobtrusive, in keeping with the growing taste for less cluttered rooms decorated in lighter colours. But once the National Grid became operational, gas lighting went into decline.

Following the discovery and exploitation of vast supplies of natural gas in the 1970s, all fittings and appliances that had been using coal-gas had to be converted. At this point only very few chose to continue lighting their homes with gas; consequently, gaslit homes are now very rare indeed.

Design of Gas Fittings

Nothing can compete with the gaselier in tawdry deformity. Bronze and ormolu constructions of leaves and chains, dog's heads and mermaids, scrolls and flowers, basket work and pebble knobs, Brummagen gone hopelessly mad and poisoning us besides.

Mrs Loftie, *The Dining Room*, 1878

Brummagen was a disparaging term used to describe the wares pouring out in the mid-nineteenth century from factories in Birmingham, then the centre of the brass trade. Virtually all gas light-fittings were made of brass, in a wide variety of styles that drew on many sources for inspiration and which expressed the rich diversity of Victorian taste. It was not uncommon for gas fittings to be decorated with a jumble of design motifs from different periods and cultures, and these were unanimously condemned by critics as all that was objectionable about British design. The manufacturers' largest group of customers was the middle class, and by satisfying its needs they were generally perceived as purveyors of vulgar and garish fittings that appealed to vulgar and pretentious people.

By the end of the century, Birmingham manufacturers had diversified into producing paraffin lamps and candlesticks as well as gas fittings. The fittings ranged from those made in chased cast brass by highly skilled craftsmen to the cheapest and flimsiest that were liable to leak. For industrial and commercial purposes gas light-fittings did not have to be concerned with aesthetics; what were required were robust, reliable fittings that were preferably cheap. On the other hand, expensive, flashy and grandiose fittings were wanted by theatres and town halls.

The domestic consumer could make his or her choice from manufacturers' catalogues that showed every type of fitting in an abundance of styles. Expensive fittings were made to appeal to wealthier consumers and some chandelier-makers, like F. & C. Osler of Birmingham, produced cut-glass gasoliers. A cut-glass gasolier is now in the Cabinet at Felbrigg Hall and another, which once hung in the mansion at Fell Foot, is in the Morning Room at Arlington Court. Few acclaimed designers appear to have produced designs for gas fittings but an exception was A.W.N. Pugin. In 1845 Pugin was commissioned to redesign and redecorate the principal rooms at Chirk Castle and a gasolier in Pugin's Reformed Gothic style can still be seen in the Cromwell Hall. Although wealthy families did buy expensive gas fittings, it was possible to have some candle and oil fittings adapted for gas lighting; examples of chandeliers formerly used

with colza or spermaceti oil are at The Argory and Castle Ward.[39] Two bronze chandeliers with 'bearded philosophers' masks' are suspended in the stairwell of the Main Staircase at The Argory and were adapted for acetylene lighting. The gilt metal 'Gothic' chandelier in the Saloon at Castle Ward probably dates from the late 1820s. In the house there are several other gaslight fittings still in situ. At Waddesdon Manor gas lighting was confined to entrance halls, corridors and domestic offices. In keeping with the exquisite furniture and *objets d'art* in the house the majority of the gas fittings in the formal parts made use of ornate mid-eighteenth-century brackets.[40]

Gas fittings had two distinct disadvantages when compared to oil lamps and candlesticks: their lack of portability and manoeuvrability. Early on, consideration was given to overcoming this problem. In 1815 Accum described and illustrated 'A stop-cock with ball and socket which, when adapted to a gas-light pipe, allows it to have an universal motion, so that the light may be turned in any direction'. The ball-and-socket joint was used with great success on wall-brackets and with gasoliers, as the joint prevented the supply pipe from fracturing should the fitting get knocked. All that remain of the gas fixtures at East Riddlesden Hall, for instance, are ball-and-socket joints that are still to be seen in some rooms.

In the late 1820s the water slide gasolier was introduced, which allowed for vertical movement. Its arrangement and use was described by Wilson; 'it is of the first importance not to have the lights too high, and yet they should be of such a height in a dwelling house as to leave head room beneath when required. For sitting rooms the gasalier, when of the sliding kind, should be, as a rule, so arranged that there is a clear height of 6ft. 4in., when the gasalier is pushed up as high as it will go, and when drawn down the burners should be about 5 feet above the floor, to give a good light for reading or working by at the table underneath.'[41]

Despite its popularity, by the end of the century even the gas press was warning against its use. In an article 'Dangerous Gas Fittings', which appeared in the *Journal of Gas Lighting* on 18 September 1900, it was stated;

> As everyone knows, the principle of this 'chandelier' is that of a water seal, which, of course, fails when there is no water in it. Few people remember to replace the water, which easily evaporates in a warm atmosphere. Even supposing, however, that there is water in the sliding tube, the chains supporting the weights which keep the pendant in position may easily get defective; and thus the bracket may drop below the water seal, and the gas be allowed to escape. This is probably what happened in Birmingham last week .... It was shown that a water slide pendant had become defective owing, not for want of water in the tube, but to flimsy chain fittings. Those defects accounted for the death of a man and very nearly that of his wife. Both had retired to bed in good health; but before morning were poisoned with escaping coal gas, which doubtless they had inhaled through most of the night...

LEFT: Cut-glass gasolier that originally hung in the mansion at Fell Foot Park on Lake Windermere in Cumbria, and now is in the Morning Room at Arlington Court.

It was just as well that some water slides were 'equipped with a whistle which sounded the alarm when gas began to escape'.[42] An early twentieth-century water slide gasolier adapted for acetylene can be seen in the Dining Room at The Argory.

Equally as dangerous were other telescopic and jointed fittings for example, the 'stuffing box' pendant that could be swung upwards when not in use. Plain pendant fittings without any manoeuvrability were also generally reserved for domestic offices. Those with two branches in the shape of an inverted 'T' were found particularly useful over kitchen tables, although more ornate varieties,

some with water slides, were used to light dining-room tables. A 'T' pendant which is still in working order can be seen in the Dining Room at A la Ronde. A pair of pendant fittings of unusual design can be found in a former boathouse, now a tea room at Fell Foot. Only one of these fittings is intact, and it has a silver ball set above the gas burners which are arranged like wheel spokes. The horizontal gas flames would have curled upwards with an effect similar to that produced by the mirrored balls that were features of many twentieth-century dance halls. It is thought that the boathouse was once a venue for parties, and around the walls are decorative iron gas brackets.

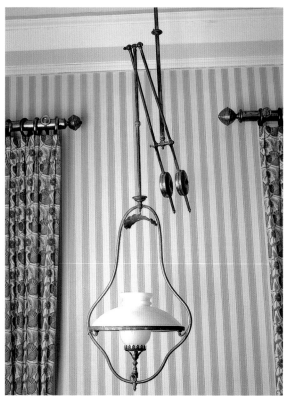

ABOVE: A Best 'Surprise' wall bracket above Captain Shelton's bed in The Argory. The counterweight, seen at the top of the fitting, allowed for directional versatility in both the horizontal and vertical planes. Below the smoke consumer is the orginal white glass shade that has gold-coloured glass bead fringing.

ABOVE RIGHT: Captain Shelton also had a Best 'Surprise' pendant lamp in his bedroom. The upper white glass shade has its glass bead fringing missing.

RIGHT: Table lamp and gas point in the Study at The Argory.

A fitting that offered all-round versatility and did not depend on water, cork or other seals was the 'Surprise' pendant, which could be described as the prototype of the electric anglepoise lamp. The pendant was invented in 1893 by a Birmingham fittings manufacturer, Robert Hall Best, and was described in an Army and Navy Stores catalogue; 'Its construction enables it to be balanced in ANY position, and to be moved with finger touch. It swings round in a 3ft. circle; measures 3ft. 6in. from ceiling plate when up, and 7ft. 10in. when down.' Albert Edward, the Prince of Wales, bought one for the King's Library at Sandringham House and in so doing ensured a period of success for the Best & Lloyd Company. A number of 'Surprise' pendants arranged as ceiling and wall-lights can be seen with their original glassware at The Argory.

Throughout the Victorian period the most decorative and expensive fittings were gasoliers. Their use was mainly confined to 'best rooms' where they could be displayed with wall-brackets of matching design and suitably ornate shades. Gas table lamps also appeared in best rooms, and in studies and bedrooms. Although it was possible for some to be attached by flexible tubing to the burners on gasoliers or wall-brackets, their use mainly relied on gas points being available. In the 1880s, William Sugg & Co. were selling mohair-covered 'nonodorous best flexible tubing' for 1s 3d per ft. The most popular fittings were wall-brackets, ranging from the overly intricate to severely functional. For porches and entrance halls gas lanterns were considered desirable. At Carlyle's

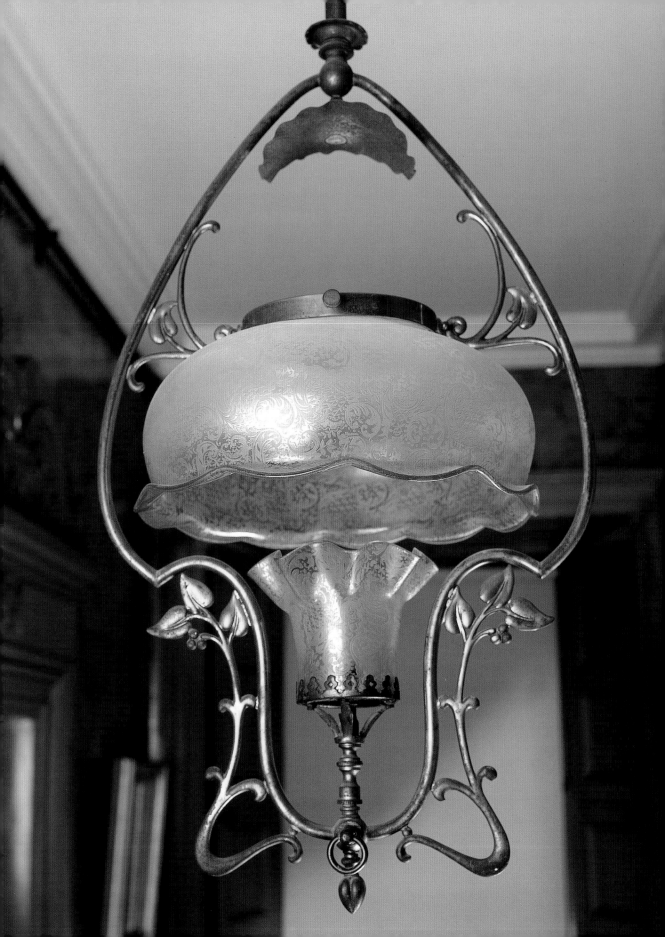

Some passageways at The Argory were lit by brass 'harp' gas pendants of Art Nouveau design. The peach flushed glass shades with etched patterns, and the smoke consumer suspended from the top of the fitting are original. The gas tap can be seen at the base of the fitting. This harp design was also popular for paraffin oil pendant lamps.

LEFT: Six-arm gasolier of 'classical' design in the Drawing Room at The Argory. The gas candles are shaded by bead fringing.

House, the Chelsea home of Thomas Carlyle, the gas lantern is still *in situ* and in the basement kitchen is a 'T' pendant for upright flat flame gas burners that was probably an original fitting *c.*1877.

For a variety of reasons some consumers chose to present their gas lighting as candles. Although in 1892 the *Journal of Gas Lighting* had been scathing about the time 'when poor ignorant gas fitters of the early Victorian period put up their glassy imitation candles, surmounted by batswing flames', 'gas candles' made a reappearance, and for a brief period were fashionable. At The Argory, a number of gasoliers have candle fittings with acetylene burners, and in the bedrooms acetylene candles are placed in silver-plated gas table lamps that are in the form of candlesticks.

Unless dimmed and shaded, the light produced by gas candles was not going to deceive the casual observer. Nevertheless some gas fittings made at the turn of the century were designed to look as if electricity, then an expensive luxury, was being used. The illusion depended largely on the effective use of shades and

An ornate three-arm
gasolier in the Study at
The Argory, with pink
flushed, etched glass shades.
The shades and their
galleries were designed to
'have the appearance of
an electrolier'.

to a certain extent of galleries (shade-holders). Fittings manufactured by the
Welsbach Incandescent Gas Light Company in 1900 claimed to have 'the
appearance of an electrolier'; fittings and shades that were probably made by
the company can be seen at The Argory.

Fittings changed dramatically in the early years of the twentieth century;
by 1910 even designs popular at the turn of the century had begun to look
old-fashioned. The introduction of incandescent mantles together with new
developments in electric lighting compelled illuminating engineers to advocate
lighting by indirect and semi-indirect methods which relied on diffusion and
reflection. The purpose of gas fittings now was solely to convey and enhance
light rather than display it, with brassware accordingly reduced to a minimum.

Once the gas companies realised the value to their businesses of having working-
class consumers, the gas industry burgeoned and for many years maintained its

A wall bracket lamp cast in the form of a mermaid, *c.*1880, at Sunnycroft, Wellington, Shropshire. The lamp was originally fitted with a flat flame burner.

competitive edge over electricity. Gas lighting and gas appliances did much to improve comfort in the home and, although many consumers gave up their gas lights as electricity became more widespread and cheaper, gas for heating and cooking remained popular. Gas fittings that were once produced in great numbers are now relatively rare as few were considered worthy of adaptation. In comparison to electric light-fittings, nineteenth-century gas lights looked unappealing and antiquated and, in the middle of the twentieth century, this was not how the majority of people wanted their homes to be presented.

CHAPTER SIX

Lighting by Electricity
Light without Flame

I have said, more than once, that at the present day we can only regard the electric light in England as a luxury, and we must pay for it as such. But there is no reason why it should always remain a luxury. There are various chances of economy which justify the conclusion that, sooner or later, the price will be brought down so as to relieve us of the use of the term 'luxury' as applied to it.

Sir William Preece, Electrician to the Post Office, 1884

Despite the hopes expressed by Preece, electric lighting remained a luxury for many years, and a house lit by electricity indicated prosperity and progressiveness. The non-inflammable nature of electric lighting provided unprecedented opportunities for decorative effects, while its combination of novelty, luxury and modernity was emphasised through the use of expensive and occasionally frivolous gadgets. Although electric lighting in the 1880s offered distinct advantages over other forms of lighting in terms of health, convenience, cleanliness, safety and aesthetic possibilities, it did not begin to provide illumination superior to that of oil lamps or incandescent gas lighting until the early years of the twentieth century. The industry was slow to develop; electric lighting only made inroads into middle-class homes after 1900 when improved technology and larger electricity supply stations made it cheaper. In 1902 Preece envisaged that electricity would soon become 'the poor man's light' but this did not become a reality until the first stage of the National Grid became operational in 1934, more than fifty years after electric lighting had first been introduced into the home.

A Brief History of Electric Lighting

For twenty years Franklin was an ardent electrician, and the leisure of seven of those years was devoted almost exclusively to the subject. He subjected electricity to every test.... He tried it on magnets. He tried it upon the sick and healthy; upon animals and men. The electricity excited by friction, the

LEFT: Tulip uplighter made by the great French glass-maker, René Lalique, in the dining room at Coleton Fishacre in Devon.

electricity drawn from the clouds, the electricity generated in the cold and glittering winter nights, the electricity of the electric eel, were all observed and compared.

The Evening Hour Library, *Benjamin Franklin 'Doer of Good' – a Biography*, n.d.

Since earliest times lightning and other natural electrical phenomena have both fascinated and perturbed human beings. In Ancient Greece the effects of static electricity were observed by Thales, who noted the attraction of small particles to amber when it was rubbed. It was therefore no coincidence when in 1600 Sir William Gilbert, physician to Queen Elizabeth I and the author of the first modern book on physics, named electricity from *elektron*, the Greek word for amber. From then onwards electricity became a subject for systematic study and experimentation. In 1663 an electricity-producing friction machine was invented by Otto von Guericke and by the middle of the eighteenth century Leyden jars were being used to store electrical charge.[1] Philosophers and natural scientists theorised, seeking to explain electricity and to find practical applications for its use. Benjamin Franklin's novel experiments with lightning and his invention of the lightning conductor are well documented, but perhaps less well known was a prototype of the electric fence that he invented to protect his privacy; 'when finding the idlers of the street were too fond of coming to a halt under one of his windows, charged the railing with his newly discovered electric fire'.[2] At the end of the eighteenth century Luigi Galvani propounded a theory of current electricity that was later revised by Alessandro Volta, whose work culminated in the invention of a chemical battery, the voltaic pile.[3]

Volta's invention subsequently enabled Sir Humphry Davy to demonstrate the prospect of incandescent and arc lighting at the Royal Institution in London. In 1802, when Davy connected the ends of a platinum wire to the terminals of a voltaic pile, the current caused the wire to glow to incandescence before oxidation broke the connection. Six years later, using an enormous battery of 2,000 cells connected in series, arcing sparks were produced; 'Charcoal pieces one inch long and one-sixth of an inch in diameter brought near each other produced a bright spark which extended over four inches when the pieces of

Caricature by L. Foy, dating from the 1790s, poking fun at the fashionable interest in electricity. A family party discovers that an electric shock may be passed along a line of people, causing mayhem. It was believed that mild shocks could improve health, persuading the 2nd Earl of Buckinghamshire in 1793 to install a Physic Closet with electrifying apparatus at his Norfolk home, Blickling Hall.

charcoal were withdrawn from each other... and by which drawing the points from each other a constant discharge took place through the heated air, in a space at least equal to four inches, producing a most brilliant ascending arch.'[4]

However, before incandescent or arc lighting could progress to become viable forms of lighting, a number of other discoveries and inventions had to be made in the generation, storage and transmission of electricity. Significant discoveries in electromagnetism and induction were made by Michael Faraday in 1821 and 1831, leading to the successful development of electric motors and dynamos.[5] In the early decades of the nineteenth century people flocked to be entertained and awed by demonstrations of electricity. A clergyman expressed concern that it was 'a phenomenon of the devil' and, as if to prove the point, Mary Shelley's eponymous hero *Frankenstein* (1818) harnessed the power of electricity to rekindle life in the dead.

In 1848 a carbon arc lamp developed by Staite and Petrie experimentally lit the portico of the National Gallery in Trafalgar Square, and although arc lighting was to be commercially uneconomic for some while, its strong, bright beams were put to beneficial use in lighthouses.[6] But by 1878 advances in technology had made arc lighting feasible and in Paris and London some streets were lit with Jablochkoff's 'electric candles'.[7] Arc lighting yielded an intense, harsh light that was prone to flicker, and it was not uncommon for the carbon rods to produce a hissing noise and a smell as they burned down. A number of museums and art galleries installed arc lamps in preference to gas lighting and in 1879 the effect of arc lighting in the Reading Room at the British Museum was reported in *The Times*: 'the electric light was turned on, and, without any apparent preparations, the spacious room was suddenly illuminated as by a magic ray of sunshine to the great satisfaction of all present'. Not all welcomed its uncompromising brilliance, as Lady Jebb recorded; 'On Wednesday we are all asked to see the Museum lit up for the Conversazione with electrical light. Mrs Brownlow asked me yesterday what she should wear. I told her if we consulted our best interests, we should wrap our faces up in some kind of head covering and look out on the world with one eye. Nothing more frightfully unbecoming than the glare of electricity having ever been discovered.'[8]

For use in the home a 'softer' light was desired and the challenge to inventors was to 'sub divide' the brightness of the arc light. Since at least 1838 several inventors had been attempting to produce incandescent lamps using platinum or carbon filaments.[9] Some claimed success, but no practical lamp had appeared on the market. Although these filaments had high melting-points, oxidation caused the filaments to burn out after a short time even when encased in glass bulbs exhausted of air. In 1875 apparatus that could produce a sufficiently high vacuum became available following Sir William Crookes's modification of Sprengel's mercury vacuum pump and it was then only a matter of time before someone produced a commercially viable lamp. The first to succeed was Joseph Swan, who had been trying to perfect a carbon filament lamp since the 1840s.[10] By February 1879 Swan had arrived at a point where he might have considered

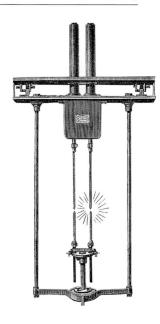

The intense light from carbons was protected by opaque glass shades. In this illustration, from R. Hammond's *The Electric Light in our Homes*, c.1882, the arc lamp's shade has been removed to reveal its carbon rods.

Incandescent lamps
illustrated in Hammond,
*op cit. c.*1882. The filament
in the lamp lower right has
a distinctive 'M' for Maxim.

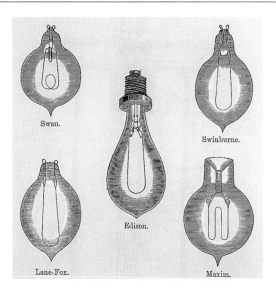

patenting his invention but did not do so immediately, believing there was 'no invention without pedigree' and that his lamp had only been made possible by the work of many others who had preceded him. This was an unfortunate business decision as later in the same year Thomas Edison perfected his incandescent lamp and immediately took out worldwide patents, an action that ensured he is remembered as the inventor of the incandescent filament lamp.[11] However, Edison's achievement was not solely confined to the production of a lamp; from the onset he envisaged and worked towards the development of centralised electricity supply stations.

In 1880 the industrialist and inventor Sir William Armstrong asked Swan to install forty-five incandescent lamps at his country home, Cragside.[12] This house already had the distinction of being the first in the world to be lit by hydroelectricity when in 1878 an arc lamp was installed to light the Picture Gallery. Armstrong wanted the arc lamp replaced and other parts of his home lit by incandescent lighting, describing the pleasing results in a letter to *The Engineer* on 17 January 1881:

> ... but the arc light, only being divisible to a small extent, could not be made nearly so serviceable for the distributed lighting of a house. Besides, the light produced by incandescence is free from all the disagreeable attributes of the arc light. It is perfectly steady and noiseless. It is free from harsh glare and shadows. It casts no ghastly hue on the countenance, and shows everything in its true colours. Being unattended by combustion, and out of contact with the atmosphere, it differs from all other lights in having no vitiating effect on the air of a room. In short nothing can be better than this light for domestic use.

At the Paris International Electrical Exhibition (1881) and the Crystal Palace Electrical Exhibition (1882) Edison's and Swan's lamps were shown alongside

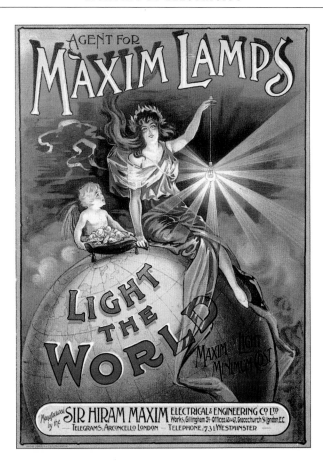

An advertisement for
Maxim lamps, c.1900.

those made by St George Lane-Fox and Hiram Maxim. Other inventors were
also bringing their lamps into the marketplace. The prospect of incandescent
electric lighting had now become a reality and this provoked an initial flurry of
investment based on false expectations that electricity would soon be as cheap as
gas. However, the abuses and exploitation of consumers by water and gas supply
companies earlier in the century had not been forgotten and as a result legal
measures were swiftly introduced to curb any excesses of the emerging electrical
industry. The effect of the first Electric Lighting Act (1882) was to inhibit investment and this caused share prices to plummet, although the subsequent Electric
Lighting Act (1888) went some way to restore confidence. Restrictive legislation
was nonetheless a key factor in the slow development of electricity supply
stations, with the result that for many years those who wanted electricity were
obliged to generate their own power. This was particularly the case for owners of
country houses.

The first public electricity supply station was established in Godalming in
1881 but the venture soon proved unprofitable.[13] Early in the following year an
electricity undertaking was set up in Brighton and so successful was the enterprise that the town can claim to have the longest continuous public electricity
supply in the world. Initially only arc lighting was available between specified

hours and consumers paid 12s a lamp a week, but these prices were soon reduced. By 1887 the cost per unit of electricity was 1s and the station was supplying continuous high-voltage power for 34 arc lamps and 1,500 incandescent lamps through a '7-gauge bare copper wire over-head mains 15 miles long'.[14] To ensure profitability electricity stations were located in affluent and densely populated areas, but supplying electricity could be a risky business. A major problem for consumers were the repercussions of over-demand at peak periods, which at worst produced a complete failure of supply, or at best caused the current to fluctuate and surge, resulting in poor-quality light or lamp breakages. Although the first electricity supply stations were not as large or imposing as gasworks their presence in a neighbourhood gave rise to complaints about the noise and vibration of the generators. In 1885 the Tallow Chandlers, disturbed by the Cannon Street installation, protested that 'the engine's intolerable noise kept the Beadle awake at night and disturbed the Court by day'.

When gas was first introduced it had been difficult for many people to understand how 'air' coming through pipes could provide light. Now they had to try to comprehend how something invisible and potentially as lethal could travel through wires and provide a light without a flame. The gas industry ensured that consumers became fully aware of the dangers of its competitor and although electrical engineers tried to reassure the public that low-voltage electricity was harmless, if certain precautions were taken, few probably went as far as William Preece who, in 1884, used his children to demonstrate its safety: 'In my house I use lamps that require only 30 volts to keep them going, with safety from shock and fire. I often put the wires into the mouths of my little children in order to illustrate practically to my guests that there is no danger. They do not much like it; but it does not hurt them.'[15]

As competition between gas and electricity suppliers intensified both industries attempted to undermine consumer confidence. A report in the gas press of 1903 discussed a fatality at the Fulham Public Baths. 'Two men went into cubicles in this establishment...and never came out alive....The most disturbing feature of these electrical accidents consists in the impossibility of foreseeing or guarding against them.'

In 1909 canvassers for electricity supply companies were being advised, 'Every prospective consumer is ready with a "no", get him to say "yes". To sell current intelligently, make yourself familiar with the other forms of lighting, heating and power. Keep track of gas explosions. Keep track of asphyxiation cases. Keep track of lamp explosions. The nearer the accident is to your territory, the better an argument it should be in your hands. Carry newspaper clippings of these if possible'.[16]

In comparison to the gas industry the electrical industry quickly set up training courses. Even so, for a number of years there was a shortage of trained electricians and engineers. Many of the first electricians had to get whatever training they could on the job through observing others, including their faults, and any formal education where it was available had to be gained in their own time. In this situation the consumer was prey to self-styled 'electricians' who were plumbers, gas fitters and house decorators by trade and about whom the *Journal of Gas Lighting* in 1904 was pleased to report, 'The most alert and up-to-date among them [ironmongers] call themselves electrical contractors. No special training is necessary for this additional branch, which any intelligent bell-hanger can pick up as he goes along.'

Bell-hangers did indeed believe they were suitably qualified as their work was concerned with laying wires for communicating systems. To some extent they were encouraged in their thinking by Colonel Crompton, who installed electric lighting in 1882 at the brewer Octavius Coope's house at Berechurch Hall near Colchester in Essex, and who noted, 'In order to deal with the novel work of wiring and fixing, I took over from the builder of the house a party of his work-men whose previous trade had been that of bell-hangers. Several of these men gradually bettered themselves, and eventually went into the business as master contractors for electrical wiring of houses'.[17]

Poorly insulated wiring or the use of wire of unsuitable gauge for the demand was generally the cause of electrical fires and it was not always in the homes wired by inexperienced 'electricians' that problems occurred. A very early installation at Hatfield House, the home of Lord Salisbury, was not without its problems:

> There were evenings when the household had to grope about in semi-darkness, illuminated only by a dim red glow... there were others when a perilous brilliancy culminated in miniature storms of lightning, ending in complete collapse. One group of lamps after another would blaze and expire in rapid succession, like stars in conflagration, till the rooms were left in pitchy blackness, and the evening's entertainment had to be concluded in the light of hastily collected bed-candles. The necessity of fuses was not yet recognised, and one evening a party of guests entering the Long Gallery found the carved panelling near the ceiling bursting into flames under the contact of an overheated wire... and with well directed volleys of sofa cushions, rendered the summoning of a fire engine unnecessary.[18]

Inventions and Developments

LAMPS

This lamp... has no mechanism about it, and when it fails, from use or accidental breakage, it is as easily replaced by a new one as a candle is placed in a candlestick.

Swan United Electric Light Company Limited, Illustrated Catalogue, 1883

In 1881 Swan's carbon filament lamps cost the enormous sum of 25s each but, as demand increased, lamp prices were reduced to 5s within a year. In 1882 Edison set up the Edison Electric Light Company in London and began legal proceedings against Swan for patent infringement, but a lengthy court battle was avoided when the companies amalgamated in 1883. Swan's original lamps produced 20 c.p. but after the amalgamation this was reduced to Edison's preference of 16 c.p (25 watts), the notional output of most flat flame gas burners. The master patent held by the Edison & Swan United Electric Light Company was ruthlessly enforced with the result that other lamp manufacturers were driven out of business and cheaper foreign lamps could not be legally sold. The consequence for consumers was that they paid an artificially high price for their lamps which, for most of the ten monopoly years, was 3s 9d each. The company's stranglehold on the industry had the effect of stultifying research in England, and Swan made only one further improvement to his original lamp in 1883 with the introduction of a filament made from 'squirted cellulose'.[19]

In 1880 Edison had designed a screw-fitting lamp-holder which, with only some slight modifications, has remained in common use, particularly in Europe and America. In comparison the Swan United Electric Light Company's Catalogue of 1883 showed six types of lamp-holders, their universal feature being that the lamp was secured into the holder by fixing the platinum loops from the bulb onto metal hooks, with contact maintained by springs pressing on to the bulb. Progress was clearly made as in the 1890 edition of the Edison & Swan United Electric Light Company Catalogue, although six lamp-holders were illustrated, only two were of the looped type. The others had Edison screw or bayonet cap

Illustration of an early lamp holder offered by Swan United Electric Light Company, from Hammond, *op cit*, c.1882.

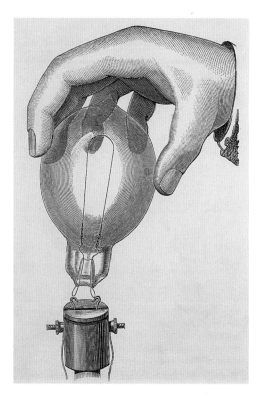

fittings, the latter having been first introduced by the Anglo-American Brush Corporation in 1883. A collection of early carbon and metal filament lamps can be seen in the Visitor Centre at Cragside. Plaster of Paris was originally used to insulate the contacts on lamps, but in 1885 this began to be replaced by 'Vitrite', a glass-like material invented by Alfred Swan, brother of Joseph.

When the Edison & Swan master patent expired in September 1893 their lamp prices were slashed to 1s 9d . From then onwards the company faced fierce competition from other manufacturers, particularly those who obtained licences to manufacture a new generation of lamps that were being developed abroad. In the late 1890s a series of lamps with metal filaments began to appear on the market, the osmium, tantalum and Nernst lamps.[20] But by the time initial difficulties with these lamps had been overcome they were almost immediately superseded by lamps with tungsten filaments, first introduced in 1909. Improvements in tungsten lamps increased efficiency and by 1914 consumers could buy 32 c.p. lamps that used the same amount of electricity as a 16 c.p. lamp.[21]

The tungsten lamp remained the mainstay of the industry for decades and even after developments in fluorescent lighting in the 1930s the lamp continued to retain its dominant position. Only now is it being challenged by a new generation of fibre optic and energy-saving lamps.

COMPONENTS AND ACCESSORIES

Perhaps the greatest change which took place in this period was shown in a loss of individuality of installation. In 1890 many components were made by the contractors as and when required on the job, while in 1900 all accessories could be purchased ready made...

J. Mellanby, *The History of Electric Wiring*, 1957

In the course of perfecting the electric lamp, Edison and his research team in the United States designed all the components and accessories that were required for a complete electrical installation, such as parallel circuits, fuses, switches and meters. In Britain, however, these products were only developed piecemeal and in the early years it was left to those responsible for installations to design and make any components. As a consequence, results were not always safe or satisfactory, although some were novel in their inventiveness. In his letter to *The Engineer* in January 1881 Sir William Armstrong described how vases in the Library at Cragside, which had previously served as bases for Duplex paraffin lamps, were converted into electric table lamps:

These vases being enamel on copper, are themselves conductors, and serve for carrying the current from the incandescent carbon to a metallic base in connection with the return wire. The entering current is brought by a branch wire to a small insulated mercury cup in the centre of the base, and is carried forward to the lamp by a piece of insulated wire which passes through a hole in the bottom of the vase, and thence through the interior of the lamp

on the top. The protruding end of this wire is naked, and dips into the mercury cup when the vase is set down. Thus the lamp may be extinguished and relighted by removing the vase from its seat or setting it down again.

It was fortunate that fuses were speedily recognised to be essential. But replacing the fuse wire required some education and in 1897 W. A. S. Benson in his *Notes on Electric Wiring and Fittings* cautioned, 'Never use a wire for fuses of a different metal or size from the one that has melted. Hair pins, nails, soda water wires etc., are made of wires which do not melt easily.'

Not only did the electrical industry incorporate into its technical language terms from the water and gas industries, but also the designs of some components from these industries were influential on early electrical accessories and fittings. The first electric switches rotated like gas taps and initially lamps on electroliers had individual switches that aimed to give the same versatility as gas taps on gasoliers. However, a problem with rotating electrical switches was that some consumers attempted to turn down their electric light as they were accustomed to do with their gas lights; this could cause arcing if the conducting wire was left bare or had been poorly insulated. It was a particular problem when accessories were made from wood or mounted on timber blocks and it was not long before porcelain and other non-conductive and non-inflammable materials were introduced. Rotating switches were in common use until the development in the late 1880s of the tumbler switch, which had an up-down action. Many switches in this period were produced with distinctive circular brass 'jelly mould' covers.[22] For those who were wealthy enough to afford something different, elaborate switch-covers provided an opportunity for a display of conspicuous consumption. Ornate switches with gilded covers dating from 1902 can be seen at Knole, and at Plas Newydd the switch-covers are cast in the form of the 6th Marquess of Anglesey's coat of arms.

Although some components, such as fuses, had to be developed specifically for the new technology, more complex accessories like plugs and points only appeared on the market as electricity became more widespread. In 1891, although Captain Ironside Bax, the Manager of the Westminster Electric Supply Corporation, considered that, 'A Wall Plug or Connector for a standard lamp is very convenient and a great luxury', it was not until appliances became commonplace – particularly electric fires and cookers which could not be plugged into lamp sockets – that wall points came to be considered essentials rather than luxuries. The first plugs were two-pin; a three-pin plug designed for the safe use of domestic appliances came onto the market in 1923 and these were not standardised until 1937. The dearth of standardised manufactured components bedevilled the electrical industry and it was largely through the efforts of Hugo Hirst, who founded the General Electric Company in 1887, that order was brought into chaos:

> Hirst's idea was simple in the extreme – to be able to supply every single
> item which went to form a complete electrical installation and to ensure

LEFT: Cloisonné vase, originally used as a base for a Duplex paraffin lamp, that Sir William Armstrong converted into an electric table lamp in late 1880, in his library at Cragside, Northumberland.

that all these components should be technically suited to each other, of
adequate quality and sold at an economic price. In the days when every
installation was a monument to the individualism of its designer, and when
the only official standard was the Imperial Wire Gauge…in this one field
of standardisation alone G.E.C. performed a service of incalculable value
to the industry.[23]

GENERATION

…in the 1890's a series of small supply stations was appropriate. But as the
economies of central generation increased and transmission costs fell, the
minimum efficient area for a supply station rose and some interconnection
became desirable.

I. C. R. Byatt, *The British Electrical Industry 1875–1914*, 1979

The best way forward for the future generation of electricity was for many years
hotly disputed by the leading electrical engineers of the day. The advocates for
direct current (DC) included Edison, Crompton and Lord Kelvin; the promoters
of alternating current (AC) were Sebastian de Ferranti, Charles Parsons and
Charles Merz. In America Edison had used to his advantage the fear held by
many of high-voltage AC by encouraging the New York Commission to consider
'Westinghouse Current' as a 'humane' form of execution. The first execution by
electric chair took place in August 1890 and Edison capitalised by advertising

Electrical bellboard,
*c.*1893, indicating which
rooms required service
at Wightwick Manor,
West Midlands. Below the
board are four distinctive,
circular brass 'jelly mould'
switch covers.

173

ABOVE: Illustration from a trade handbook produced by Merryweather & Sons, promoting their products for supplying water and electric lighting to 'Estates and Villages', *c.*1900.

LEFT: The former accumulator house at Baddesley Clinton, Warwickshire.

the safety of his DC system in comparison to the 'lethal' AC electricity produced by his competitors, Westinghouse. Both systems had advantages and disadvantages. DC was safer as at this time only low voltages were produced for domestic use and the current could be stored in batteries (accumulators), but the system lost power over distance. Although AC could not be stored, transformers enabled the current to be transmitted at very high voltages over long distances without losing power. For large-scale generation DC eventually lost out to polyphase AC, a development of the 1890s, but for the smaller individual installation of the domestic consumer low-voltage DC continued to be preferred.

A tantalising glimpse of what the future held came with the development of Deptford Power Station on the south bank of the Thames between 1887 and 1889, masterminded and designed by Sebastian de Ferranti.[24] The station was built with the capacity to supply thousands of London customers, but potential numbers had been overestimated and two disastrous fires at the Grosvenor Street substation interrupted the supply for three months, losing the company valuable business. Although the Deptford venture was a commercial failure, significant discoveries were made, not least being Ferranti's development of high-voltage cable. Deptford's legacy was to inspire others and in the 1890s large-scale generation over a wide area became economically feasible following Nikola Tesla's work on polyphase AC frequencies and Charles Parsons's inventions of steam turbines and radial-flow turbo alternators.[25] In the early years of the twentieth century 'cathedrals of power' began to be established. With greater economies of scale and increased competition between supply companies, the price of electricity decreased annually from 1900 until 1914, enabling middle-class householders to become the new consumers of electricity.

Until 1900 virtually all demand for electricity had been for domestic lighting, as power for industrial uses continued to be supplied by steam and gas engines. The development of power stations, however, made electricity an attractive and cost-effective proposition for industry. This change was recognised in legislation that was adjusted to take account of industrial demands which required supply of higher voltage. By 1909 many power stations were supplying 200–250 volts and this was to have implications for domestic consumers in terms of the lamps and appliances they could use. Despite these shifts in demand electricity supply continued to be unco-ordinated and fragmented. In this haphazard situation the supply industry had to be taken in hand and in 1925 the Weir Committee recommended standardisation and the setting-up of a 'national gridiron'. The first stage of construction of the National Grid was completed in 1934, but 'it took about twenty-five years to complete standardisation, involving the conversion of three quarters of a million DC consumers and two and a half million non-standard AC consumers'.[26]

It has been variously estimated that by 1920 between a half and one million homes had electricity, and of these very few were working-class. Although meters were used to measure consumption, pre-payment meters did not come into widespread use until after the National Grid became operational and poorer homes began to get connected. The network of power supply made possible by the Grid dramatically affected the numbers of connected houses, which rose from 31 per cent in 1931 to 65 per cent in 1938. Ten years later this had increased to 85 per cent.[27] By the time the newly elected Labour government nationalised the industry in 1948, electric lighting was no longer considered a luxury.

APPLIANCES AND NOVELTIES

Everything electrical will make a house a home.
Leaving restless husbands little wish at night to roam,
Electric lights with pretty shades improve a wifey's looks,
Cooking is an art she no longer learns from books.
Touch a little button and the dinner soon is done
Roasting things electric'ly is really lots of fun
If laundry prices make you frown, a cure you can rely on
Consists of nothing more than this – your own electric iron.
If the day is damp and dreary and your nerves begin to twitch
Then hurry to the ideal home, that little house in which
You can 'keep the home fires burning' by turning on a switch!

Electrical Development Association promotional literature, *c.*1920

Electricity used for lighting only was unprofitable and it made sound financial sense to suppliers if demand could be spread more evenly. In his presidential address at the Institution of Electrical Engineers in 1895, Crompton underlined the urgent need for the industry to diversify and it was during this decade that electrical appliances and gadgets began to appear on the market. Electricity offered far more scope for novelty applications than gas and some manufacturers quickly exploited this potential by producing small luxury items like electric clocks, cigar lighters and dinner gongs, whilst others supplied very wealthy consumers with passenger lifts and electric cars. Some early, interesting electrical appliances can be seen at a number of National Trust houses – dinner gongs at Cragside, Bakelite electric hot-water bottles at Kingston Lacy and Chastleton House. At Plas yn Rhiw there is a small collection of electrical items that includes a kettle, toaster, iron, radios and fires. In the purchase of larger electrical items, few could outdo Maurice, the future 4th Baron Egerton, who liked to drive around the estate at Tatton Park in an electric 1900 Benz Comfortable; an electric brougham can also be seen in the carriage collection there. Large establishments found passenger and luggage lifts useful, and a number survive in National Trust houses. An Otis lift, thought to be the first in England, was imported from America and installed at Waddesdon Manor for the visit of Queen Victoria in 1891.

Affluence and modernity could be displayed by the acquisition of electrical products and at Castle Drogo, built for Julius Drewe between 1910 and 1930, the architect Edwin Lutyens incorporated state-of-the-art technology into his

plans. Those who knew the house before the Second World War remembered that this technology included a centralised vacuum cleaning system and the provision of 332 sockets into which were plugged 'hundreds of electric fires'.

In the eighteenth century electricity had been thought beneficial to health. Some were persuaded to remedy infertility by trying out James Graham's 'Celestial' electrical bed at the Temple of Health in the Royal Terrace in London. One of Graham's attendant nymphs was Emma Hart, the future Lady Hamilton and Nelson's 'Bequest to the Nation'.[28] However, suspicions of lewd practices and quackery brought electro-therapy into disrepute, although it gained some credibility and respectability towards the end of the nineteenth century. One advocate of electrical treatments was the research chemist Otto Overbeck, who patented an electrical rejuvenator that he believed could 'cure all illnesses. . .with the exception of malformation and germ diseases'. Lady Diana Cooper remembered electricity being used to cure a debilitating childhood illness; 'The minimum exercise, no getting up in the morning, and Dr Coleman to come every day when the family were in London to treat me with galvanism. For several years I had treatment – a big box of plugs and and wires and Ons and Offs and wet pads clamped upon me that I might tingle and jerk'.[29]

The development of appliances, together with increasing numbers of consumers, compelled the electricity industry to take steps to educate their customers. Local supply companies began to target affluent homes with informative educational magazines, and electricity showrooms were set up in town centres, staffed by demonstrators who helpfully showed and advised customers how to make best use of 'electric servants' who were 'ready to give instant response to your wishes day and night'. In the early years of the twentieth century, as people were becoming less inclined to find work as domestic servants, the wealthy were urged to invest in 'labour-saving' appliances, which they were told would save on servant costs and make positions in their homes more appealing to potential employees. Middle-class women were made to feel that household tasks were less demeaning when the work was being done by a costly electrical appliance. To promote the wider use of electricity the Electrical Development Association was founded in 1919 and much of its promotional literature was aimed specifically at women.

Lighting the Home

The rich man with a very large establishment will almost certainly declare in favour of electricity, which in his case will probably give the lowest working costs, while his less wealthy neighbour will most likely install air-gas or acetylene. . . . The amount of attention required to operate an air-gas or acetylene plant is very small, and it is not unusual to make it part of the housemaid's duty. In the case of electric light the writer has never heard of

LEFT: The architect Edwin Lutyens installed sophisticated electrical technology into the 'Norman' Castle Drogo he built for the Drewe family in Devon in the early years of the twentieth century. The Switch Room, which is still in operation, housed terminals for electricity brought direct to the castle from two turbines harnessed to the River Teign, as well as more conventional alternating current supply.

this being done; male attention of some sort appears to be required, even if it is only such the bootboy can give. Gardeners can usually undertake the work quite successfully.

Maurice Hird in Weaver, The House and its Equipment, c.1910

For many years the use of electric lighting was largely confined to those living in urban areas. The only option for anyone who wanted electricity but lived outside the boundaries of a local supply station was to have their own generating systems installed.[30] Despite the fact that early installations were very expensive and could be problematical, electric lighting did have an immediate appeal for some householders, particularly those with scientific interests like Sir William Armstrong. Others, like the Robartes at Lanhydrock whose property had suffered a devastating fire, were persuaded that electricity was infinitely the safest option.

In the 1880s several firms were established that specialised in providing country-house owners with complete electrical installations. One such firm was Drake & Gorham. Bernard Drake wrote and lectured on the benefits of electric lighting, and in an article in Country Life in 1899 he appeared to be attempting to drum up more business for the firm by playing on social pride; 'In every well-appointed country house the electric lighting is now considered to be of scarcely less importance than the water supply, the drainage, and other necessaries. In town it is a recognised fact that a house without electric light will not let, and in the country the hostess has been forced to appreciate that her house parties are not considered up-to-date if her friends have to return to the dingy candle during their stay.'

However, electricity did not always live up to expectations. Lady Newton at Lyme Park, where electricity was installed in 1904, wrote: 'A feature of these rooms, and indeed all rooms on the first floor, is their loftiness; they measure from fifteen to twenty feet in height. How can they have been lit, in the days when rushlights and candles were the only means of lighting, passes comprehension, as even with electricity of the present day it is difficult to obtain sufficient brilliancy.'[31]

The costs of an electrical installation, lamps, fittings and accessories could be enormous. In a letter to The Times on 29 January 1884, Octavius Coope, MP detailed the costs of having electric lighting at Berechurch Hall, where the installation amounted to £1,490 8s and the running costs for the year came to £359 18s 9d. Although Coope was very pleased with his electric lighting he reported some difficulties; 'a little temporary trouble... occasioned by the drunkenness of the engine driver who had to be summarily dismissed... who by his carelessness weakened the carbon filaments... and caused them to break sooner than they would otherwise have done'. The price of the engine driver's carelessness amounted to £75, the cost of renewing 300 lamps at 5s each; a considerable sum when compared to the annual wages of the engine driver and his lad, which totalled £79 14s.

For house owners who wanted the luxury of electricity but also wanted to economise, a variety of cost-cutting steps could be taken, although in effect many of these savings turned out to be either unsafe or false economies. Money could be saved by having lamps wired in series. In this arrangement all lamps on a circuit would extinguish if one lamp failed, and as carbon lamps were sensitive to fluctuations in current this would not be rare. Considerably more expensive and satisfactory was wiring in parallel, the system advocated by Edison, where lamps were wired separately, even though some eminent electricians like Crompton initially dismissed parallel circuits as wasteful. Expense could also be spared in the laying of wires. The costly option was to conceal them in walls, which entailed not only channelling into plaster but also the expense of redecoration. A much cheaper and safer option, particularly given the poor insulation of early wiring, was to lay wires on the surface and cover with wooden or metal casing, a feature that can still be seen in a number of houses.[32]

Many private householders chose to have low-voltage DC installations. Perhaps intended as a cost-saving measure, some had generating sets and accumulators that proved inadequate with maximum load. In this situation, if the system did not break down completely, the level of illumination was dramatically reduced. A report in *The Times* on 23 January 1900 describes the effect; 'of all the lights in use, the electric light is the most irritating and depressing when the supply is insufficient.... Electric light with insufficient voltage acquires an abominable orange tinge, which may be warranted to give the most tastefully decorated drawing room the aspect of a dungeon.'

A 100-volt DC system was the first to be installed at Baddesley Clinton and, even though it was improved in 1940, Mr Ferrers-Walker recalled, 'The old original supply was indeed limited and it was not possible to have electric current available for more than two or three rooms and to operate equipment. This was inevitably difficult when showing people around the house and entertaining'.[33] Similarly a visitor to Wimpole Hall in the 1930s described, 'those scarce flickering lights which progressively dimmed as the load on the ancient batteries increased'.

One problem encountered with carbon lamps was that, as a perfect vacuum could not be achieved in production, during the course of usage the filament gradually deposited carbon particles on the inside of the lamp which caused blackening. Although consumers were advised to change their lamps when this started to happen, high replacement costs were a deterrent and many continued to burn their dimly glowing lamps with expensive electricity until the filament broke completely. Apparent economies could also be made by using fewer lamps; 'A sixteen candle power lamp is usually found sufficient for a room 10 feet long and 10 feet wide.... The author knows of one particular instance in which great disappointment was experienced by a consumer, in a large establishment, who had substituted for upwards of 1,000 gas jets only 120 electric lights of sixteen candle-power each.'[34] Given that a 16 c.p. lamp is approximately equivalent to 25 watts, this recommended level of illumination would be considered very low by today's standards. The *Journal of Gas Lighting*, never one to pull its punches, was happy to report on 13 September 1898 that 'One big consumer after another grows tired of the costly little lamps with filaments that glow like newly burnt-out matches, the while his neighbour and rival makes a blaze with incandescent gas burners'.

Problems of insufficient and poor-quality lighting were further exacerbated by the use of an 8 c.p. lamp that was attractive to many consumers because it was cheaper to buy and consumed less electricity. The *Journal of Gas Lighting* described this lamp as having the effect of 'darkness made visible'. When Lord Scarsdale had electricity installed at Kedleston Hall by Drake & Gorham in 1898 for the grand sum of £1,917, of the 487 lamps supplied 231 were 8 c.p. and 36 of 5 c.p. Many of the lower candle-power lamps had the appearance of 'imitation wax candles' and were for use in converted antique fittings and those made in historical styles.[35]

Guidance for consumers on how they might control and restrict their electric lighting, particularly in the servants' quarters, could be found in advice manuals. Borlase Matthews, writing in 1909, was very helpful in this respect;

> The lighting of servants' bedrooms is a debatable point, as it encourages reading there, and consequent long hour burning. Servants are also apt to learn a little electrical engineering, just sufficient to be able to change the low for high candle-power lamps from other parts of the house. Still, the fire risk is greatly reduced if electric light is installed in these rooms, and therefore it may be wise to do so on this account. In some houses the lights in the servants' bedrooms are so wired that they can be controlled by a switch in the dressing room or similar place, so that the consumer can extinguish their lights when he goes to bed himself.[36]

In many households indoor and outdoor servants were generally the last to benefit from any new advances in lighting. At Tatton Park, for example, electricity was first installed for a visit of the Prince and Princess of Wales in 1887, but the workers who lived in the Old Hall on the estate did not have electricity until 1958. This was, however, not the case at Wimpole Hall, where it was observed, 'Oddly enough, the servants' quarters were fully electrified while the rest of the house was not'.[37]

During the nineteenth century unshaded lighting in formal rooms had come to be considered vulgar, yet when electricity was first introduced consumers rarely shaded their incandescent carbon lamps. This was partly to do with display; proud owners of electric lighting wanted everyone to 'see' the new technology unadorned and in so doing marvel at its flameless light and mysterious wiring. But there were also more practical reasons, as shading the lamps would further reduce what was already a poor light, especially if only a few lamps were used and the voltage was insufficient. Interior decoration also affected light levels and in a lecture given in 1903 the speaker, A. T. Cooper, estimated that 'Dull and dark walls reflect only about twenty per cent, middle tints forty to fifty

RIGHT: Carbon lamp with a 'hairpin' filament in one of the lanterns in the Great Kitchen at Saltram in Devon. The late eighteenth-century lantern, originally for candle-light, was copied from the design of the fittings in the Prince Regent's state-of-the art kitchen at the Royal Pavilion in Brighton.

Catalogue illustration of a cut glass lamp from 'Fancy Lamps', 1 February 1893, from the Edison & Swan United Electric Light Company.

per cent, while white walls and mirrors reflect eighty to ninety per cent of the light cast upon them'.[38]

Another, not insignificant problem was that lamps were often hung at the same low level as pre-electric fittings, as remarked upon by an illumination engineer: 'In many houses the old positions which were allocated to gas or oil, permanently fixed with a view to being within easy reach, must be retained. For the owner, having adapted himself to the general arrangement, will insist upon the new lights being in the same position as the old. Many absurdities of lighting to-day are due to this.'[39]

Nonetheless the unshaded lamp was an important element in creating a new aesthetic for electric lighting and was used by a number of leading designers. These included C. R. Ashbee, one of the foremost members of the Arts and Crafts Movement, who waxed lyrical about the lamp: 'Indeed, one feels that this exquisite pear shaped lobe is final in design; like a violin or a ship, its shape appears to conform so perfectly to the union of the two wires, that nothing further in the shaping of the glass is to be done. This, then, is the designer's first limitation. He should in almost all cases, let it hang, and hang in repose.'[40]

It is hardly surprising that in consequence of using unshaded lamps many consumers complained of eye strain and headaches, and opinion was divided as to whether electric lighting was intrinsically damaging to eyesight. A contemporary description of unshaded lamps was given at a meeting at the Architectural Association in 1898; 'In that room they had an illustration of placing the lights above their heads with the most glaring and unsatisfactory result. The lights looked like red-hot hairpins; and they fixed themselves on the retinas of the eye'.[41] One solution to prevent eyestrain and help consumers avoid the 'red-hot hairpin' effect was to use frosted or obscured lamps. During the early years of their monopoly the Edison & Swan Company introduced a range of 'Ornamental bulbs and fancy lamps', the most expensive of which were made of cut-glass and sold from 8s each.

Some women considered there was a distinct disadvantage to downward shining light: Mrs J. E. H. Gordon, one of the earliest writers on electricity, was clear in her advice on the subject:

> There was a round table seating ten guests, and ten lamps with lemon yellow shades were hung just above their eyes, so that the light focussed into the eyes and face of everyone sitting at table... showing every wrinkle and line in the face. No one over the age of eighteen should be asked to sit beneath such a light! Light like sympathy should be unobtrusive to be pleasant, and soft reflected rays fall more kindly than direct light on tired eyes and on the faces and figures of those who have passed the 'half-way house of life'.[42]

The celebrated actress Ellen Terry, performing with Henry Irving at the Lyceum Theatre in London, was totally unimpressed by electric lighting, as she recorded in her memoirs; 'I entreated Henry to have the gas restored, and he did... until

Punch cartoon, 1889, showing the disadvantages of the new, bright electric lighting – parasols, part of fashion for all things Japanese, shade the ladies from the glare.

we left the theatre for good in 1902. . . . The thick softness of gaslight, with the lovely specks and motes in it, so like natural light, gave illusion to many a scene which is now revealed in all its naked trashiness by electricity.'[43]

Although Ellen Terry may have had her way at the Lyceum, most major theatres installed electric lighting at the earliest opportunity as fires were a constant hazard. The first theatre to have incandescent lighting was the Savoy in December 1881, lit by a total of 1,194 lamps supplied by Swan. When Richard D'Oyly Carte staged *Iolanthe* in 1882 Swan created some spectacular lighting effects for the Fairy Queen and her chorus who, with miniature lamps in their hair, 'glittered like a swarm of fireflies.'[44] The miniature lamps made by Swan not only were adapted for beneficial use in medical instruments but also gave rise to a fashion for electric jewellery. Mrs Gordon was one of the first to wear electric jewels, but this could be potentially dangerous and expensive, as she discovered 'Sometimes the battery heated, and leaked, and once I well remember, the old lamps having worn out, I had some new ones given to me that were a wrong resistance for the battery. It heated, and we barely had time to cast the battery into the bath before the gutta-percha sides gave way, and the acids poured out, taking off all the paint. So having spoilt a dress, a carpet, and a bath, I abandoned personal electric light decorations.'[45]

In America one of the very first to make a show with personal electrical adornment was Mrs Cornelius Vanderbilt who, in 1883, had an 'Electric Light' ballgown in blue velvet and satin designed by Frederick Worth. A newspaper report recorded, 'hidden in [the] bodice was a convenient little battery which did not interfere with dancing in the least'.[46] Another dress which, although it did not incorporate electricity, was intended to be seen by electric light was worn by Mary, Lady Curzon, wife of Lord Curzon, the Viceroy of India, at the ball which followed the Coronation Durbar in Delhi in 1903. This dress was 'embroidered

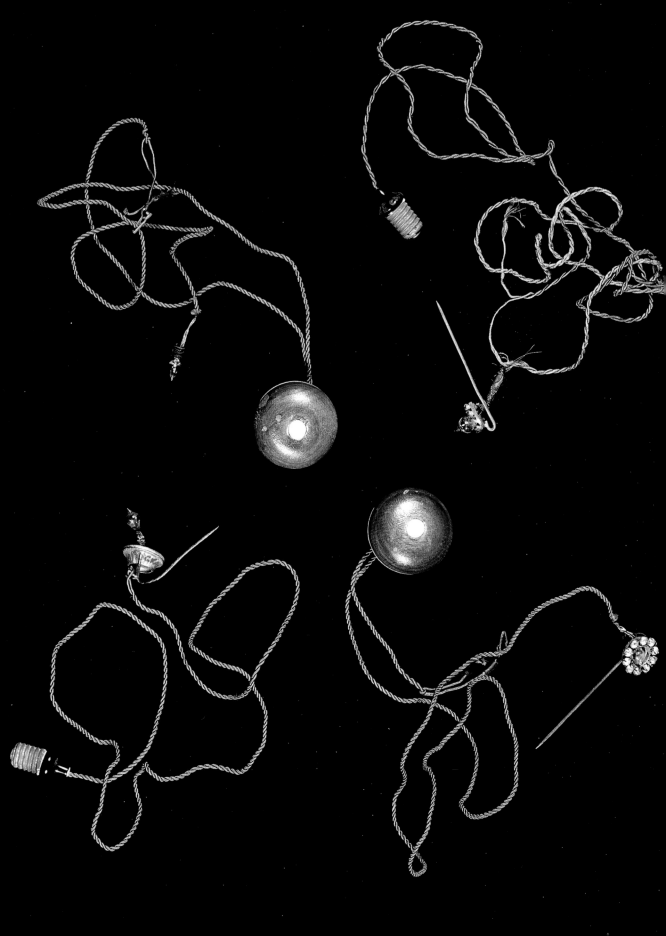

FAR LEFT: Electric
jewellery in the form of scarf
pins and lapel decorations,
from Cragside.

LEFT: Mrs Cornelius
Vanderbilt in all her
luminous glory in 1893,
wearing an 'Electric Light'
ballgown designed
by Frederick Worth.

by Indian craftsmen in metal thread and jewels on cloth of gold in a pattern of peacock feathers so that it would glisten in a room lit by electricity'.[47]

Electric jewellery was only one of a number of inventions that were developed to show the novelty of the new technology. Electric tablecloths also enjoyed some popularity and were used by the Drewe family at their home at Wadhurst Place in East Sussex, and later at Castle Drogo, as recalled by Frances Drewe:

> My father was very proud of an electric cloth which was put under the damask cloth and they put candle sticks at the four corners which pricked in with little connections... for lighting the table candles... it was very effective unless something wet was spilled when there would be a brief panic in case the moisture short-circuited the cloth and blew the fuses; the whole contraption would be turned off while a plate was put under the damask table-cloth to prevent the wet seeping through and children usually had a sheet of some water-proof material placed in front of them under the two cloths.[48]

Apart from electric candlesticks that could be pronged into the tablecloth, manufacturers also produced other ornamental fixtures which in 1909 included 'quaintly illuminated insects... and flowers and fruit'. The seemingly limitless possibilities were considered by Mrs Gordon in her book *Decorative Electricity*; 'little lamps may be lowered as water-spirits into the vases, and flowers arranged above.... Electric lights may be nestled in plants themselves; growing strawberry plants look charming with little lights beneath their leaves; so do dwarf orange and lemon trees, the fruit scooped out and the lamps hung inside the empty rinds'.[49] Richard Grant, chef at Petworth House in the 1930s, went one better, decorating a cake, in celebration of the coronation of George VI and Queen Elizabeth, that featured bunches of roses lit by tiny bulbs.

An interesting effect was achieved in the Sitting Room at Mount Stewart, where the cut-glass chandelier in the shape of a galleon was suspended so to appear to be floating on the waters of Strangford Lough beyond, giving the impression of a ghost ship.

The advice against the use of overhead lighting was particularly heeded by wealthy householders who could afford the luxury of shaded table and standard lamps, recreating the pools of light once given by candles and oil lamps. Nostalgia was also apparent in the taste for electric candles that were used in candelabra and wall-sconces. This was commented upon in an article in the *Architectural Review* in 1901; 'In drawing rooms... there is a singular form of applying the light which consists of imitation wax candles, a tribute to the past and implying regret, for what could be pleasanter to the eyes than the soft blaze of wax lights.'

Earlier, in 1897, and not altogether unsurprisingly, the *Journal of Gas Lighting* also had something to say about electric candles: 'we were scandalised to see in a most conspicuous position an elaborate brass chandelier, fitted all over with imitation candles terminating in imitation candle flames made of twisted glass bulbs enclosing incandescent filaments.... Some martyr to the cause of Truth and Art will be haled before a Magistrate for the offence of demolishing a set of sham electrical candles; and he will go away with a halo round his head.'

With the introduction of 32 c.p. tungsten lamps, shades became essential as light was not only brighter but also of an entirely different quality. 'When the sun has set, one desires, as a continuation of the light of the departing day, the warm tone which the artificial illuminants of today provide. From this standpoint the old carbon filament lamp, with its yellow rays, gives greater satisfaction and a more pleasing effect than the white light of the metal filament lamp.'[50]

Early in the twentieth century, as electricity became cheaper and more widely available, middle-class households could contemplate the luxury of electric lighting and it became a selling-point in newly built homes. Typical usage was electricity for lighting formal rooms, if not every room, and gas for cooking and heating water. In an effort to prevent loss of revenue gas companies responded aggressively by introducing a standing charge for homes supplied with both electricity and gas and initially this charge did deter some on limited incomes from having electricity. In 1920, when the Straw family moved into their

LEFT: Cut-glass chandelier in the form of a galleon, hanging in the Sitting Room at Mount Stewart County Down.

Edwardian house at 7 Blyth Grove, Worksop, only the ground and first floors had electricity, and although gas was supplied it was used for cooking only. However it was not all plain sailing in the household, as when a lamp unceremoniously fell onto William Straw's plate at dinner, he vowed never to replace it. Problems also occurred with the electric lamps at George Bernard Shaw's home, where a generator was installed *c.*1930. Violet Liddle, who was a housemaid at Shaw's Corner, remembered when 'an electric bulb would burst... caused by a surge of electricity current going through the generator', an incident that continued to have a lasting effect as, 'even today when I need to replace a bulb I turn my head away when I switch the light on'.[51]

Before the National Grid became operational only very few working-class families had electricity despite schemes to recruit consumers by making the lighting affordable. In 1909 the Fixed Price Light Company offered to supply electricity to working people in parts of London. Lamps had to be purchased from the company and if the consumer exceeded the agreed load lights flashed until it was reduced. Some local authorities also operated schemes; one of the earliest was in 1899 in Shoreditch, where council tenants were given the option of having electricity supplied for an extra 8d or 10d a week, depending on the size of their accommodation. In 1903 in Battersea the tenants on a newly built council estate were not given a choice as all the flats had electric lighting. In this scheme the council, who owned the electricity station but not the gasworks, provided tenants with pre-payment meters and fittings. The council charged its tenants 4d a unit for their electricity, which led the *Journal of Gas Lighting* to claim that the low prices were being subsidised through the rates.

Some years later, in 1934, a resident in the Battersea area wrote to the Electrical Association for Women about his inability to get electricity; 'I have been waiting for over twelve months trying to get the electric light laid on.... Just fancy asking us working-class people to pay £1 a point. This is outside my reach, as my weekly pay does not come to 50s.... The mains DC and AC run down each side of Wandsworth Road not 200 yards from my door. I can see Battersea Power Station from my front window. So here we are surrounded by Power Stations and yet cannot get the light'.[52]

By the time of nationalisation in 1948, the majority of the population lived in homes lit by electricity. When the McCartney family moved into 20 Forthlin Road in 1955, electric lighting was just one of a number of amenities that council tenants could expect to find in their new homes.

LEFT: Electrolier with two lamps in the Front Room at 7 Blyth Grove, Mr Straw's House in Worksop Nottinghamshire.

Design of Fittings

No progress has been made in realising a style of interior fitting distinctive of electricity. From hall-lanterns to drawing room standard lamps, the fittings ape gas or oil where they do not caricature candles.

'The Season's Electric Light Appliances', *Journal of Gas Lighting*, 10 December 1901

Until manufacturers were secure in the knowledge that electric lighting had a future, very few companies produced fittings specifically designed for electricity. Initially the market for fittings was small and those who could afford electricity often already had expensive fittings that could be easily converted, even though these were designed for use with technologies where the light shone upwards. It was not only antique light-fittings that wealthy householders converted to electricity. At Anglesey Abbey, for example, Ming figures have been used as table lamp bases and at Mount Stewart decorative nineteenth-century tea canisters were similarly employed. Perhaps the most bizarre conversion, also at Mount Stewart, is a ceramic fox that has been fitted with an internal lamp which illuminates its eyes.

Before 1900 many manufacturers were content to sell their gas fittings as electroliers rather than to develop designs more suitable for electricity, and of this practice it was commented: 'The easy simple and common method of making an electric fitting has been, to take a Gasolier pattern, turn the arms upside down – and presto – the thing is done'.[53]

One of the first firms to go into electric light-fitting production was F. & C. Osler, who by 1904 were said to have 'worked up something like two thousand patterns' for the electric light and about whom the *Birmingham Magazine of Arts and Industries* commented, 'on the advent of the electric light, they recognised that this new illuminant needed special fittings, and hence they laid themselves out for the supply of such delicate and artistic fittings as so beautiful a light demanded'.[54]

Fittings that offered consumers the best of both worlds and which might be considered essential for those whose lighting supplies were unreliable was the combination fitting with upright gas burners and descending electric lamps. Although these potentially lethal fittings do not appear have been popular in Britain, judging by how few are seen in British manufacturers' catalogues, they were fairly commonplace in America.

The designs of many early electric fittings were based on historical styles and both larger manufacturers like G.E.C. and more specialist upmarket firms catered for the growing numbers of wealthier consumers who wanted electric fittings that harmonised with their antique furnishings and period interiors. Even manufacturers producing fittings in designs that did not have historical precedent were involved in this profitable line of business. W. A. S. Benson, for example, who was firmly associated with the avant-garde (see below), designed a pair of large electroliers based on Dutch-style brass chandeliers that hang in the Great Parlour at Wightwick Manor (see frontispiece illustration).

One of the novelties of incandescent lighting was the electric wiring, and some designers like C. R. Ashbee felt that little more was needed for the display of electric lighting than the wires and the unadorned lamp. Consequently many fittings designed by Ashbee and others in the Art and Crafts Movement deliberately emphasised these features that other lighting technologies did not share. At Wightwick Manor, where electricity was installed when the house was built

ABOVE: A catalogue illustration of a gas and electric combination fitting, offered by Charles Smith, Sons & Co., 1898.

LEFT: A gilded chinoiserie girandole in the drawing room at Lyme Park. This eighteenth-century fitting, originally designed for candles, has been converted to electricity and has mother-of-pearl shades.

ABOVE AND RIGHT:
One of Philip Webb's copper bracket lamps in the drawing room at Standen, Sussex. In a letter dated 7 July 1894, the architect explained to Margaret, wife of his patron James Beale, that the design for the pendant light brackets should be 'embossed copper sconces standing on the picture rail', and drew a sketch to show the effect.

in 1888, Ashbee's influence can clearly be seen on the plain bracket lamps in the Great Parlour that were designed by George Jack. At Standen, built in 1894, the architect Philip Webb designed the copper bracket lamps in the Drawing Room, using straw-coloured glass spirals to decorate the wires. For a short period around 1900 cord ornaments came into vogue and were sold by leading manufacturers. Some of these can be seen at Cragside, where the lighting was upgraded in 1894 with highly decorative electric fittings supplied by Lea, Sons & Co. Electric wires were also exploited to give fittings directional versatility; very popular lights for use over dining- and dressing-room tables were rise-and-fall pendants, which continued in production until at least the 1920s. Several examples of these can be seen at Lanhydrock.

Perhaps the most celebrated designer of electric light-fittings in this period was W. A. S. Benson, whose fittings were described in the *Magazine of Art* in 1897 as 'palpitatingly modern'. The popularity of his designs can be gauged by the

A rise and fall pendant with delicate wrought iron decoration in the library at Cragside. This fitting, along with several others, was supplied in 1894 by Lea, Sons & Co. of Shrewsbury, as illustrated in their catalogue.

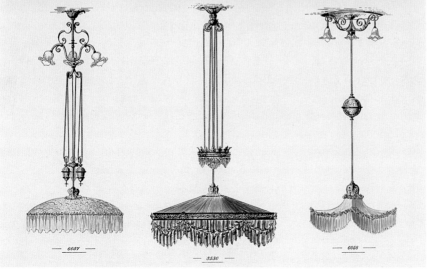

ABOVE: Brass electric lamps by W. A. S. Benson, which he designed so that they could be used as a table lamp or wall light. Both are shown here in the Willow Bedroom at Standen.

extent to which they were widely copied by other manufacturers. Standen and Wightwick Manor have superb examples of Benson electric lamps and electroliers. Despite the views and objections of leading Arts and Crafts designers towards Art Nouveau, the style was used extensively by manufacturers for their electric fittings, the New Art perhaps considered eminently appropriate for the new technology. In America light-fittings designed by Tiffany were used for decorative display, accentuating and focusing attention upon the exquisite beauty and craftsmanship of the shades and metalwork. Two Tiffany table lamps were brought back from America by Rudyard and Carrie Kipling and can be seen in the Parlour of their home, Bateman's.

As early as 1883 shades were being produced based on scientific principles that both protected the eye and enhanced and diffused light without significant loss of illumination. In that year Alexander Trotter, a distinguished electrical engineer and inventor, patented his 'Dioptric' shades which enclosed the light-source in a glass shade composed of a multiplicity of prisms.[55] Trotter had initially designed his dioptric prismatic reflectors for use with arc lamps but they were soon advocated for use with incandescent lamps, and later incandescent gas mantles. Trotter's invention seems originally to have come too soon and he had no commercial success. However in 1895 the dioptric shade resurfaced as the 'Holophane' system, proclaimed as a new invention by Blondel and Psaroudaki.[56] After the introduction of tungsten lamps holophane shades became increasingly popular and their use was recommended in educational and

RIGHT: A pewter table lamp and shade in Art Nouveau style in the Portico Room at Arlington Court. The lamp was produced by a large German domestic metalwork company, Wurrtembergische Metallwarenfabrik (WMF), c.1900.

promotional literature sent out by electricity supply companies. The following example is taken from an article, 'An Illuminating Conversation about Light', that appeared in the *Watford Bulletin c.*1913:

> MRS. N. '... until the electrical man gave us a hint, "A lamp is not meant to be seen but to give you light to see other things by". Sounds quite elementary doesn't it? But even Jack confessed he had not thought of it that way. He was intending to hang the lamps low down, just where the gas lamps used to be. That is what Mr. and Mrs. H. did and the result is that they have had a brilliant light glaring into their eyes, spoiling their sight and giving them headaches.'
>
> MRS. L. 'That is all very well but think of the light you waste if you put the lamps high.'
>
> MRS. N. 'That is what I said at first; and Jack's remark was that we would need twice the number of lamps if we had them near the ceiling. But the electrical man induced us to try an experiment with some new prismatic reflectors that he sells. They are beautiful pieces of glass, and you can get them in various shapes, and with a satin finish if you want it. But the great point about them is that they throw the light downwards, so that although you put the lamp high, you get even more light on your table or your work than if you had a bare lamp low down, glaring into your eyes.... Jack says that a lamp without a prismatic reflector is like a woman without a husband – incomplete and useless.'

The progressive design and indisputable benefits of holophane shades ensured that their popularity endured. They were used on some fittings designed by the Modernist architect Ernö Goldfinger for his London home at 2 Willow Road, completed in 1939.[57]

In 1891 Mrs Gordon, who had advanced views on lighting the home, accurately predicted the developments that lay ahead. 'I believe that, whatever the illuminant used, the light of the future will be a reflected light. What we have to aim at is, that the room should be flooded with a warm, soft radiance, and that we should be unconscious of the source from which it proceeds. This can only be attained by the use of reflected lights.'[58]

The Society of Illuminating Engineers, founded in 1908, aimed to make a contribution to the science of illumination. Through their journal *Illuminating Engineer* they were early advocates of systems of lighting that relied on reflected light, with the mantra 'Light on the object, not in the eye'.[59] Indirect and semi-indirect systems shielded the eye from the glare of lamps by reflecting and diffusing light from ceilings and walls. Perhaps one of the finest examples of indirect lighting is to be found at the home built by Stephen and Virginia Courtauld in 1936 at Eltham Palace, in south London. In some rooms the lighting is concealed by a cornice and reflected from ceilings. A particularly dramatic effect can be seen in the Dining Room, where a large panel in the ceiling is covered in aluminium leaf.[60]

LEFT: One of the Tiffany table lamps brought to England from America by Rudyard and Carrie Kipling, and shown in the Parlour at Bateman's, Sussex.

Uplighter with a holophane shade, one of several light fittings designed by Ernö Goldfinger for his home, 2 Willow Road, in Hampstead.

Art Deco honeycomb ceiling light designed in 1925 for Rupert and Lady Dorothy D'Oyly Carte and installed in the first floor corridor at Coleton Fishacre.

Initially wall and pendant fittings for semi-indirect lighting were made from expensive materials like alabaster and marble; fine examples can be seen at Anglesey Abbey and Kingston Lacy. At Coleton Fishacre, a house completed in 1926 for Rupert D'Oyly Carte, many of the original light-fittings remain, including glass wall-lights made by Lalique. The fittings for the new lighting systems were sold under names that suggested their benefits; for example, G.E.C. sold 'Dalite' fittings with 'Superlux' glassware, and British Thomson-Houston offered the 'Eye-Rest' system with X-ray reflectors and 'Alabas' and 'Veluria' glassware. To make semi-indirect light-fittings more affordable, manufacturers were soon producing fittings in glass streaked with coloured veins to resemble marble and alabaster. These glass bowl fittings suspended on chains became ubiquitous and remained a feature of many sitting and dining rooms until the early 1960s. For example, one can be seen at 20 Forthlin Road.

In the last twenty years new lighting systems have been developed, from environmentally friendly energy-saving lamps to lighting that is considered to be as close as it is possible to get to the bright, clear light provided by sunshine. The quest for 'artificial sunshine' has indeed come a long way from the firelight that our ancestors once found adequate to lighten the hours of darkness. In this century, we must hope that discoveries will be made that not only continue to brighten our lives but also do not cause damage to our fragile planet.

The artificial production and supply of light during the absence of the sun, unquestionably holds a distinguished rank among the most important arts of life.

Frederick Accum, *A Practical Treatise on Gas-Light*, 1815

At the end of the nineteenth century it would still have been possible for a visitor to Britain to see all the lighting technologies described in this book: from lighting that had its origins from a time before the Roman invasion to that with which we are familiar today. Therefore looking back from the beginning of the twenty-first century, when electricity has become an indispensable adjunct to modern living, we can only but wonder at the close proximity of a way of life that has all but disappeared.

The words of Sir Joseph Swan introduced this book; by the end of his long life he had witnessed many changes and remarkable inventions that radically and permanently transformed society. It is perhaps fitting to close with Sir Joseph's reflections in 1906 on the remarkable time in which he had lived.

> If I could have had the power of choice of the particular space of time within which my life should be spent I believe I would have chosen precisely my actual lifetime. What a glorious time it has been! Surely no other 78 years in all the long history of the world ever produced an equal harvest of invention and discovery for the beneficial use and enlightenment of mankind.

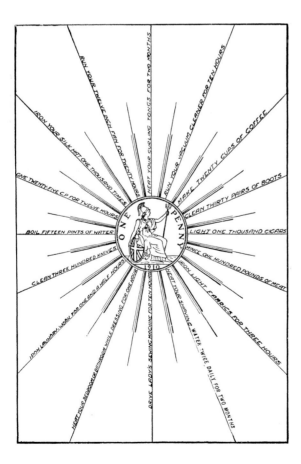

'One Penny or Two Cents' Worth of Electricity – What it Will Do', from *Electric Cooking, Heating, Cleaning ... being a Manual of Electricity in the Service of the Home*, edited by M. and E.W. Lancaster, 1914.

Notes

Details of books given here in abbreviated form will be found in the Select Bibliography.

INTRODUCTION

1. 'Joseph Wilson Swan', *Electrician*, 10 November 1893, p.38.
2. Information from Murray, p.216.
3. An analysis of Gregory King's statistics is given in Falkus, p.6.
4. Statistics quoted in Davidoff, pp.60-61. Between 1837 and 1911 460 new peers were created, of whom only ten had origins in the nobility and 31 in the gentry; the overwhelming majority had backgrounds in industry and commerce.
5. Statistical information supplied by the Office for National Statistics and from Briggs and Burnett.
6. £160 per annum was the point at which income tax was paid. See Burnett p.189.
7. Quoted in Burnett, p.188.
8. Quoted in Briggs, p.259.
9. 'Electric Lighting of Villages', *Country Life*, 1905, 18, p.173.
10. The last of the London link boys was reported to have retired in 1840.
11. Carrier and Dick, pp.10-11.
12. Statistics from Burnett, pp.140-41.
13. Richards, *The Gas Consumer's Guide*, p.12.
14. Quoted from *The Illustrated Police News*, 17 November 1888 (Great Newspapers Reprinted No. 25, Peter Way Ltd, 1974), pp.2-3.
15. For further information see 'Utilizing the Waste Heat of Gas-Lamps', *Journal of Gas Lighting*, 21 September 1897 and 'The "Pluto" Patent for Utilizing the Waste Heat of Gas-Lamps', *Journal of Gas Lighting*, 12 July 1898.
16. In a survey of 1,000 towns in 1920 Evetts found that 87 per cent of street lighting was gas; Evetts, p.1. Many gas lights are still in use in London, for example in the Royal Parks, outside Buckingham Palace and the Palace of Westminster.
17. Quoted in Chandler and Lacey, p.1.

CHAPTER ONE

1. Quoted from George Smith, pp.36-7.
2. George Cavendish, *The Life and Death of Thomas Wolsey*, ed. F. S. Ellis, 1908.
3. Candle-fir was abundant in Scotland and Northern Europe, where most of these fittings originated. Peerman have similarities in design to rushlight-holders and could be either floor-standing or, more usually, table lights.
4. Quoted in the Kingston Lacy Guide Book, The National Trust, 1994, p.32.
5. The design of the torchères is based on the Barbarini candelabrum in the Vatican Museum which was illustrated by C. H. Tatham in his *Ancient Ornamental Architecture*, 1799.
6. At Felbrigg Hall Katherine Windham noted in her account book for 1687-8 that £44 had been spent on silver andirons, with matching dogs, shovel and tongs.
7. Quoted in O'Dea, p.237, whose book offers a comprehensive international overview of the history of lighting.
8. Other houses have equally fine displays of their fire-fighting equipment, for example Powis Castle and Kingston Lacy.

CHAPTER TWO

1. Quoted in O'Dea, p.232.
2. At Aberconwy House there are examples of both types of rushlight-holders. Other examples can be seen at Bateman's, Florence Court and Plas yn Rhiw.
3. Grissets can be seen at Tŷ Mawr Wybrnant, Moseley Old Hall, Aberconwy House, East Riddlesden Hall and Snowshill Manor.
4. Briggs, p.160.
5. The duty charged on tallow candles in the period 1711-1830 can be found in Mitchell. In this study the details of duty on wax candles were not given, as the amount was small in comparison to tallow candles.
6. Quoted from Phillips, p.72.

7. Bunches of old, yellowed dip candles can be seen at Hill Top and Rufford Old Hall.
8. The objects in the collection at the Elizabethan House Museum are on loan from the Norfolk Museum Service, who manage the house on behalf of the National Trust. Some single pendants, which could also be fixed to walls, had length-adjustable mechanisms and examples can be seen in 'Top Gallant' at Snowshill Manor.
9. This room is so called because it is believed that Oliver Cromwell met with his army officers and sealed the fate of King Charles I.
10. Early light-fittings are considered in depth and detail in Caspall.
11. Quoted from Mrs B. Palliser, *History of Lace*, 1902, in Horn, p.110.

CHAPTER THREE

1. Quoted in Bourne and Brett, p.94.
2. Quoted in Phillips, p.69.
3. Quoted in Dummelow, p.16.
4. In the Army and Navy Stores General Catalogue, 1882, the cost of 6lbs of best candles in sizes 4 and 6 to the pound were: wax 12s 9d, spermaceti 9s 3d, composition 3s 9d, paraffin 3s 6d; a 3lbs packet of size 8 tallow moulds was 1s 6d and 12lbs of tallow dips 5s 6d.
5. Blackamoor candlestands from the seventeenth century can also be seen at Ham House and Knole.
6. Venice had a virtual monopoly on all mirror glass until Louis XIV encouraged the establishment of a mirror-making industry in France. In 1665 the Manufacture des Glaces de Venise was opened, employing the services and skills of Venetian craftsmen. The factory soon came under royal patronage and was renamed Manufacture Royale des Glaces de Miroirs and, using new production methods, it became possible to make larger mirrors. In the same period in England the Duke of Buckingham set up a glasshouse at Vauxhall but the mirrors could not compete in size with those made in France.

7. The glass tax was doubled in 1777 and as it was imposed on the raw materials of glass-making, the attendance of an exciseman at all glass-making premises was required for some procedures. In 1780 Ireland was granted freedom from the tax and many glassmakers went there to work. The important glass-making centres established in Waterford and Cork enjoyed considerable prosperity, particularly as English customers could enjoy the benefit of a superbly crafted chandelier without paying additional tax. However, Irish lead crystal glass became subject to the tax in 1825 and, after pressure from English glassmakers, the tax was halved in 1831. A pair of late eighteenth-century Irish crystal glass chandeliers hangs in the Great Hall at Dyrham Park.

8. Yet another of Charles Paget Wade's amazingly diverse collections contains a very important group of court clothes from the eighteenth century. This collection is not kept at Snowshill for conservation reasons, but at Berrington Hall. Scholars wishing to inspect costumes from this collection are advised to contact the property manager at Berrington.

9. Quoted in Fowler and Cornforth, p.221.

10. Quoted in A. Cleminson, 'Christmas at Kingston Lacy: Frances Bankes's Ball of 1791', *Apollo*, December 1991, pp.405–9.

11. Quoted in The Museum of Costume and Assembly Rooms, Bath, The Official Guide, 1994.

12. William Parker set up in business in 1762 and was one of the most famous chandelier-makers of the eighteenth and nineteenth centuries, supplying fittings for the Prince Regent at Carlton House. In 1802–3 Parker's amalgamated with Perry & Co., established in 1756. In 1835 the firm, renamed Perry & Co., supplied Buckingham Palace with seven chandeliers for the Throne Room. An intriguing and rare Perry & Co. chandelier from this period, which is made of sculpted glass and has no cut-glass decorations, hangs at Buscot Park. Other later Perry & Co. chandeliers can be seen in the Saloon at Coughton Court.

13. Cord tassels were illustrated in the 1762 edition of Thomas Chippendale's *The Gentleman and Cabinet Maker's Director*. Since the seventeenth century, however, it was not unusual for suspension chains, rods and cords to be covered with material and decorated with bows or tassels.

14. Erddig Guide Book, The National Trust, 1995.

15. Swift, pp.36–37.

16. Lady Morley and her brother's observations are taken from the Saltram Guide Book, The National Trust, 1998. A pair of Regency 'tent-and-waterfall' chandeliers was later introduced into the Saloon; one weekend a year they are lit for the enjoyment of visitors.

17. Kedleston Hall Guide Book, The National Trust, 1999.

18. Quoted in Thornton, *Authentic Decor*, p.319.

19. Osterley Park Guide Book, The National Trust, 1998.

20. Calke Abbey Guide Book, The National Trust, 1998.

21. J. Joll, 'A Pugin Commission', *The Decorative Arts Society 1850 to the Present*, No.24, 2000, pp.6–19.

22. Augustus Welby Northmore Pugin (1812–52) was only fifteen when he supplied designs for metalwork and Gothic furniture for Windsor Castle. However, he is now chiefly remembered for his writings and designs for the interiors of the new Palace of Westminster and for the Mediaeval Court at the Great Exhibition. Pugin became a Roman Catholic and subsequently through his work and writings advocated the Reformed Gothic, or what is now usually termed the Gothic Revival, style as the true Christian style, embodying the spirituality and craft of the medieval cathedral builders. Pugin viewed the Neo-classical style, based on classical Greek and Roman architecture and design, as pagan. Following his publications, which were influential on Ruskin and Morris, the so-called 'Battle of the Styles' was a much debated topic. In 1838 Pugin persuaded a Birmingham button manufacturer, John Hardman, to set up a 'medieval'

metalwork venture and subsequently Hardman's cornered the market in producing ecclesiastical brassware.

23. Seventeenth-century Dutch-style brass chandeliers can also be seen at Bateman's, Clevedon Court and Springhill and numerous examples from this and later periods are to be found in many other National Trust houses.

24. Matthew Boulton (1728–1809) was born in Birmingham, the son of a button and buckle manufacturer. He went into partnership with John Fothergill c.1762 and the Soho Silver Manufactory was erected between 1759 and 1766. The business was initially concerned with the 'toy' trade, making buttons, buckles and small objects. However, under Boulton's direction the enterprise diversified into making ormolu for mounts and candle-branches and larger pieces of silverware to the designs of Robert Adam, John Flaxman and James Wyatt. Boulton, along with Josiah Wedgwood, was one of the earliest manufacturers to use mass-production, and eventually the firm was producing goods of varying quality and prices to appeal to a wide range of customers. In 1773 Boulton went into partnership with James Watt to produce Watt's steam engines, appointing William Murdoch in 1777 as the engineer to oversee the work. William Murdoch was later to develop successfully a viable system of gas lighting (see Chapter Five). In 1784 Boulton was approached by Ami Argand for support to patent his lamp, and although Boulton went on to manufacture many of these lamps, he gave Argand little support in his patent battles (see Chapter Four).

25. Robert Adam also worked at Saltram, where there are five Boulton candelabra with bluejohn feldspar bodies, each with six ormolu branches. These cost £31 14s in 1772 and are a version of a design made for George III. A 'King's pattern' candelabrum can also be seen at Hinton Ampner.

26. Less ornate silver chandeliers can be seen in the Blue Drawing Room at Powis Castle, where there are three five-branched chandeliers made c.1905. In the same room are ten silver sconces of a similar date that are replicas of 1710 originals, of which two are in the

National Museum of Wales, Cardiff. A massive, late nineteenth-century silver-plated chandelier of a seventeenth-century French design is in the Central Hall at Polesden Lacey.
27. Other work by Storr is to be found at Tatton Park and Petworth House.
28. Giltwood chandeliers at Upton House are typical of those made in 'historical' styles in the early years of the twentieth century. The giltwood chandeliers in the Long Gallery at Lyme Park are of interest as being not only similar in design to a chandelier illustrated in the 1762 edition of Chippendale's *Director*, but also identical to those that hang in the Long Gallery of Sudbury Hall. The latter were supplied in the 1920s by the interior decorating firm of Lenygon and Morant, who specialised in decorating historic properties. Both properties have authentic early Georgian giltwood chandeliers which were probably used as precedents for the choice of the new fittings.
29. For a comprehensive account of this specialised subject see Mortimer.
30. Glass chandeliers were also imported but for the most part did not compare in delicacy and elegance to the late eighteenth-century chandeliers being produced in England and Ireland. During the late Middle Ages Italy, Bohemia, Germany and Austria were important glass-making centres but in the Renaissance period Venice rose to prominence, producing fine and luxurious glassware. The glass was made at Murano, an area of Venice dedicated to glass-making since 1292. As an important trading centre for goods from the East and West, Venetian glassmakers were particularly influenced by the design and decoration of glassware coming from Byzantium.
31. Petworth House Guide Book, The National Trust, 1999.

CHAPTER FOUR

1. Chandler and Lacey, p.38.
2. James Young (1811-83) had leased a small petroleum spring in Derbyshire and obtained two kinds of oil from the crude petroleum, one useful for illumination, the other for lubrication. When this source ceased he used his process of distillation on bitumous shale found in the Scottish lowlands and paraffin was produced. Young set up his own company, which was later absorbed by British Petroleum.
3. François-Pierre-Ami Argand (1750-1803) was born in Geneva, then French territory, where he studied physics and chemistry under the tutelage of de Saussure and later with Lavoisier in Paris.
4. The Soho Manufactory was painfully slow in producing the lamps and there were continual shortfalls in production. This resulted in Argand and Parker having to find additional lamp suppliers. Moreover, there were problems both in making the lamp leakproof and with the wick mechanism, which underwent a number of improvements. A full and comprehensive account of Argand's work and life is in Wolfe.
5. National Encyclopaedia, *A Dictionary of Universal Knowledge by Writers of Eminence in Literature, Science and Art*.
6. Sir Benjamin Thompson, Count Rumford (1753-1814) was born in Woburn, Massachusetts. Thompson worked as a schoolmaster in Rumford (now Concord), New Hampshire, but an advantageous marriage provided the means to pursue his various scientific interests and to travel. As an Anglophile, he fought on the side of the British in the American War of Independence and for his services was knighted by King George III in 1784. Thompson travelled in Europe and spent some years in Bavaria as Grand Chamberlain and Minister of War and Police. In these positions he introduced a number of important military, administrative and social reforms for which he was ennobled as a Count of the Holy Empire in 1791. In 1796 Rumford was elected a Fellow of the Royal Society and he played an active role in founding the Royal Institution. He had a particular interest in lighting, heating and ventilation and his discoveries and inventions did much to improve domestic comfort. His *Rules* for the construction of fireplaces were generally adopted throughout the United Kingdom and perhaps his greatest invention was the cooking-stove.
7. In tests carried out in 1819 at the Apothecaries' Hall it was found that the costs per hour of an Argand lamp burning sperm oil was 3d, tallow mould candles 3½d and beeswax candles 14d.
8. Schivelbusch, p.167.
9. Rowell and Robinson, p.120.
10. A bronze and ormolu chandelier with combined lighting can be seen in the Dining Room at Killerton. This chandelier is very close in design to an eighteen-branch candle chandelier in the Palladio Room at Clandon Park.
11. Hardyment, p.174.
12. Penrhyn Castle Guide Book, The National Trust, 1991, p.31. In the archives at Kedleston Hall there is an account dated May 1878 from Miller & Son for £5 3s 6d for 'Lamp oil and cleaning lamps'.
13. O'Dea, p.226.
14. Taylor, pp.111-12.
15. A. Vallance, 'The Furnishing and Decoration of the House, VI – window blinds, lighting and accessories', *Art Journal*, 1892, p.374.
16. Felbrigg Hall Guide Book, The National Trust, 1999.
17. Cooper, p.35.
18. Waterson, p.176.
19. Other examples can be seen at Blickling Hall, Buckland Abbey, Hill Top and Plas yn Rhiw. At Mount Stewart a crusie lamp has been adapted to electricity by having an electric candle placed in the centre of the bowl. Some properties have examples of early lamps; terracotta spout lamps can be seen at Arlington Court, Felbrigg Hall and Kingston Lacy, and bronze lamps at Castle Coole, Hardwick Hall, Kedleston Hall and Moseley Old Hall.
20. Quoted in Temple Newsam Country House Studies No.4, *Country House Lighting 1660-1890*, 1992, p.75.
21. The lamp is fully described ibid., pp.29-30.
22. Another pair of 'Michaelangelo' lamps is in the Picture Gallery at Stourhead. Unfortunately these have lost their covers, as have a smaller pair

of black basalt-ware lamps that are shown with them. In the Print Room at The Vyne is a 'Michaelangelo' lamp and another Wedgwood black basalt lamp *c*.1780 where the reservoir is supported by three female terms.

23. Examples are to be seen at Snowshill and at Standen.

24. Examples of minimalist dish fittings can be see in the East Ante Room at Attingham Park, the Little Dining Room at Petworth House and the Library at Castle Coole.

25. Chandeliers of bronze, ormolu or a combination of both materials can be seen at The Argory, Arlington Court, Dunham Massey, Ickworth House, Lyme Park, Nostell Priory and Tatton Park. All the chandeliers mentioned have been converted to electricity with the exception of those at The Argory, which were adapted for acetylene gas. A few of the chandeliers have had their centre reservoirs removed.

26. See J. Lomax, 'Piranesi, Mr Messenger and the Duke of Newcastle', *Leeds Arts Calendar*, 1986, pp.26-32.

CHAPTER FIVE

1. William Murdoch (1754-1839) was born at Bello Mill, Old Cumnock, Ayrshire. When he came to England he spelt his name with a 'k', believing it would help in pronunciation; consequently his name is seen with either spelling. A number of books consider the history of the gas industry; of particular interest is Chandler, *Lighting by Gas*.

2. Frederick Winsor (1763-1830), formerly Winzer, variously said to be Moravian or Prussian, had realised the potential of gas lighting when he was in Paris and had seen the 'thermolamps' which provided both heat and light, invented by the French gas pioneer, Philippe Lebon. Although he spoke little English, Winsor came to London in 1803 and tried to sell lamps he had copied from Lebon. He hired the Lyceum Theatre and, with the aid of an interpreter, demonstrated gas lighting.

3. Chandler and Lacey, p. 36.

4. For a comprehensive history of the company see Everard.

5. The first municipal gasworks was in Manchester in 1843. For further information see M.E. Falkus, 'The British Gas Industry before 1850', *Economic History Review*, second series No.20, 1967, pp.494-508 and Wilson, *Lighting the Town*.

6. Quoted from Everard, p.102.

7. See King, p.18.

8. Quoted in Sampson, p.132.

9. In 1823 Charles MacIntosh patented a process for waterproofing fabric using rubber dissolved in coal-tar naptha. In the mid-nineteenth century aniline and many other chemicals were distilled from coal-tar and used to make the deep-coloured dyes that became very fashionable for clothing and furnishings.

10. Samuel Clegg (1781-1861) had been Murdoch's assistant at Boulton & Watt's factory, which he left in 1805 to work on his own account. Clegg was an important figure in the gas industry; before 1820 he had invented the first 'wet' and 'dry' gas meters, a horizontal rotary retort, a pressure regulator and had improved the process of gas purification by the use of wet lime.

11. Quoted from Everard, p.68.

12. W.J. Liberty, 'A Centenary of Gas Lighting and its Historical Development', *Illuminating Engineer*, 1913, 6, pp.175-231.

13. Williams, p.47.

14. The struggles of the Gasworkers' Union to improve working hours and conditions is told by their leader, Will Thorne, in his book *My Life's Battles*, originally published in 1925.

15. Bankes and Watkin, p.92.

16. Other National Trust properties once lit by acetylene are, for example, St Michael's Mount and Farnborough Hall. The pipe used for acetylene gas was considerably smaller in diameter than that for coal-gas; a section of this slender pipe can be seen in the Servery at Dunster Castle. In the corridor of the Entrance Hall at Oxburgh Hall can just be seen a wall-bracket in Art Nouveau style that was used with acetylene.

17. William Sugg (1832-1907) was a gas fittings manufacturer who made a number of important inventions that improved gas lighting. Sugg's incorrodible burner tips, introduced in 1858, were made from steatite, a type of soapstone that he described as, 'in its natural state, softer than ivory. It admits of being worked to a very fine polish; but after it has been burned in a kiln it becomes harder than the hardest steel and will resist a very high temperature... it is also unaffected by the action of damp, being perfectly incorrodible. Gas burners made of this material will remain in constant use for more than twenty years without deterioration.' In 1869 Sugg invented the 'London' Argand burner that was adopted by the Gas Referees as the standard test burner for measuring the luminosity of gas.

18. Chandler, p.105.

19. Carl Auer von Welsbach (1858-1929) was born in Vienna. He trained as a chemist and was a pupil of Professor Robert Bunsen, the inventor of the aerated burner. It was this invention that made possible the successful development of the incandescent mantle. In 1887 Welsbach set up a company to produce mantles and burners, the burners costing 1 guinea and the mantles 5s each; at that time an electric lamp cost 5s. However, prices were reduced dramatically as sales increased in the 1890s.

20. The difference between the incandescent mantle and flat flame and gas Argand burners was that the mantle was dependent on heat for its illumination, whereas in other burners luminosity was dependent on the intrinsic illuminating quality of the gas. The luminous gas flame contained carbon particles which glowed during combustion. However, if the carbon was not fully consumed escaping soots and other by-products damaged furniture and decorations. By 1920 it was recognised that the future for gas was to be in cooking and heating rather than illumination, and from then onwards it was mandatory for gas companies to declare the calorific value of their gas rather than the candle power.

21. 'The Incandescent Gas Light Company Ltd Improved Welsbach System', p.6.

22. The first patent for an inverted burner was taken out by H. A. Kent in 1897, although others developed the technology further, for example Bernt and Cervenka who patented an 'inverted gas mantle burner' in 1900 and Ahrendt in 1903.

23. Throughout the nineteenth century most ignition systems relied on pilot lights and later developments made use of electric igniters. Sir Edmund Elton of Clevedon Court, who has already been mentioned in connection with his 'Sunflower' art-pottery, was co-inventor of the Elton-Stephens automatic ignition device patented in 1906. Sir Edmund's son Ambrose was a director of the Clevedon Gas Company and he refused to have electricity at Clevedon Court. During the Second World War, when the house was leased to British Petroleum, electric lighting was installed in some of the main rooms but Sir Ambrose continued to light his own apartments with gas until he died in 1951.

24. Reported in the *Journal of Gas Lighting*, 24 October 1899.

25. J. O. N. Rutter, *Advantages of Gas-Light in Private Houses*, 1846, p.7.

26. King, p.19.

27. Edis, p.277.

28. Frederick Accum (1769-1831) was born in Westphalia. He had been an assistant to Humphry Davy and, as the first chemist appointed to the Gas Light and Coke Company, was an early supporter of Winsor's gas lighting. Some of the fittings illustrated in Accum's book were used to light Rudolph Ackerman's Repository of Arts in the Strand that had a private gasworks installed by Clegg in 1812. Ackerman estimated that he saved £119 a year by lighting with gas rather than candles and oil and in using superior cannel coal found, 'when contrasted with our former lights [it] bears the same comparison to them as a bright summer sunshine does to a murky November day'.

29. Quoted in Barty-King, p.41.

30. Brown, p.55.

31. Other National Trust country house properties that were thought to have once been connected to a town supply include Dunham Massey, East Riddlesden Hall, Knole, Melford Hall and Sudbury Hall. Although Dunster Castle was lit by acetylene at the beginning of the twentieth century, coal-gas was supplied to the castle in 1907 by the Minehead Gas Light and Coke Company. In the Drawing Room is a highly ornate brass gasolier that probably dates from *c.*1875; it now has candle-branches inserted into the burners of its eight arms and is converted to electricity.

32. Saltram was originally supplied by the local Plympton Gas Company but the supply was insufficient to meet the demands of the house and a gasworks was built. In the Green Dressing Room there are four swing wall-brackets, one of which still retains its batswing burner. At Kedleston Hall there was a gasholder on the estate in 1862. However, in 1878 the local gas company agreed to supply gas to the property. In all there were over 130 gas lights which were located mainly in the domestic offices and servants' quarters; many of the formal reception rooms were not gaslit.

33. The mansion at Fell Foot was demolished in 1907. The coal for the gasworks was brought by train and ferried across Lake Windermere, and the former gas house is now the home of the Park Manager. Some gas fittings can still be seen in the boathouses. The *Britannia* was 49 tons, 96 ft long, had two masts and could carry 122 passengers. The Colonel, who was an enthusiastic sportsman, used the yacht to convey his dogs up and down the lake. The yacht was sold in 1907 and used as a passenger ferry until 1915.

34. Miss Pole was quoted in Hallam, p.24.

35. Hughes, pp.97-98.

36. King, p.27.

37. Liberty, p.186.

38. Gas lighting was not introduced into the interior of the Royal Pavilion until after the property was sold to the town corporation in 1850. For further information about the gas installation at the Brighton Pavilion see Jessica Rutherford's article in Temple Newsam Country House Studies Number 4, *Country House Lighting 1660-1890*.

39. Castle Ward had its own gasworks, now demolished, that were adjacent to the Coal Quay where deliveries of coal were unloaded, having been ferried across Strangford Lough.

40. There was once a gasworks on the estate at Waddesdon Manor. On the Royal Lodge Gates, gas lamps with flat flame burners continue to be lit every night.

41. R. Wilson, p.75.

42. Best, p.117.

CHAPTER SIX

1. Leyden jars used by Sir William Armstrong for his electrical experiments can be seen in the recreation of his laboratory in the Visitor Centre at Cragside.

2. Benjamin Franklin (1706-90), born in Boston, the son of a tallow chandler. Franklin's inquiring mind led him to make a number of important discoveries and he is credited with having invented bifocal spectacles. The quotations are from The Evening Hour Library, *Benjamin Franklin 'Doer of Good' – a Biography*, n.d.

3. Aloysius Galvani (1737-98), Professor of Anatomy in Bologna. His theory of 'animal magnetism' was disproved by Alessandro Volta (1745-1826), Professor of Natural Philosophy, Pavia.

4. Sir Humphry Davy (1778-1829), born in Penzance, the son of a woodcarver. Despite having a poor early education, Davy became a great scientist and is perhaps best remembered for his invention of the miner's safety lamp. He was knighted in 1812 and became President of the Royal Society in 1820. The quotation is from Schivelbusch, p.52.

5. Michael Faraday (1791-1867). It was through Davy's influence that Faraday was appointed a chemical assistant at the Royal Institution in 1813 and twenty years later he became Professor of Chemistry. Although small dynamos began to be made after 1831, none could generate electricity cheaply enough for industrial use. This situation changed after 1871 when Gramme produced a dynamo with a ring-shaped armature.

6. In 1858 Professor F. H. Holmes experimentally lit the South Foreland lighthouse, Kent. In 1871 the Souter lighthouse, Tyne and Wear, was the first in the world to be lit by Holmes's alternating current magneto-electric generator.

7. Paul Jablochkoff (1847-94) was a Russian telegraph engineer who, while working in Paris in 1876, invented his 'candles'. Instead of carbon rods pointing upwards and downwards towards each other, as was the usual arrangement in arc lamps, Jablochkoff placed his rods in parallel. Arc lighting never completely ousted cheaper gas lamps for street lighting although arc lamps were found useful for large industrial areas, like dockyards.

8. Lady Jebb quoted in Evans, p.92.

9. Throughout the text the term lamp is used rather than bulb. Electric lamps were not generally referred to as 'bulbs' until the twentieth century.

10. Sir Joseph Wilson Swan (1828-1914), born in Sunderland, the son of an anchorsmith. He received little formal education. He had become inspired to perfect an incandescent lamp after having seen a demonstration by Staite of an arc lamp in 1847. Swan's notable inventions before the incandescent lamp included the Autotype process for photographic printing and bromide photographic printing paper. In recognition of his work Swan became a Fellow of the Royal Society in 1894 and he received a knighthood in 1904.

11. Thomas Alva Edison (1847-1931), born in Milan, Ohio. From an early age Edison demonstrated impressive entrepreneurial skills and he made a number of significant inventions which included the phonograph before turning his attention to incandescent lighting. Edison had established a research laboratory at Menlo Park, New Jersey, where he employed about a hundred people, and in October 1878 announced that he had solved the problem of electric lighting 'indefinitely'. In the event, Edison's claim was premature but it did not prevent him from maximising publicity by issuing regular bulletins in the American press.

12. Sir William Armstrong (1810-1900). Born in Newcastle upon Tyne, he started out in life as a solicitor, before becoming an industrialist, engineer and inventor who built up a considerable business in armaments and engineering on Tyneside. He was created 1st Baron Armstrong in 1887. Armstrong was a man of many talents, a keen scientist with a particular interest in hydraulics. He invented an hydraulic crane, locks, lifts and moving bridges. In 1863 Armstrong built a small country retreat at Rothbury and in 1869 commissioned the architect Norman Shaw to enlarge it into a magnificent country mansion, Cragside. Armstrong wanted the most up-to-date services for his home with all the convenience and luxury that technology could provide and consequently Cragside was known as 'the Palace of a Modern Magician'. Armstrong's research into hydraulics enabled him to harness power from damming water in lakes created on the estate to convert into energy that could be put to practical use at the mansion. For the first electrical installation in 1878, Armstrong coupled a Vortex turbine to a Siemens dynamo on Debdon lake that provided the power to light the carbon arc lamp in the Picture Gallery. The electrical installation was upgraded and refined several times, a new powerhouse was built a mile downstream from Tumbleton lake and a gas-powered generator and second generator were installed in 1895. Today visitors can walk the Power Circuit in the grounds and see the water turbine and other installations.

13. The Godalming station began as a hydroelectric scheme but because of insufficient water supply a Siemens alternator was later installed and Alexander Siemens took over the supply contract. Electricity was supplied for both public and private lighting but by 1884 had failed to become profitable for Siemens, who estimated that he needed 'a load of 400-500 private lights and could only find 100'. For further information see Bowers, *A History of Electric Light and Power*. The first municipal electricity station was in Bradford, in 1889.

14. See Central Electricity Generating Board, *1882-1982 Brighton and the Electric Revolution*, 2M/1/85.

15. 'Mr Preece on Domestic Electric Lighting', reported in the *Journal of Gas Lighting*, 21 October 1884, p.716.

16. The Fulham Public Baths electrocutions were reported in the *Journal of Gas Lighting*, 6 January 1903, p.20. The advice to canvassers is from Matthews, p.270.

17. Colonel R. E. B. Crompton (1845-1940) was born into a Yorkshire gentry family and educated at Harrow. He served in the Army in India, where he designed a massive steam tractor to haul wagon trains. He returned to England in 1875 to work as a mechanical engineer and by 1880 had established his own factory in Chelmsford to make electrical plant for arc lighting. Crompton's equipment came to the attention of Swan and he became Chief Engineer to Swan's company in 1880. Crompton subsequently became the first British manufacturer to make machinery specifically for incandescent electric lighting. In 1882 he won the contract to light the newly built Royal Courts of Justice, the Strand, London, with a mixture of arc and incandescent lighting and this was among the first of many large contracts he secured. For further information see his *Reminiscences*, 1928. The quote is from Bowers, *A History of Electric Light and Power*, p.126.

18. Robert Cecil, 3rd Marquess of Salisbury (1830-1903) was a keen amateur electrician and, like Armstrong, had a hydroelectric system and used arc lighting before incandescent lamps became available. The Hatfield House installation dates from February 1881 and Salisbury was advised by Mr W. Sykes, electrician to the London, Chatham & Dover Railway Co. Quote from Cecil, pp.6-7.

19. The cellulose filament thread was further developed by two of Swan's assistants, Charles Stearn and Fred Topham, who later sold their process of making 'artificial silk' to Courtaulds.

20. The osmium lamp was invented in 1897 by Auer von Welsbach of incandescent gas mantle fame. G.E.C. obtained the sole selling rights in Britain

and when the lamp was first introduced it could only be used with voltages below 110 volts and was more reliable with direct current. Nernst lamps were named after their inventor, Professor Walter Nernst of Göttingen. Although the filament did not require a vacuum, a heater was necessary for starting the lamp. Professor Nernst demonstrated his lamp at the Royal Society of Arts in 1899. Tantalum, a very scarce metal, was developed for use in lamps by von Bolton in 1905. The German manufacturers Siemens and Halske gained control of all world sources and, like the osmium lamp, it was only available for use with a low voltage supply. For a comprehensive account of electric lamp developments see Bowers, *Lengthening the Day*.

21. In 1909 an American, Dr William Coolidge, discovered how to make tungsten ductile. The tungsten vacuum lamp was introduced in 1911 but was superseded by a lamp developed by Irving Langmuir, who coiled the tungsten filament and placed it in a gas-filled bulb. A more efficient lamp with a coiled coil was introduced in 1934.

22. Brass 'jelly mould' switches can be seen at Hughenden Manor, Lanhydrock and Wightwick Manor. At Tatton Park there are a number of these switches and other ornate switches cast in the shape of bows.

23. Mellanby, p.28.

24. Sebastian Ziani de Ferranti (1864-1930) was born in Liverpool and was largely self-educated. At the age of seventeen he went to work at Siemens Brothers & Co., at Woolwich and soon afterwards was supervising the company's electrical installations. He set up his first company in 1882 and in the following year established with Robert Hammond the Ferranti Hammond Electric Light Co., manufacturing generators, arc lamps and meters, which collapsed two years later. Ferranti then set up another business in his own name as a manufacturing engineer and brought onto the market his mercury-motor meter which was the foundation of his commercial success. For a comprehensive account of Ferranti's

life and work see J. F. Wilson, *Ferranti and the British Electrical Industry 1864-1930*.

25. The Hon. Charles Parsons, later Sir Charles (1854-1931), was the youngest son of the 3rd Earl of Rosse, a noted astronomer. After taking mathematics at Cambridge Parsons became an apprentice at Lord Armstrong's engineering company on Tyneside and in 1889 started his own company.

26. Quotes from Hannah, p.44.

27. Consumer statistics can be found in Bowers, *A History of Electric Light and Power*, Byatt, Chant and Hannah.

28. James Graham was born in 1745 in Edinburgh and went to America, where he practised as a physician. There he became aware of Franklin's electrical experiments. When he returned to England he set up the Temple of Health, equipped with an 'electrical throne' as well as his Celestial bed. The bed had an electrified headboard on which was written 'Be fruitful. Multiply and Replenish the Earth' and the tilting mattress was stuffed with stallion's hair. The bed cost up to £100 to rent for the night and reputedly cost Graham £10,000 to build.

29. Otto Overbeck's electrical rejuvenator can be seen at Overbeck's Museum and Garden, Devon. The quote is from Cooper, p.43.

30. Many National Trust properties had their own electricity installations that remained in use until handed over to the Trust. At Castle Drogo the Switchroom is still operational. A distribution board of gargantuan proportions can be seen in the lecture room at Waddesdon Manor. At Bateman's a water turbine made by Gilbert Gilkes & Co. can be seen in the Mill dam. It was rebuilt by the Royal Engineers with a generator designed by Christy Bros & Middleton supplying power through a 250-yard length of deep-sea cable to the accumulator house.

31. Quoted from Newton, p.280. In a footnote Lady Newton recorded the benefits of electric lighting in Egyptian tombs which 'has arrested the further destruction of the paintings by the tourists' torches, to say nothing of its

being the means of getting rid of the clouds of bats which infested these temples'.

32. Stannos wiring, developed by Siemens Brothers & Co. in 1909, was considered ideal for country-house owners who were operating their own plant. According to Mellanby, Stannos wiring was 'a well thought-out system, the cables, though small in size, were robust . . . and lent themselves admirably to inconspicuous surface wiring, and neatness was further enhanced by a special tumbler switch, only 15/8 in diameter'. Stannos wiring was installed at Dunster Castle in 1922.

33. I am grateful to Mr T. W. Ferrers-Walker for this information. The installation remained in operation until 1979 at which time the National Trust had the property connected to the mains supply. Mr Stan Walford, who continues to work at the house as a volunteer, vividly recalls the system in operation.

34. Bax, pp.26-7.

35. Kedleston Hall was rewired between 1974 and 1977 to 240 volts with the exception of the chandelier in the Drawing Room which remained at 110 volts. Drake & Gorham also installed electricity at Ickworth House between 1907 and 1909; the estimate for the first phase of the work in the East Wing amounted to £1,787 10s. A total of 721 lamps were supplied to the East Wing and Round House and of these 343 were of 16 c.p., 161 of 8 c.p. and 217 of 21 c.p. tantalum metal filament lamps. The house was fitted with 354 switches and 171 points. Drake & Gorham also installed lighting at Lanhydrock in 1884, although the original installation was probably upgraded in 1896.

36. Matthews, p.15.

37. Quoted in Wimpole Hall Guide Book, The National Trust, 1999.

38. 'The Practical Application of Electricity to Buildings', *Birmingham Magazine of Arts and Industries*, 1901-1903, 3, p.186.

39. W. R. Rawlings, 'Private House Lighting by Electricity', *Illuminating Engineer*, 1912, 5, pp.242-3.

40. C. R. Ashbee, 'Suggestions for Electric Light Fittings', *Art Journal*, 1895, pp.91-3.

41. Mr G. H. Fellowes-Prynne in a discussion at the Architectural Association following the reading of a paper, 'Another View of Lights and Lighting'. Carbon lamps with 'hairpin' filaments can be seen working in the Great Kitchen at Saltram.

42. Mrs. J. E. H. Gordon, *Decorative Electricity with a Chapter on Fire Risks*, p.103.

43. Quoted in Barty-King, p.160.

44. For further information see Swan, and M. Dillon, '"Like a Glow-worm who had lost its glow", the Invention of the Incandescent Electric Lamp and the Development of Artificial Silk and Electric Jewellery', *Costume*, 2001, 35, pp.76-81.

45. Mrs. J. E. H. Gordon, op cit., pp.121-4.

46. Quoted in Moss, p.123.

47. Kedleston Hall Guide Book, The National Trust, 1999.

48. From notes made by Miss Frances Drewe (1907-1981) held in the National Trust Regional Office, Devon and kindly made available by Mr Hugh Meller. Although the electric tablecloth no longer survives at Castle Drogo, the silver-plated electric candlesticks remain in place on the dining-room table.

49. Mrs. J. E. H. Gordon, op cit., p.54.

50. W. R. Rawlings, 'Private House Lighting by Electricity', *Illuminating Engineer*, 1912, 5, p.237.

51. I am grateful to Mrs Liddle for this information.

52. Scott, p.105. The Electrical Association for Women was founded in 1924 by Caroline Haslett, an engineer. The Association aimed to educate women in the use of electrical appliances and lobbied manufacturers and electricity companies to take into account women's views on products and where points should be located in newly built homes. The Association also campaigned vigorously to get electricity into working-class homes.

53. 'An Ancient Art', *Birmingham Magazine of Arts and Industries*, 1897-8, 1, p.70. Typical of many gasoliers that were adapted for electricity by the simple expedient of rotating the arms downwards, are those in Gothic Revival style hanging in the Dining Room and Great Hall at Knightshayes Court, a property that never had a gas supply. The fittings were acquired by the National Trust.

54. F. & C. Osler built up a considerable reputation in the nineteenth century as chandelier-makers and were responsible for making the Crystal Fountain which was the centrepiece at the Great Exhibition in 1851. Oslers continued

to produce chandeliers and sconces in historical styles and examples of their work can be seen at Ickworth House. For a comprehensive history of the company see J. P. Smith.

55. Alexander Pelham Trotter (1857-1947) made many valuable contributions to electrical engineering and to the science of illumination. He was educated at Harrow, took Natural Sciences at Cambridge and then became apprenticed to an engineering company. In 1886 he went into partnership with W. T. Goolden and worked on the design and manufacture of generators. In 1890 he became Editor of the *Electrician*.

56. The Holophane Company eventually acknowledged Trotter's earlier invention. Holophane shades can be seen at Hughenden Manor and Wallington.

57. Ernö Goldfinger (1902-1987) was born in Budapest. He studied architecture in Paris under the guidance of Auguste Perret and in 1934 settled in England. Goldfinger was particularly interested in the science of illumination and he designed innovative schemes to maximise light unobtrusively.

58. Mrs. J. E. H. Gordon, op cit., p.102.

59. The Society was based upon and shared the same objectives as the Society of Illuminating Engineers founded in New York in 1906.

60. The property is in the care of English Heritage.

Select Bibliography

ACCUM, F., *A Practical Treatise on Gas-Light; Exhibiting a Summary Description of the Apparatus and Machinery best calculated for Illuminating Streets, Houses, and Manufactories, with Carburetted Hydrogen, or Coal Gas; with remarks on the Utility, Safety, and General Nature of this New Branch of Civil Economy* (Hayden, 1815).

BACOT, H. Parrot, *Nineteenth Century Lighting, Candle-powered Devices; 1783-1883* (Schiffer Publishing Ltd, 1987).

BANKES, V. and WATKIN, P., *A Kingston Lacy Childhood* (Dovecote Press, 1986).

BARTY-KING, H., *New Flame* (Graphmitre Ltd, 1984).

BAX, E. Ironside, *Popular Electric Lighting; being Practical Hints to Present and Intending Users of Electricity Energy for Illuminating Purposes* (Biggs & Co., 1891).

BEARD, G., *Craftsmen and Interior Decoration in England 1160-1820* (John Bartholomew & Son, 1981).

BEARD, G., *The Work of Robert Adam* (John Bartholomew & Son, 1978).

BENSON, W.A.S. & Co., *Notes on Electric Wiring and Fittings* (London, 1897).

BEST, R.D., *Brass Chandelier, a Biography of R. H. Best of Birmingham by his son R. D. Best, with an Introduction by P. Sargant Florence* (George Allen & Unwin Ltd, 1940).

BILLS, D.M., GRIFFITHS, E. and GRIFFITHS, W.R., *Kinver Rock Houses* (Elda Publications, n.d.).

BOURNE, J. and BRETT, V., *Lighting in the Domestic Interior, Renaissance to Art Nouveau* (Sotheby's, 1991).

BOWERS, B., *A History of Electric Light and Power* (Peter Peregrinus Ltd, 1982).

BOWERS, B., *Lengthening the Day, a History of Lighting Technology* (Oxford University Press, 1998).

BRIGGS, A., *A Social History of England* (Weidenfeld & Nicolson, 1983).

BROWN, J., *Instructions to Gas Consumers on the Economical Management of Gas; the Properties and Process of its Manufacture; the Principle and Mechanism of the Meter; and the Advantages of Coal Gas over all other Means of Artificial Illumination* (Longman & Co., 1852).

BURFORD, E.J., *Royal St James's, Being a Story of Kings, Clubmen and Courtesans* (Robert Hale, 1988).

BURKE, T., *English Night Life* (Batsford, 1941).

BURNETT, J., *A Social History of Housing, 1815-1985* (Methuen University Paperbacks, second edition, 1986).

BYATT, I.C.R., *The British Electrical Industry 1875-1914* (Clarendon Press, 1979).

CARRIER, R. and DICK, O.L., *The Vanished City* (Hutchinson, 1957).

CASPALL, J. *Fire and Light in the Home pre-1820* (Antique Collectors' Club, 1995).

CECIL, G., *Life of Robert, Marquess of Salisbury*, Vol. III (1931).

Central Electricity Generating Board, *1882-1982 Brighton and the Electric Revolution* (CEGB, South Eastern Region, 2M/1/85).

CHANDLER, D., *Lighting by Gas: an Outline of its History* (Chancery Lane Printing Works, first edition 1936 or second edition 1956).

CHANDLER, D. and LACEY, A.D., *The Rise of the Gas Industry in Britain* (British Gas Council, 1949).

CHANT, C. (ed.), *Science, Technology and Everyday Life 1870-1950* (Routledge, in association with the Open University, 1989).

CLOUTH, D., *Joseph Swan 1828-1914, a Pictorial Account of a North Eastern Scientist's Life and Work* (Gateshead Metropolitan Borough Council, n.d.).

COOPER, D., *The Rainbow Comes and Goes* (Rupert Hart-Davis, 1958).

CROMPTON, R.E.B., *Reminiscences* (Constable & Co., 1928).

DAVIDOFF, L., *The Best Circles, Society, Etiquette and the Season* (The Cresset Library, 1973).

DAVIDSON, H.C. (ed.), *The Book of the Home, a Practical Guide to Household Management*, Vol. 2 (The Gresham Publishing Co., 1900).

DAWES, F.V., *Not in Front of the Servants, a True Portrait of Upstairs, Downstairs Life* (Century in association with the National Trust, 1989).

DELIEB, E., *The Great Silver Manufactory, Matthew Boulton and the Birmingham Silversmiths 1760-1790* (Studio Vista, 1971).

DUMMELOW, J., *The Wax Chandlers of London* (Phillimore, 1973).

EDIS, R.W., *Decoration and Furniture of Town Houses* (Macmillan, 1881).

Electricity Council, *Electricity Supply in the United Kingdom – A Chronology – From the Beginnings of the Industry to 31st December 1985* (The Electricity Council, fourth edition, 1987).

EVANS, J., *The Victorians* (Cambridge University Press, 1966).

EVELEIGH, D.J., *Candle Lighting* (Shire Album 132, Shire Publications Ltd, 1985).

The Evening Hour Library, *'Benjamin Franklin "Doer of Good" – a Biography'*, W.P. Nimmo (Hay & Mitchell, n.d.).

EVERARD, S. *The History of the Gas Light and Coke Company, 1812-1949* (Ernest Benn, 1949).

EVETTS, G., *The Administration and Finance of Gas Undertakings* (Benn Bros. Ltd, 1922).

FALKUS, M., *Britain Transformed, an Economic and Social History 1700-1914* (Causeway Press Ltd, 1997).

FLETCHER, R., *The Parkers at Saltram, 1769-89, Everyday Life in an Eighteenth-century House* (British Broadcasting Corporation, 1970).

FOWLER, J. and CORNFORTH, J., *English Decoration in the 18th Century* (Barrie & Jenkins, 1974).

FREEMAN, L., *New Light on Old Lamps* (Century House, 1968).

GENTLE, R. and FEILD, R., revised and enlarged by B. Gentle, *Domestic Metalwork 1640-1820* (Antique Collectors' Club, 1994).

GIROUARD, M., *Life in the English Country House* (Penguin Books, 1980).

GLEDHILL, D., *Gas Lighting* (Shire Album 65, Shire Publications Ltd, 1987).

GORDON, Mrs J.E.H., *Decorative Electricity with a Chapter on Fire Risks by J.E.H. Gordon* (Sampson, Low Marston, Searle & Rivington, 1891).

GORDON, J.E.H., *A Practical Treatise on Electric Lighting* (Sampson, Low Marston, Searle & Rivington, 1884).

HALLAM, W.E., *The Story of Sudbury* (Derbyshire Countryside Ltd, 1972).

HAMMOND, R., *The Electric Light in our Homes* (Frederick Warne, n.d. c.1882).

HANNAH, L., *Electricity Before Nationalisation* (Macmillan Press, 1979).

HARDYMENT, C., *Behind the Scenes* (The National Trust, 1997).

HEDGES, K., *Useful Information on Electric Lighting* (E. & F.N. Spon, third edition, 1882).

HEDGES, K., *Precautions to be Adopted on Introducing the Electric Light with Notes on the Prevention of Fire Risks* (E. & F.N. Spon, 1886).

HENNESSY, R.A.S., *The Electric Revolution* (The Scientific Book Club, 1972).

HOLLINGSHEAD, J., *Ragged London in 1861* (Dent, 1986).

HORN, P., *Labouring Life in the Victorian Countryside* (Gill & Macmillan, 1976).

HUGHES, M.V., *A London Child of the 1870's* (Oxford University Press, 1984).

JEKYLL, G., *Old English Household Life* (Batsford, 1975).

KETTON-CREMER, R.W., *Felbrigg, the Story of a House* (The National Trust, 1976).

KING, G., *Advice to Gas Consumers on Gas Economy, or How to Keep Down High and Extravagant Bills* (Martin Billing & Son, 1875).

KLEIN, D. and LLOYD, W. (eds), *The History of Glass* (Tiger Books International, 1997).

LAING, A., *Lighting* (HMSO, 1982).

LANCASTER, M. and LANCASTER, E.W. (eds), *Electric Cooking, Heating, Cleaning etc. being a Manual of Electricity in the Service of the Home* (Constable & Co., 1914).

MACKINTOSH, I., *Pit, Boxes and Gallery, the Story of the Theatre Royal, Bury St Edmunds* (The National Trust, 1979).

MATTHEWS, R. Borlase, *Electricity for Everyone* (Electrical Press, 1909).

MEADOWS, C.A., *Discovering Oil Lamps* (Shire Publications, no. 145, reprinted 1987).

MELLANBY, J., *The History of Electric Wiring* (Macdonald, 1957).

MICHAELIS, R.F., *Old Domestic Base-Metal Candlesticks from the 13th to 19th Century* (Antique Collectors' Club, 1978).

MITCHELL, B.R., *British Historical Statistics* (Cambridge University Press, 1988).

MORTIMER, M., *The English Glass Chandelier* (Antique Collectors' Club, 2000).

MOSS, R.W., *Lighting for Historic Buildings, a Guide to Selecting Reproductions* (Preservation Press, John Wiley & Sons, 1988).

MURRAY, V., *High Society in the Regency Period 1788-1830* (Penguin Books, 1999).

National Encyclopaedia, *A Dictionary of Universal Knowledge by Writers of Eminence in Literature, Science and Art*, 14 vols (William Mackenzie, c.1886).

NEWTON, Lady, *The House at Lyme* (William Heinemann, 1917).

NICOLSON, G. and FAWCETT, J., *The Village in History* (Weidenfeld & Nicolson, 1988).

NIXON, N. and HILL, J., *Mill Life at Styal* (Willow Publishing, 1986).

O'DEA, W.T., *The Social History of Lighting* (Routledge & Kegan Paul, 1958).

PHILBRICK, N., *In the Heart of the Sea* (Harper Collins, 2000).

PHILLIPS, G., *The Tallow Chandlers Company, Seven Centuries of Light* (Granta Editions, 1999).

PONDER, S. (comp.), *Wightwick Manor The Morris and De Morgan Collections* (The National Trust, n.d.).

REES, T., *Theatre Lighting in the Age of Gas* (The Society for Theatre Research, 1978).

REEVES, M. Pemberton, *Round about a Pound a Week* (Virago, 1979).

RICHARDS, W., *The Gas Consumer's Guide: containing Instructions on the Management of Gas; the Means of Economizing Gas; Popular Description of the Gas Meter, with Full Directions for Ascertaining the Consumption by Meter; Ventilation etc.* (E. & F.N. Spon, 1866).

RICHARDS, W., *The Gas Consumer's Handy Book* (E. & F.N. Spon, 1877).

ROUTLEDGE, R., *Discoveries and Inventions of the Nineteenth Century* (Bracken Books, 1989).

ROWELL, C. and ROBINSON, J.M., *Uppark Restored* (The National Trust, 1996).

RUBINSTEIN, S., *Historians of London* (Peter Owen, 1968).

RUTTER, J.O.N., *Advantages of Gas-Light in Private Houses* (John W. Parker, 1846).

SAMPSON, J., *All Change* (Kingston-upon-Thames, St Lukes Church, 1985).

SCHIVELBUSCH, W., *Disenchanted Night: the Industrialisation of Light in the Nineteenth Century*, translated from the German by Angela Davis (Berg, 1988).

SCOTT, P., *An Electrical Adventure* (Electrical Association for Women, 1934).

SMITH, G., *Essay on the Construction of Cottages* (1834).

SMITH, J.P., *Osler's Crystal for Royalty and Rajahs* (Mallet, 1991).

South Metropolitan Gas Company, *A Century of Gas in South London* (South Metropolitan Gas Company, 1924).

SWAN, K.C., *Sir Joseph Swan and the Invention of the Incandescent Lamp* (The British Council and Longmans, Green & Co., 1946).

SWIFT, J., *Directions to Servants* (Antony Blond, 1965).

TATHAM, C.H., *Ancient Ornamental Architecture* (1799).

TAYLOR, A., *Quench the Lamp* (Brandon, 1990).

Temple Newsam Country House Studies Number 4, *Country House Lighting 1660-1890* (Leeds City Art Galleries, 1992).

THORNE, W., *My Life's Battles*
(Lawrence & Wishart, 1989).

THORNTON, P., *Seventeenth-Century
Interior Decoration in England
France and Holland* (Yale University
Press, 1983).

THORNTON, P., *Authentic Decor, the
Domestic Interior 1620-1920*
(Weidenfeld & Nicolson, 1984).

TIMMINS, S., (ed.), *Birmingham and
the Midland Hardware District* (Frank
Cass & Co. Ltd, new impression
1967). First published by Hardwicke
in 1866 under the title *The Resources,
Products, and Industrial History of
Birmingham and the Midland
Hardware District: a Series of Reports
Collected by the Local Industries
Committee of the British Association of
Birmingham, in 1865.*

Tyne and Wear County Council
Museums Service, *The History of
Domestic Lighting* (information
sheet, n.d.).

WATERSON, M., *The Servants' Hall,
a Domestic History of Erddig*
(The National Trust, 1990).

WEAVER, L. (ed.), *The House and its
Equipment* (Country Life, c.1910).

WILDHIDE, E., *The Fireplace* (Little,
Brown & Co., 1994).

WILLES, M., *Scenes from Georgian Life*
(The National Trust, 2001).

WILLIAMS, T.I., *A History of the British
Gas Industry* (Oxford University
Press, 1981).

WILSON, J.F., *Ferranti and the British
Electrical Industry 1864-1930*
(Manchester University Press, 1988).

WILSON, J.F., *Lighting the Town, a Study
of Management in the North West Gas
Industry 1805-1880* (Paul Chapman
Publishing, 1991).

WILSON, R., *Common Sense for
Gas Users. Being a Catechism of
Gas-Lighting. For Householders,
Millowners, and other Large Consumers,
Gas-Fitters, Architects, Engineers, etc.*
(Crosby Lockwood & Co., 1877).

WOLFE, J.J., *Brandy, Balloons, &
Lamps: Ami Argand, 1750-1803*
(Southern Illinois University Press,
1999).

WOODFORDE, J., *The Truth about
Cottages* (Routledge & Kegan Paul,
1979).

National Trust
Guide Books

National Trust guide books proved
invaluable when researching material
for this book. Quotations have been
taken from those listed below.

Barrington Court, 1997
Calke Abbey, 1998
Castle Drogo, 1995
Cliveden, 1994
Erddig, 1995
Felbrigg Hall, 1999
Ham House, 1999
Hardwick Hall, 1999
Kedleston Hall, 1999
Kingston Lacy, 1994
Knole, 1999
Museum of Costume and Assembly
Rooms, Bath, 1994
Osterley Park, 1998
Penrhyn Castle, 1991
Petworth House, 1999
Saltram, 1998
Snowshill Manor, 1998
Wimpole Hall, 1999

Journal Articles

ALCORN, E.M., 'The Hanover
Chandelier', *The Burlington Magazine*,
Vol. CXXIX, 1997, pp.40-43.

'An Ancient Art', *Birmingham Magazine
of Arts and Industries*, 1897-8, 1, p.70.

ASHBEE, C.R., 'Suggestions for Electric
Light Fittings', *Art Journal*, 1895,
pp.91-3.

CLEMINSON, A., 'Christmas at
Kingston Lacy: Frances Bankes's Ball
of 1791', *Apollo*, December 1991,
pp.405-9.

COOPER, A.T., 'The Practical
Application of Electricity to
Buildings', *Birmingham Magazine of
Arts and Industries*, 1901-1903, 3, p.186.

DILLON, M., '"Like a Glow-worm who
had lost its glow", the Invention of the
Incandescent Electric Lamp and the
Development of Artificial Silk and
Electric Jewellery', *Costume*, 2001, 35,
pp.76-81.

DRAKE, B., 'Electric Lighting of
Country Houses', *Country Life*, 1899,
6, p.472.

'Electric Lighting of Villages', *Country
Life*, 1905, 18, p.173.

ELVILLE, E.M., 'The History of the
Glass Chandelier', *Country Life
Annual*, 1949.

FALKUS, M.E., 'The British Gas Industry
before 1850', *Economic History Review*,
second series No. 20, 1967, pp.494-508.

The Illustrated Police News, 17 November
1888 (Great Newspapers Reprinted
No. 25, Peter Way Ltd, 1974), pp.2-3.

JOHNSTON, J.W., 'Light from the
Earliest Times', *Illuminating Engineer*,
5, 1912, pp.425-9.

JOLL, J., 'A Pugin Commission',
*The Decorative Arts Society 1850 to the
Present*, 24, 2000, pp.6-19.

'Joseph Wilson Swan', *Electrician*,
10 November 1893, p.38.

'Mr Preece on Domestic Electric
Lighting', *Journal of Gas Lighting*,
21 October 1884, p.716.

'The "Pluto" Patent for Utilizing the
Waste Heat of Gas-Lamps', *Journal
of Gas Lighting*, 12 July 1898.

'The Season's Electric Light
Appliances', *Journal of Gas Lighting*,
10 December 1901, p.1516.

'Utilizing the Waste Heat of Gas-
Lamps', *Journal of Gas Lighting*,
21 September 1897.

LIBERTY, W.J., 'A Centenary of Gas
Lighting and its Historical
Development', *Illuminating Engineer*,
1913, 6, pp.175-231.

LOMAX, J., 'Piranesi, Mr Messenger and
the Duke of Newcastle "Supereminent
art applied to industry"', *Leeds Arts
Calendar*, 1986, pp.26-32.

LOMAX, J., 'Parsimony by Candlelight,
Lord Warrington's Silver Lighting
Equipment', *Apollo*, April 1993,
pp.244-7.

PAGET, J.C., 'The Abuse of Electric
Lighting', *Architectural Review*, 1901,
9, p.62.

RAWLINGS, W.R., 'Private House
Lighting by Electricity', *Illuminating
Engineer*, 1912, 5, pp.242-3.

VALLANCE, A., 'The Furnishings and
Decoration of the House, VI – window
blinds, lighting and accessories', *Art
Journal*, 1892, p.374.

WEBBER, W.H.Y., 'Private House
Lighting by Gas', *Illuminating
Engineer*, 1912, 5, pp.250-58.

Gazetteer

This is by no means an exhaustive list of all the light-fittings, accessories and installations to be found in National Trust properties but the list will provide the reader with a selection of properties that have examples of lighting described in this book.

Firelight

CENTRAL HEARTHS
Alfriston Clergy House, East Sussex
Tatton Old Hall, Cheshire

Fire Appliances and Fire-fighting Equipment

Calke Abbey, Derbyshire
Castle Ward, County Down
Cotehele, Cornwall
Dunham Massey, Cheshire
Erddig, Wrexham
Felbrigg Hall, Norfolk
Ham House, London
Kingston Lacy, Dorset
Lanhydrock, Cornwall
Lavenham Guildhall of Corpus Christi,
    Suffolk
Lyme Park, Cheshire
Powis Castle, Powys
Saltram, Devon
Tatton Park, Cheshire

Rushlight-holders and Accessories

Aberconwy House, Conwy
Bateman's, East Sussex
Cotehele, Cornwall
East Riddlesden Hall, Yorkshire
Elizabethan House Museum, Great
    Yarmouth, Norfolk
Florence Court, Fermanagh
Ightham Mote, Kent
Moseley Old Hall, Staffordshire
Oakhurst Cottage, Surrey
Plas yn Rhiw, Gloucestershire
Snowshill Manor, Gloucestershire
Tŷ Mawr Wybrnant, Conwy
Townend, Cumbria

Candle Fittings and Accessories

WROUGHT-IRON CORONA
Anglesey Abbey, Cambridgeshire
Sizergh Castle, Cumbria

BRASS CHANDELIERS
Bateman's, East Sussex
Clevedon Court, Somerset
Hardwick Hall, Derbyshire
Lindisfarne Castle, Northumberland
Snowshill Manor, Gloucestershire
Springhill, Londonderry
Treasurer's House, York

BRASS SCONCES
East Riddlesden Hall, Yorkshire
Hardwick Hall, Derbyshire
Wightwick Manor, Staffordshire

IRON LANTERNS
East Riddlesden Hall, Yorkshire
Hardwick Hall, Derbyshire
Knole, Kent
Rufford Old Hall, Lancashire
Snowshill Manor, Gloucestershire

PEWTER FITTINGS
Arlington Court, Devon
Buckland Abbey, Devon
Cotehele, Cornwall
Snowshill Manor, Gloucestershire

IRON, BRASS AND TIMBER
CANDLE FITTINGS
Cotehele, Cornwall
East Riddlesden Hall, Yorkshire
Hardwick Hall, Derbyshire
Ightham Mote, Kent
Lindisfarne Castle, Northumberland
Mount Stewart House,
    County Down
Rufford Old Hall, Lancashire
Snowshill Manor, Gloucestershire

ENAMEL CANDLESTICKS
Montacute House, Somerset
Sizergh Castle, Cumbria
Waddesdon Manor, Buckinghamshire

SILVER CHANDELIERS
Anglesey Abbey, Cambridgeshire
Polesden Lacey, Surrey
Powis Castle, Powys

SILVER SCONCES
Anglesey Abbey, Cambridgeshire
Attingham Park, Shropshire
Belton House, Lincolnshire
Chirk Castle, Wrexham
Dunham Massey, Cheshire
Erddig, Wrexham
Knole, Kent
Polesden Lacey, Surrey
Powis Castle, Powys

SILVER CANDELABRA, CHAMBERSTICKS
AND CANDLESTICKS
Attingham Park, Shropshire
Belton House, Lincolnshire
Ickworth House, Suffolk
Kedleston Hall, Derbyshire
Kingston Lacy, Dorset
Lyme Park, Cheshire
Petworth, West Sussex
Saltram, Devon
Shugborough, Staffordshire
Tatton Park, Cheshire
Wallington, Northumberland

SILVER CANDLESTANDS
Knole, Kent
Waddesdon Manor, Buckinghamshire

GILT METAL CHANDELIERS, SCONCES
AND CANDELABRA
Belton House, Lincolnshire
Chastleton House, Oxfordshire
Clandon Park, Surrey
Ham House, London
Hatchlands, Surrey
Hughenden Manor, Buckinghamshire
Ickworth House, Suffolk
Penrhyn Castle, Gwynedd
Powis Castle, Powys
Tatton Park, Cheshire

GILTWOOD CHANDELIERS, SCONCES
AND GIRANDOLES
Antony, Cornwall
Berrington Hall, Herefordshire
Blickling Hall, Norfolk
Hughenden Manor, Buckinghamshire
Kedleston Hall, Derbyshire
Knole, Kent
Lyme Park, Cheshire
Mount Stewart House, County Down
Osterley Park, London
Sudbury Hall, Derbyshire
Waddesdon Manor, Buckinghamshire

CUT-GLASS CHANDELIERS, SCONCES
AND CANDLESTICKS
Bath Assembly Rooms, Somerset
Blickling Hall, Norfolk
Buscot Park, Oxfordshire
Clandon Park, Surrey
Dyrham Park, Gloucestershire
Ickworth House, Suffolk
Kedleston Hall, Derbyshire
Kingston Lacy, Dorset
Mount Stewart House,
　County Down
Oxburgh Hall, Norfolk
Saltram, Devon
Stourhead, Wiltshire
Tatton Park, Cheshire
Uppark, West Sussex
West Wycombe Park, Buckinghamshire

CANDLE VASE LAMPS
Antony, Cornwall
Castle Coole, Fermanagh
Chirk Castle, Wrexham
Dyrham Park, Gloucestershire
Erddig, Wrexham
Gawthorpe Hall, Lancashire
Hardwick Hall, Derbyshire
Lacock Abbey, Wiltshire
Nostell Priory, Yorkshire

GILT METAL HALL LANTERNS
Attingham Park, Shropshire
Basildon Park, Berkshire
Cliveden, Berkshire
Lyme Park, Cheshire
Uppark, West Sussex

WALL-LANTERNS
Erddig, Wrexham
Nostell Priory, Yorkshire
Wallington, Northumberland

PORCELAIN CANDLESTICKS AND
CANDELABRA
Castle Coole, Fermanagh
Clandon Park, Surrey
Fenton House, London
Lanhydrock, Cornwall
Lyme Park, Cheshire
Upton House, Warwickshire
Waddesdon Manor,
　Buckinghamshire

SPRING-LOADED CANDLESTICKS
The Argory, Armagh
Arlington Court, Devon
Canons Ashby, Northamptonshire
Carlyle's House, London

CANDLE BRACKETS
Elizabethan House Museum,
　Great Yarmouth, Norfolk
Felbrigg Hall, Norfolk
Speke Hall, Liverpool

CANDLESTANDS
Beningbrough Hall, Yorkshire
Hardwick Hall, Derbyshire
Knole, Kent

TORCHÈRES
Ardress House, Armagh
Castle Coole, Fermanagh
Felbrigg Hall, Norfolk
Kedleston Hall, Derbyshire
Osterley Park, London
Saltram, Devon

French Candle Fittings

CHANDELIERS, SCONCES,
CANDELABRA AND
CANDLESTICKS
Attingham Park, Shropshire
Berrington Hall, Herefordshire
Buscot Park, Oxfordshire
Castle Coole, Fermanagh
Chirk Castle, Wrexham
Hatchlands, Surrey
Hinton Ampner, Hampshire
Petworth House, West Sussex
Tatton Park, Cheshire
Waddesdon Manor, Buckinghamshire

CANDLESTANDS
Knole, Kent
Waddesdon Manor, Buckinghamshire

Italian Candle Fittings

VENETIAN MURANO GLASS
CHANDELIERS
Buscot Park, Oxfordshire
Castle Drogo, Devon
Gawthorpe Hall, Lancashire
Ickworth House, Suffolk
Lacock Abbey, Wiltshire

VENETIAN LANTERNS
Berrington Hall, Herefordshire
Clandon Park, Surrey
Dunster Castle, Somerset
Snowshill Manor, Gloucestershire

GIRANDOLES
Clandon Park, Surrey

CANDLESTANDS
Charlecote Park, Warwickshire
Kingston Lacy, Dorset

BLACKAMOOR CANDLESTANDS
Dunster Castle, Somerset
Dyrham Park, Gloucestershire
Ham House, London
Kingston Lacy, Dorset
Knole, Kent

Oil Fittings

CRUSIE LAMPS
Moseley Old Hall, Staffordshire
Mount Stewart House,
　County Down
Plas yn Rhiw, Gwynedd
Snowshill Manor, Gloucestershire

FLOATING-WICK LAMPS
Castle Ward, County Down
Snowshill Manor, Gloucestershire
Standen, West Sussex

SPOUTED LAMPS
Arlington Court, Devon
Calke Abbey, Derbyshire
Castle Coole, Fermanagh
Kingston Lacy, Dorset
Osterley Park, London
Saltram, Devon
Snowshill Manor, Gloucestershire
Springhill, Londonderry
Stourhead, Wiltshire
The Vyne, Hampshire
Wightwick Manor, West
　Midlands

ARGAND LAMPS AND
CHANDELIERS
The Argory, Armagh
Arlington Court, Devon
Calke Abbey, Derbyshire
Charlecote Park, Warwickshire
Dunham Massey, Cheshire
Gawthorpe Hall, Lancashire
Hatchlands, Surrey
Hinton Ampner, Hampshire
Ickworth House, Suffolk
Kingston Lacy, Dorset
Lyme Park, Cheshire
Penrhyn Castle, Gwynedd
Petworth, West Sussex
Stourhead, Wiltshire
Tatton Park, Cheshire
Uppark, West Sussex

ANNULAR LAMPS
Arlington Court, Devon
Killerton, Devon
Uppark, West Sussex

MODERATOR, CARCEL AND
SINUMBRA LAMPS
Calke Abbey, Derbyshire
Waddesdon Manor, Buckinghamshire

PARAFFIN LAMPS AND
CHANDELIERS
Arlington Court, Devon
Erddig, Wrexham
Florence Court, Fermanagh
Saltram, Devon
Speke Hall, Liverpool
Wallington, Northumberland

LAMP ROOMS AND OIL STORES
Calke Abbey, Derbyshire
Florence Court, Fermanagh
Penrhyn Castle, Gwynedd
Speke Hall, Liverpool
Uppark, West Sussex

Gas Lighting

PROPERTIES ONCE LIT
ENTIRELY OR PARTLY
BY COAL GAS
A la Ronde,* Devon – has working
    gas lights
Ascott, Buckinghamshire
Buscot Park,** Oxfordshire
Carlyle's House,* London
Castle Ward,*** County Down
Chirk Castle,*** Wrexham
Clevedon Court,* Somerset
Cliveden,*** Berkshire
Cragside,* Northumberland
Crown Liquor Saloon,* Belfast –
    continues to be lit by gas
Dudmaston, Shropshire
Dunham Massey,**** Cheshire
Dunster Castle,* Somerset
East Riddlesden Hall,* Yorkshire
Elizabethan House Museum,*
    Great Yarmouth, Norfolk
Fell Foot,*** Cumbria
Lavenham Guildhall of Corpus Christi,*
    Suffolk
Holy Austen Rock Houses,* Kinver
    Edge, Staffordshire
Knole,* Kent
Melford Hall,* Suffolk
Penrhyn Castle,* Gwynedd
Petworth,* West Sussex

Quarry Bank Mill,*** Styal, Cheshire
Saltram, Devon
Sudbury Hall,* Derbyshire
Sunnycroft,* Wellington, Shropshire –
    has working gas lights
Theatre Royal,* Bury St Edmunds,
    Suffolk
Waddesdon Manor, Buckinghamshire –
    Royal Lodge Gates lit by gas
Wimpole Hall,*** Cambridgeshire

* supplied by local town gasworks
** the estate had a distillery 1869–79
    for which a gasworks was built
*** some remains of gasworks
**** may have had own gasworks

ACETYLENE LIGHTING
The Argory, Armagh – complete
    installation
Dunster Castle,* Somerset
Farnborough Hall,* Warwickshire
Oxburgh Hall,* Norfolk
St Michael's Mount,* Cornwall

* no plant remaining

AIR-GAS LIGHTING
Rufford Old Hall, Lancashire –
    complete installation

GAS LIGHT FITTINGS
Arlington Court,* Devon
Castle Ward, County Down
Chirk Castle, Wrexham
Cragside, Northumberland
Dunster Castle, Somerset
Elizabethan House Museum,
    Great Yarmouth, Norfolk
Felbrigg Hall,* Norfolk
Fell Foot, Cumbria
Knightshayes Court,* Devon
Quarry Bank Mill, Styal, Cheshire
Saltram, Devon
Wimpole Hall, Cambridgeshire

* no history of gas lighting – fittings
    introduced

Electricity

ELECTRICITY INSTALLATIONS –
PRE-1920
Baddesley Clinton,* Warwickshire
Bateman's, East Sussex
Berrington Hall,* Herefordshire
Buscot Park,* Oxfordshire
Castle Ward,* County Down

Chirk Castle,* Wrexham
Cliveden,* Berkshire
Cragside, Northumberland
Dunham Massey, Cheshire
Dyrham Park,* Gloucestershire
Ham House,* London
Hatchlands,* Surrey
Hughenden Manor,* Buckinghamshire
Ickworth House,* Suffolk
Ightham Mote,* Kent
Kedleston Hall,* Derbyshire
Killerton,* Devon
Kingston Lacy,* Dorset
Knole,* Kent
Lanhydrock,* Cornwall
Lyme Park,* Cheshire
Melford Hall,** Suffolk
Montacute,* Somerset
Petworth,* West Sussex
Powis Castle,* Powys
Standen,* West Sussex
Mr Straw's House,** Nottinghamshire
Wightwick Manor,* West Midlands

* no plant remaining
** supplied by local electricity company

BATTERY ROOM
Souter Lighthouse, South Tyneside

FUSE BOXES
Dunham Massey, Cheshire
Tatton Park, Cheshire

SWITCH ROOMS
Castle Drogo, Devon – operational
Waddesdon Manor, Buckinghamshire

WATER TURBINE AND
GENERATOR HOUSE
Bateman's, East Sussex
Cragside, Northumberland

EARLY ELECTRIC
LIGHT-FITTINGS
Arlington Court, Devon
Bateman's, East Sussex
Cragside, Northumberland
Dunham Massey, Cheshire
Ham House, London
Ickworth House, Suffolk
Kingston Lacy, Dorset
Lanhydrock, Cornwall
Petworth, West Sussex
Standen, West Sussex
Stourhead, Wiltshire
Tatton Park, Cheshire
Wightwick Manor, West Midlands

List of Plates

The author and publisher would like to thank the institutions and individuals who have granted permission to reproduce their material in these pages.

Please note that figures in **bold** refer to page numbers.

NTPL – National Trust Photographic Library
NT – National Trust Archives and Regional Libraries

Lighting Societies, Restorers and Suppliers

This list is selective, and is correct
at time of going to press.

United Kingdom

HISTORICAL LIGHTING SOCIETIES

The Historic Lighting Club
publishes quarterly *The Midnight Oil*.
For further information contact:

The Membership Secretary,
PO Box 25,
Wotton-under-Edge.
Gloucestershire GL12 7YS

The Institution of Gas Engineers
History Fund publishes
quarterly *Historic Gas Times*.
For further information contact:

The Institution of Gas Engineers
and Managers
www.igem.org.uk

RESTORATION AND REFURBISHMENT OF PERIOD LIGHTING

Chandelier Cleaning and
Restoration Services Ltd,
Gypsy Mead,
Fyfield,
Essex CM5 0RB

Chelsom Ltd,
Heritage House,
Clifton Road,
Blackpool,
Lancashire FY4 4QA

Delomosne & Sons Ltd,
Court Close,
North Wraxall,
Chippenham,
Wiltshire SN14 7AD

Rupert Harris Conservation,
Studio 5,
1 Fawe Street
London E14 6PD

Quantum Lighting Ltd,
106 Albion Street,
New Brighton,
Wallasey,
Wirral CH45 9JH

W. Sitch & Co. (est. 1776),
48 Berwick Street,
Oxford Street,
London W1V 4JD

Sugg Lighting Ltd,
Sussex Manor Business Park,
Gatwick Road,
Crawley,
West Sussex RH10 2GD

Wilkinson plc,
5 Catford Hill,
London SE6 4NU
Glass restorers to HM The Queen

Christopher Wray,
591-3 King's Road,
London SW6 2YW

ANTIQUE AND REPRODUCTION LIGHT-FITTINGS AND ACCESSORIES

Many towns have shops that
sell antique and reproduction
lighting. The list below details
some of the largest or specialist
companies.

Best & Lloyd Works,
William Street West,
Smethwick,
West Midlands B66 2NX

Chandelier Cleaning and
Restoration Services Ltd,
Gypsy Mead,
Fyfield,
Essex CM5 0RB

Chelsom Ltd,
Heritage House,
Clifton Road,
Blackpool,
Lancashire FY4 4QA

Delomosne & Sons Ltd,
Court Close,
North Wraxall,
Chippenham,
Wiltshire SN14 7AD

Hamilton Litestat Group,
Quarry Industrial Estate,
Mere,
Wiltshire B12 6LA

Lamps and Candles Ltd,
22 Royce Road,
Peterborough PE1 5YH

Quantum Lighting Ltd,
106 Albion Street,
New Brighton,
Wallasey,
Wirral CH45 9JH

W. Sitch & Co. (est. 1776),
48 Berwick Street,
Oxford Street,
London W1V 4JD

Starlight Lighting Specialists,
16 London Road,
Wansford-in-England,
Peterborough PE8 6JB

Sugg Lighting Ltd,
Sussex Manor Business Park,
Gatwick Road,
Crawley,
West Sussex RH10 2GD

Wilkinson plc,
5 Catford Hill,
London SE6 4NU

Christopher Wray,
591-3 King's Road,
London SW6 2YW
Has branches throughout the
country.

United States and Canada

HISTORICAL LIGHTING SOCIETIES

The Rushlight Club, founded
in 1932, publishes a journal
of lighting history, *The Rushlight*.

For information contact:

The Corresponding Secretary,
PO Box 75, Southampton,
New York, NY 11969
USA

The Historical Lighting Society
of Canada

For information contact:

The Membership Secretary,
PO Box 561,
Station 'R', Toronto, Ontario
Canada M4G 4E1

RESTORATION AND REFURBISHMENT OF PERIOD LIGHTING

Michael Dotzel & Son Inc.,
402 East 63rd Street,
New York, NY 10021
USA

Grand Brass Lamp Parts, Inc.,
221 Grand Street,
New York, NY 10013
USA

Restoration and Design Studio,
249 East 77th Street,
New York, NY 10021
USA

ANTIQUE AND REPRODUCTION LIGHT-FITTINGS AND ACCESSORIES

Details of some of the largest
or specialist companies.

Barry of Chelsea Antiques,
154 Ninth Avenue,
New York, NY 10011
USA

Empire Lighting,
8400 Woodbine Avenue,
Markham,
Ontario,
Canada L3R 4N7

Fischer Gambino,
637 Royal Street,
New Orleans,
USA

Gaslight Time,
5 Plaza Street West,
Brooklyn,
New York, NY 11217
USA

House of Lights,
49560 Van Dyke,
Utica,
MI 48317
USA

Irreplaceable Artifacts,
14 Second Avenue,
New York,
NY 10003
USA

Lighting Inc.
6628 Gulf Freeway,
Houston,
TX 77087
USA

Michigan Chandelier,
190 Last Maple,
Troy,
MI 48083
USA

Nesle,
151 East 57th Street,
New York, NY 10022
USA

Newel Art Galleries,
425 East 53rd Street,
New York, NY 10022
USA

Period Lighting Fixtures Inc.,
River Road,
North Adams,
MA 01247
USA

Price Glover, Inc.,
59 East 79th Street,
New York, NY 10021
USA

Richardson Lighting,
7070 San Pedro,
San Antonio,
TX 78216
USA

Unilight Ltd,
5530 St-Patrick Street,
Montreal,
Quebec,
Canada H4E 1A8

Australia

HISTORIC LIGHTING SOCIETIES

Australian Lamplighters' Guild.
For further information contact:

Secretary,
PO Box 129,
Gisborne,
Victoria 3437

ANTIQUE AND REPRODUCTION LIGHT-FITTINGS AND ACCESSORIES

Custom Lighting Designers
of Light Pty Ltd,
Melbourne Office:
1167 High Street,
Armadale,
Victoria 3143

Sydney Office:
18–20 York Street,
Sydney,
New South Wales 2000

Mondoluce
Suite 9,
Plaistowe Mews,
City West Business Centre,
West Perth
Western Australia 6005

Equivalent Values of the Pound

This statistical series shows changes in the value of money since the fifteenth century, giving the amount of money required at March 2000 to purchase goods bought at £1 at the dates shown on the table.

The retail price index is based on the combined cost of a number of specified goods, and does not, for example, take into account the cost of real property or the level of wages.

UNIT	DATE	TODAY'S EQUIVALENT
£1	1470	£410·25
£1	1520	£410·25
£1	1570	£149·18
£1	1620	£86·37
£1	1670	£74·59
£1	1720	£74·59
£1	1770	£56·59
£1	1820	£33·49
£1	1870	£41·03
£1	1920	£18·23
£1	1970	£8·87
£1	1980	£2·46
£1	1990	£1·30
£1	2000	£1·02

Equivalent Illumination Values

Until the early years of the twentieth century, the luminosity of gas burners and electric lamps was measured in candle power (c.p.). This was the equivalent to the light produced by one spermaceti candle weighing two ounces and burning 120 grains an hour. The luminosity of paraffin oil lamps was measured as 'line' (''').

The measurements are approximates.

CANDLE POWER EQUIVALENT TO LINE		
10'''	=	22 c.p.
15'''	=	40 c.p.
20'''	=	50 c.p.
30'''	=	100 c.p.

CANDLE POWER EQUIVALENT TO WATTS		
8 c.p.	=	10 watts
16 c.p.	=	25 watts
25 c.p.	=	36 watts
50 c.p.	=	60 watts

Index